From the Margins to the Cutting Edge

Community Media and Empowerment

INTERNATIONAL ASSOCIATION FOR MEDIA AND COMMUNICATION RESEARCH

This series consists of books arising from the intellectual work of IAMCR members, sections, working groups, and committees. Books address themes relevant to IAMCR interests; make a major contribution to the theory, research, practice and/or policy literature; are international in scope; and represent a diversity of perspectives. Book proposals are refereed.

IAMCR Publication Committee: Annabelle Sreberny, UK

IAMCR Book Series Editor: Thomas Tufte, Denmark

IAMCR Publication Committee Members:

Valerio Cruz Brittos (Brazil), Arnold de Beer (South Africa), Andrew Calabrese (USA), Joseph Man Chan (PRC), Marjan de Bruin (Jamaica), John Downing (USA), Cees Hamelink (Netherlands), Todd Holden (Japan), Shelton Gunaratne (USA), Rosa Mikael Martey (USA), Davina Frau Miegs (France), Virginia Nightingale (Australia), Francisco Sierra (Spain), Ruth Teer-Tomaselli (South Africa), Janet Wasko (USA), Robert White (Italy)

Titles

From the Margins to the Cutting Edge

Community Media and Empowerment

edited by

Peter M. Lewis
London School of Economics and Political Science

Susan Jones
Free Radio Freudenstadt

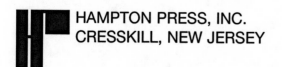
HAMPTON PRESS, INC.
CRESSKILL, NEW JERSEY

Printed in the United States of America

Library of Congress Cataloging-in-Publication-Data

From the margins to the cutting edge : community media and empowerment /
    edited by Peter M. Lewis, Susan Jones
        p. cm. -- (The IAMCR book series)
    Includes bibliographic references and index.
    ISBN 1-57273-717-4 -- ISBN 1-57273-718-2
        1. Community radio--Europe. 2. Radio broadcasting--social aspects--
Europe. 3. Internet radio broadcasting--Social aspects--Europe. 4. People
with social disabilities--Europe--Information services. 5. Social
participation--Europe. I. Lewis, Peter M. II. Jones, Susan, 1947- III. Title:
Community media and empowerment.

    ✓ HE8697.95.E85F76 2006
    384.54--dc22

                                                            2006045844

Hampton Press, Inc.
23 Broadway
Cresskill, NJ 07626

Contents

Acknowledgements

Many of the ideas for this book and much of the energy was generated in a series of meetings whose main purpose was planning and evaluating the projects—*Creating Community Voices* and *Digital Dialogues*, described in Chapter 1. Besides the meetings in Turku, Finland, others were hosted by colleagues in Leipzig, Sheffield, Connemara and Panni in South Italy. To them, grateful thanks are due, as also to those who contributed ideas and work but whose names will not be found in the book, especially Sangita Basudev, Mary Dowson, Rhadia Tarafder and Mary Ruddy. Thorsten Müll's skill in the technical design of the Digital Dialogues web site made it easier for us editors—and all who visit the site—to access the documents and handbooks referred to in the book.

Finally, our thanks to Jan Servaes and Publications Committee of the IAMCR for their review which helped to improve our work, and at Hampton Press, Mariann Hutlak, our production editor, and Barbara Bernstein, our patient and understanding editor.

Section I

Development, Community, and Learning

1

About this Book

Turku, Finland, December 1996: a group of ten people meet to pool their experience and brainstorm ideas about a project they want to launch with funding from the European Commission. They come from across Europe and most of them work in community radio; several have moved to university teaching where they reflect and write about their experience and encourage their students to study and experiment with this form of broadcasting. All are witnesses to the educational process involved in community radio, for one of its essential features is the involvement of ordinary people, non-professional broadcasters whose acquisition of broadcasting skills brings with it a new and more confident idea of themselves and a changed view of the social reality of their lives.

Out of this meeting *Creating Community Voices* was born, a two-year training project funded under the EC's Socrates program for adult education. It was followed by a second two-year project, *Digital Dialogues*, which extended and developed the first. Both were led by Traudel Günnel, for many years on the staff of *Radio Dreyeckland*, one of Europe's oldest and most successful community radio stations, and now a lecturer at Freiburg's University of Education. It was Günnel who brought together the original group in 1996, and her energy and inspiration that sustained the projects and ensured that the complex bureaucratic requirements of such an endeavor did not obscure the work of training, evaluation and reporting, and that communication among the project partners was enriched by convivial exchanges among colleagues who became friends. Moreover it was Günnel's own intellectual and professional journey–during the course of the projects she was awarded a doctorate for her thesis on "Community Radio in the Context of Media Politics, Communication Science, and Education" [1] which provided an important theoretical and pedagogical rationale for the projects and a stimulus for this book.

The final meeting of the *Digital Dialogues* partnership took place, like the first brainstorming, in Turku, where another long-standing community radio station, *Radio Robin Hood*, was host. Robin Hood, in English legend, robbed the rich to give to the poor. Nowadays different methods effect, and another discourse describes, this rearrangement of wealth: taxation, welfare, social services. But even in the wealthiest parts of the world, official arrangements have not eliminated poverty or social disenfranchisement.

The authors of a UNESCO handbook on ICT innovations for Poverty Reduction describe poverty as

> a complex condition that involves issues of voice, empowerment, rights and opportunities as well as material deprivation. The core issues of poverty go beyond issues of material deprivation to include education and literacy, aspirations, women's rights, freedoms and safety, and social participation. The common "poverty indicators" such as health and education facilities are widely raised, but they are part of a more complex and diverse picture of poverty. Moreover, even material deprivation is generally identified in ways that are specific to a location and culture. (Slater & Tacchi, 2004, p. 38)

The comment puts into context a phrase which risks becoming a cliché: the "information-poor," as if we could confine poverty to being a metaphor in mediacentric discourse. Instead it must be seen as an aspect of social reality for a very large proportion of the world's population, including Europeans. Whether it is the villagers of Panni in South Italy, or the metalworkers in Turku, the young musicians in Freiburg, or the asylum-seekers brought to Northeast England, they have this in common with the youngsters who have to walk for two hours to use the internet at *Kothmale Community Radio* in central Sri Lanka: escape from their material conditions is only possible if a vision of alternatives is accompanied by an experience that helps them see that change is possible, in themselves as well as in the world around them.

It is the argument of this book that the educational approach it describes—holistic, student-centered, linking learning with doing—provides just such a catalyst.

Slater and Tacchi's comment draws attention, then, to two points that are important to stress at the outset of this book. First, the ability and means to communicate in the modern world are fundamental in aiding people to escape material poverty and dependence and to speak for themselves in civil society. Second, material deprivation, specific to a location and culture, is relative. The social contexts described in this book and the media training designed to help people improve those contexts have relevance the world over. Although the experience described comes from Europe, the issues encountered—urban versus rural, young versus old, migration, the need to acquire new skills in order to get employment—can be found in all parts of the world where there is poverty, marginalization, and exclusion.

The book had its origins in community radio, but it is about much more than just radio—inevitably, because during the period of its gestation and the progressive development of the projects it describes, the internet has become a hugely important research tool for broadcasters as for all researchers, and the growth of web radio has been one aspect of increasing technological convergence.

But it is the social implication of convergence that is our starting point—the fact that the digital and web skills needed, not just for contemporary broadcasting, but for participation in modern society, are beyond the reach of those who are socially marginal. "Marginal," as the reader can find in the chapters that follow, can mean for women the habitual giving way to a man to start or fix a piece of technology; it can mean the feeling that the story of your life is untellable because in the city, where power and wealth reside, no one is interested; it can mean being cut off from home and everything that gives meaning to your life by a language and customs that are incomprehensible.

Migration and diaspora, story-telling and autobiography, partnerships between media trainers and practitioners and the representatives of groups and associations in civil society, new understandings of community reached via the internet and email—these are some of the themes with which this book engages. A common thread is the internet and sound—sound —edited, mixed, and recorded digitally, as well as broadcast live. The internet in its own right—as a research resource, a means of political coordination and of program distribution, and as a broadcasting medium—is becoming increasingly important in the community media sector. And despite the fact that more academic notice is being taken of community and alternative media, what has not so far been documented or discussed is the training that is the fundamental precondition for access and participation. And, as this book shows, more than any technical training, it is the relationship of community media projects to their communities and the kinds of partnership formed that allow a dialogue to take place and ensure that the training is targeted and effective.

The community radio stations from which these projects drew their inspiration, committed as they are to principles of access and participation, have had a quarter of a century's experience in the training needed for the effective use of radio by social groups whose voices and opinions are rarely heard in mainstream media. Community radio is also potentially a means to bridge the "digital divide," offering, as most stations now do, access to digital and web technology.

But technical skills are not in themselves sufficient to bring people across this bridge. Those whose opinions are rarely given a hearing may have forgotten, or never learned, how to express them. If technical training is combined with research, production, and presentation skills, which community radio routinely offers, the experience can also equip people with a self-confidence that is motivating. It can lead to employment—not necessarily in the media—and a fuller participation in today's information society. Yet those who could most benefit from this training often do not think of becoming involved in using the internet or in community radio. A survey of European community radio in the mid-1990s found that the group taking most advantage of this outlet was the young, employed male volunteer, making radio programs as a spare-time hobby (Lewis, 1994). Affirmative action is needed to create the conditions that will make the training experience attractive for those who most need it. The excitement of broadcasting, unashamedly exploited by community radio, is one such attraction; the "web adventure" is another. Although this approach is often successful in equipping non-professionals with technical skills, the motivation to use them for socially relevant purposes comes from a process of critical reflection that allows participants to see the link between community media and relations of power in their community and in society at large.

Finally, there are ethical and aesthetic components involved in almost any media activity. Progressing from a conventional consumer status to an active, decision-making role in media production, however modest its scope, can bring awareness of how and why decisions about information are made. Selection of themes, emphasis, and presentation style not only influence public opinion and political developments (as every spin doctor knows). They also provide the basis for fundamental cultural and social attitudes: for realistic self-images, communicative habits, mutual respect and tolerance, or, when treated less responsibly, for prejudicial clichés on matters of ethnics, gender, religion, and any number of volatile issues confronting the public.

Given the overbearing thrust of today's mainstream media and the oversimplified images they often propagate, even the most elemental forms of differentiation and self-articulation take on enhanced meaning. Taking responsibility for the *gestalt* of a published media product becomes an exercise in self-determination.

PROJECTS ON WHICH THIS BOOK IS BASED

Creating Community Voices: Community Radio and New Technologies for Socially Disadvantaged Groups (CCV) was designed to develop training materials and skills to facilitate increased involvement of socially disadvantaged adults in European-based community radio (CR) stations. Launched in September 1998 and completed two years later, the project included activities in five countries—Austria, Finland, Germany, Ireland, and the United Kingdom. Its main aim was to develop models of good practice in training that would assist access to CR stations by disadvantaged groups and to disseminate them in the form of guidelines to the CR sector and relevant adult education circles.

The second two-year project, *Digital Dialogues: Networking Community Media* (DD), followed in 2002. Nine actions involving eleven partners took place in six countries—to the five in CCV mentioned above was added Italy. The activities covered website creation, digital audio editing, live broadcasting of local events, the creation of local sound archives for music, webcasting, community radio training for refuges and asylum seekers, an internet course for mothers and daughters, and the creation of oral archives in an Italian village. (See Figure 1.1 for a summary of the information available at http://www.digital-dialogues.de.)

FIGURE 1.1. Access to Project Outcomes via Internet
http://www.digital-dialogues.de

At this internet address, the *Digital Dialogues* partners have published background information on their work, descriptions of project activities, and various aids for training and evaluation processes in community media. Each of the partners is presented, as are their activities and results, along with links, occasional photographs or sound files.

In the following chapters of this book, reference is frequently made to the descriptive and reflective texts written by trainers and coordinators during the course of the projects. On this website, these texts are available in several languages for use by community media colleagues. The material is copyrighted but can be downloaded free of cost for learning applications or reference.

These papers can be accessed from each of the corresponding "partner" and "action" pages, i.e., in the context of their origin, or simply by moving directly to the "database" entry in the navigation strip on the left of the screen. "Training aids & handbooks" gives an overall list of instructional materials, with direct links to the relevant files. "Concepts and outcomes" cross-references this information, listing each of the activities individually with all documents or products made available by its partners. In turn, these documents provide information on further sources. The handbook on webcasting (Action 6), for example, lists the URLs of a number of audio archives used by grassroots groups and media activists worldwide (as of 2004).

Training aids from the previous project, *Creating Community Voices*, can best be located via "database" and "previous project." This opens a sitemap of the former CCV website where, for example, handbooks on digital audio editing, *tandem training*, or introducing women to radio can be readily accessed.

From the opening "home" page or the "contact" page, a click onto the European flag will lead to information about the EU Education and Training program that supported these projects, Socrates-Grundtvig.

This book is structured in three parts: two introductory chapters are followed by examples of the training and activities in different places, contexts, and media; the final part includes a chapter on project evaluation and a postscript discussing the global context of alternative and community media.

Section I: Development, Community, and Learning

In the introductory Chapter 2, *Community Media: Giving "a Voice to the Voiceless,"* Peter Lewis sketches a brief history of community media theory and practice in order to explain the background of experience on which the CCV and DD partners drew and which is assumed by the majority of authors whose chapters follow. This is mainly, he acknowledges, North American and European experience, and the rich history of Latin American work on participatory media, as well as the German media and pedagogical theory summarized by Traudel Günnel in the following chapter was until recently largely unknown to English-speaking readers.

Lewis argues that training in participatory media owes much to the critical pedagogy of Paulo Freire, though the debt is not always consciously acknowledged. The motivation to create "alternative" media starts from a shared critical appraisal of mainstream media whose values, agenda, and assumptions are conventionally made to seem natural and commonsense. Questioning this "reality," then taking the opportunity to "name" their own reality, is what community radio uniquely offers participants.

Action-orientated media pedagogy (AOMP) is now an essential element in contemporary education and training. In Chapter 3, *Action-oriented Media Pedagogy: Theory and Practice*, Traudel Günnel takes up some issues often overlooked in theoretical discussion: how practice can enlighten method, the necessity of situational adjustment to participating groups, and the significance of media training programs for structural development and vocational advancement. She concludes with a critique of some of the theoretical elements underpinning AOMP.

Section II: Examples of Praxis

A fundamental characteristic of community radio, as of the training projects associated with it, is a partnership between the station, or core project, and groups or organizations in the community served. In Chapter 4, *Organic Radio: The Role of Social Partnerships in Creating Community Voices*, Caroline Mitchell and Ann Baxter draw on experience in Northern England, in Turku, Finland, and in Vienna. At the University of Sunderland, the student radio station's links with a Women's Education Center, and, in a separate project in Bradford, cooperation with minority ethnic women's groups on radio training and broadcasts illustrate one type of partnership. *Radio Robin Hood*'s relationship with a trade union in Turku is quite different, the union being a cofounder of the station. Yet another type of partnership, and one which influenced approaches throughout the two projects, was that of *Radio Orange 94.0*, Vienna, where what the station calls "tandem training" was organized with three organizations working with, respectively, senior citizens, working-class apprentices, and homeless people. This chapter also reflects on the value of participatory research approaches.

In Chapter 5, *Digital Skills and Networking*, Karin Eble and Traudel Günnel use the example of three projects, all based in Freiburg, Germany, to illustrate that media competence and digital skills are not purely technical matters but figure within the broader totality of an individual's repertoire of skills, life circumstances, and social reality. First, they describe a project that developed instructional software on digital editing, now standard practice in radio production, and emphasize that a precondition for its use is familiarity and confidence with computer skills. An interesting aspect of this project was the extent to which evaluation was closely woven into the development of the training materials.

In the second example, an all-women's team of media educators and trainers organized workshops to support mothers and daughters in overcoming generation and gender gaps, and to help them discover how they can use the internet responsibly and autonomously. Surprisingly—even for the participants themselves—coming together over technical topics released considerable creative energy and also new interactive impulses among family members. Mutual recognition of interests and skills emerged as an immediate outcome and as a basis for self-confidence in ongoing activities involving sounds and images, computers, and the internet.

The third example describes how four organizations collaborated in the launch of an audio platform, *soundnezz.de,* to encourage publication and webcasting opportunities for children, young people, and students. Workshops were conducted in cooperation with youth groups, but also within a school situation and as an elective for teacher trainees. The authors discuss the organizational and ethical problems of providing access while ensuring accountability and responsibility.

Chapter 6, *Networking Community Media: Web Radio as a Participatory Medium* by Caroline Mitchell and Susan Jones, draws together the experiences in Freiburg, Sunderland, Vienna, and other locations to consider the wide spectrum of internet applications that can complement and supplement conventional radio broadcasting. As an effective means for the distribution and reception of audio material, the internet can support program sharing along new paths, linking communities and interest groups on any level, from the local to the global. Webcasting, mutual cultivation of archives, exchange of current news reports and commentaries can be particularly significant toward empowering smaller groups, because regulation and bureaucratic hurdles are minimized. For those living far away from their culture of origin, as an example of work with refugees and asylum seekers in Sunderland, UK, shows, even a basic introduction to the realm of exchange through media can be of great value for their own self-definition and free expression.

Live Broadcasting of Public Events, Chapter 7, by Susan Jones, discusses the live broadcasting experience that was gathered in a small German city with a rural environment, Freudenstadt in the Black Forest. Community radio stations normally broadcast from their studios; here *Freies Radio Freudenstadt* organized broadcasts from external venues, working together with other local organizations and civic groups which thus had an opportunity to present themselves in the public forum. This is of particular advantage for partner organizations not regularly involved in community media activity. In Freudenstadt, the *Digital Dialogues* project enabled members of many social groups to participate in live broadcasts of local events and thus about their own lives. Young people and members of minority groups are integrated into the broadcasting teams and thus come into contact with established local organizations and leading community figures while preparing and producing the broadcasts. This experience improves their social integration and also their communicative skills and self-confidence.

The chapter discusses the necessary components of a successful broadcast—public relations, teamwork, logistics, training on the selection of proper equipment, coordination at the site of the event, testing and trouble shooting, as well as editorial concerns, such as the preparation of interviews, presentation, and the use of music. It also examines the significance of live broadcasting events as a form of linkage between active local groups with disparate interests and a way of helping media volunteers to maintain close contact with their audience and their social and political environment.

In Chapter 8, *Telling it Like it Is: Autobiography as Self-Definition and Social Identification*, Beatrice Barbalato and Karin Eble discuss two rather different projects that have an important common theme: encouraging people to value their own skills, experience, and personal history. In Panni, a small town in the province of Foggia in the Italian Apennine Mountains, Barbalato collected the stories of a town that has lost many of its inhabitants through emigration to other countries, or through the drift of young people toward cities in search of employment. The stories of both young and old, of those that remain and those who have left, and of some who have returned, are recorded in a newsprint magazine subscribed to locally and from abroad, and in an audio archive that can be accessed globally through the internet. The experience of gathering these interviews and stories is contextualized within the tradition of autobiographical narrative, which by its very nature intermingles fact and personal fiction, and in doing so can give valuable insights into social traditions and the weight they bear.

The Panni experience is contrasted with another Freiburg project in which a local sound archive is being developed that aims to help developing listening awareness of the personal, cultural, and local soundscapes in which people live. The starting point was a project with young, regionally active music ensembles that helped them record their own sound and music productions and upload them onto a website. Parallel to the studio sessions in small groups and the publication of the completed takes on the internet, meetings and events involving larger circles of participants aimed at personal encounter and accountability. A major facet of participants' interest was their motivation to tell about their everyday lives through music and lyrics and to take a position in relation to styles and social expectations.

Section III: Discussion

In Chapter 9, *Monitoring and Evaluation*, Peter Lewis discusses the issues and problems relating to the monitoring and evaluation of the CCV and DD projects. That evaluation of community-based projects should be itself be participatory is increasingly recognized in rural development programs, but within the community radio movement participatory monitoring and evaluation (PM&E) has yet to be seen as a logical component of participatory media. Lewis discusses the extent to which ethnographic methods accord with the action research approach and the evaluation of the CCV and DD projects in relation to the pedagogical theory summarized by Günnel.

Local and Global Participation, Chapter 10, reflects on some issues related to pedagogical theory and adult education raised in the preceding chapters, as well as on the reasons why community radio deserves more attention for its contribution to nonformal adult education. In a global postscript, we explore the connection between local struggles that use community media in search of democracy and the global debate that demands a voice for civil society in the World Summit on the Information Society.

NOTE

1. The full title of the thesis (in English) is "Experimenting with an Editorial Group from the Working World: Community Radio in the Context of Media Politics, Communication Science, and Education." For the original German title see in References Günnel (2003).

REFERENCES

Günnel, W. (2003). *Experiment Arbeitsweltsredaktion: Bürgerradio im Kontext von Medienpolitik, Kommunikationswissenschaften und Pädagogik*. München: Kopaed.

Lewis, P.M. (1994). *Community radio: Employment trends and training needs. Report of a transnational survey*. Sheffield: AMARC-Europe.

Tacchi, J., & Slater, D. (2004). *Research on ICT innovations for poverty reduction*. Paris: UNESCO. Available at http://cirac.qut.edu.au/ictpr/downloads/research.pdf

2

Community Media: Giving "a Voice to the Voiceless"

Peter M. Lewis

INTRODUCTION: COMMUNITY RADIO

The two projects, *Creating Community Voices* and *Digital Dialogues*, whose activities are discussed in this book, had their origins in community radio experience in Western Europe. As will have been clear from the preceding introductory chapter, the activities themselves covered a wider range of media than simply radio, but community radio experience was their inspiration and many of the "actions" in the two projects were managed by community radio broadcasters.

It is the purpose of this chapter to situate that experience within a theoretical and historical context. This will involve locating the place of community radio and community media within the wider field of alternative media, a task that immediately confronts the geographical and historical specificity of community media in Western Europe from its appearance in the late 1960s. In other regions of the world, opposition or alternatives to mainstream media arose in different circumstances, developed different forms, and acquired different labels. There are, however, in these initiatives across the world a sufficient number of features in common to make generalizations possible and, where radio is concerned, the existence of the World Association of Community Radio Broadcasters, known by its French acronym AMARC since its formation in Montreal in 1983, has led to some clarification and definitions that are incorporated in its several Charters and Declarations.[1] AMARC uses English, French, and Spanish as official languages but, even so, the different historical paths and positions that led to this international self-recognition are still not widely known across language barriers. To take two examples, Gumucio Dagron complains with reason about the English/Spanish divide in the literature on communication for development (Gumucio Dagron, 2001, p. 7), and the theorists of action-oriented media pedagogy cited by Traudel Günnel (see Chapter 3 and footnote 2 therein) are little known in the parallel anglophone field, which draws on quite different sources to underpin similar practice. These differences are complicated and made more interesting by the fact that, as I have remarked elsewhere (Lewis, 1993, p. 21), theory in this field was slower in developing than practice. To adapt and invert Marx's famous saying, people first used these media to change the world, and only afterwards have "philosophers" in various ways attempted to interpret the results.

Before discussing these interpretations, it may be helpful first to provide some snapshots of community radio for the benefit of readers who may not have encountered the phenomenon.

KPON-FM, Columbia, Missouri, USA, 1977. The station provided a programming alternative to what was available in the area; it involved a wide range of people in production, but discriminated positively in favor of women and minority ethnic groups. Seventy percent of income was raised through listener subscriptions and donations (Lewis, 1977, p. 8).

Radio Quartiere, Bologna, Italy, 1977. The station was unlicensed; 45 hours a week of programming included regular programs for and by trade unions, women's groups, medical students, prisoners, naturists, the police, with jazz, rock, and ethnic music. Seventy people, all volunteers, formed a general assembly that appointed a production committee. Start up and two years' running costs were met by ARCI, a communist sporting and cultural organization (Postgate, Lewis, & Southgate, 1979, p. 70).

Vancouver Co-op Radio, Vancouver, Canada, 1986. Licensed from 1974, a co-operative of shareholders, each with one vote, elects a nine-member Board that appoints 4-5 paid staff. Programming aims to be a radical alternative to local mainstream outlets. The station attempts to depend on not more than 10 percent from any one source of funding (Lewis & Booth, 1989, p. 124).

Radio Asé Pléré An Nou Lité, Martinique, 1991. Surviving jamming and electricity cuts by the authorities, the station, whose name in Creole means "Enough Crying, let's get on with our struggle!," could be heard throughout the island, promoting the Creole language and music not heard on the main stations. Listener access to the airwaves was a top priority. With no government support, funding came from donations and (one third) from membership fees to an organization supporting the station (Girard, 1992, p. 158).

Radio Mallku Kiririya, Irupata, Potosí, Bolivia, 1992. The station belonged to a Quechua-speaking community high in the Andes and was "run by peasants for peasants," broadcasting only at weekends when they are free from their normal work. Messages, notices, music and other programs were presented live from the premises built by the local community (Reyes Velásquez in Lewis, 1993, p. 87).

Bush Radio, Salt River, Cape Town, South Africa, 2000. With origins in CASET, a group using cassettes to distribute information before the end of apartheid, Bush Radio began broadcasting in 1993 and was officially licensed two years later. The station broadcasts in Xhosa, Afrikaans, and English, and has played a leading role in the development of community radio in South Africa and in training for the sector. It operates an open access policy expressed in monthly open forums (Girard, 1992, p. 201; Gumucio Dagron, 2001, p. 211).

What these examples have in common is that the community or communities for whom the station exists manage the policy, make the programs, and deliberately choose to broadcast content suited to their needs and not obtainable from mainstream outlets. There are many variant forms of community radio, but none aim to make a profit for private or corporate gain. In this they can be distinguished from commercial radio, even though some commercially funded stations do broadcast programming *for* "the community". Similarly, the local stations in state-controlled or public radio systems broadcast programming intended to meet local needs—but planned, produced, and presented by professionals.

By contrast, community radio has been described as radio *by* the people *for* the people. The voices heard are those from social groups not usually given space in mainstream media, unless edited as "vox pops" or framed in a professional discourse. Community radio since the latter half of the 20th century has set itself the mission of giving just such voices and opinions airtime, of giving "a voice to the voiceless." This has involved more than simply widening the range of speakers and interviewees heard on the radio: it has meant handing over the microphone, the tape recorder, and the studio to nonprofessionals, to communities that in fact control station policy and schedules.

Such a shift of control has always required training, but for people to speak for themselves in a digital world, new skills are needed. In the last decade, digital and web technology have extended the reach of community radio but also made it technically more difficult to achieve access, especially for the marginalized. So it was the purpose of the projects discussed in this book to pilot approaches to training that would enable disadvantaged groups in Europe to bridge what has been called the digital divide and continue to take advantage of community radio's presence in the continent. That presence is considerable and must total several thousand stations. The exact number at any one time is impossible to know because this type of enterprise is often of brief or intermittent duration—the reason that the examples above are marked with a specific date. The reader will have noticed, too, that no European station was included in the list, chosen deliberately to illustrate the global relevance of the media training described in this book. Poverty and unequal access to resources, including communication, exist in Europe as elsewhere in the world. The transition to democratic governance and the accompanying challenge for an emerging civil society can be found in parts of this region as in other regions. If an emphasis on radio needs justification, Gumucio Dagron's list of its advantages over other media as a tool for social change and participatory communication underlines its importance as a subject of study:[2]

- It is cost-efficient.
- Conveying spoken language, it can reach "the huge illiterate population that still remains marginalized especially in rural areas of the Third World."
- It is relevant to local practices, traditions, and culture.
- Sustainability is feasible.
- Its outreach and geographic coverage are better than those of other media.
- The convergence between radio and the Internet produces many advantages. (Gumucio Dagron, 2001, p. 19)

It must be emphasized that although much of the discussion in the chapters that follow necessarily focuses on media, whether radio or not, the driving force and rationale of the training the projects offered, and for the community media movement as a whole, was and is *not* media-centric. Rather, the motivation is social, cultural, and political experience — experience that has been unable to find expression in mainstream media. The particular needs and conditions of the social groups whose training in and use of media is the book's scope will be clear from the accounts in subsequent chapters.

The word *training* suggests a much more limited experience than that which actually occurred in the projects. Like all genuine educational experiences, these were liberating and empowering, but although the skills acquired are nowadays useful at home and widely transferable into conventional work situations, including mainstream media, the actual setting in which they were practiced was that of community or alternative media. Some projects related to radio, others to uses of the internet, a few to both, and a prerequisite for using both media effectively is computer competence. The training these projects provided took place outside mainstream educational systems and therefore should be categorized as nonformal education. Since people of all ages were involved, "lifelong learning" better describes the process than "adult education," although the latter is the heading under which funding was provided by the European Commission's Socrates and Grundtvig programs.

HISTORY

What follows is, first, a brief summary of the history of community media practice to illustrate the terminology that described the field before it entered the academic theoretical agenda. This is followed by a brief historical survey of the theoretical development of the field before, finally, a discussion of theoretical concepts that apply to the case studies discussed in subsequent chapters.

Although the first models of alternative radio (KPFA in California, USA, and Radio Sutatenza in Colombia) date from the late 1940s, it was the use of video in radical alternative media projects in North America that first made an impression across the Atlantic. The Canadian National Film Board's *Challenge for Change* experience was an important influence in Britain and, through its francophone Quebec project, *Societé Nouvelle*, on mainland Europe also. The prefix "community" had been in use in North America in the late 1960s in relation to community TV on cable and signified (for example, in usage by the Canadian regulatory body, the CRTC) local community involvement in ownership and production — programming by the community in contrast to local programming about local people and events. The experience of *Challenge for Change* in community video was important in helping the CRTC to frame regulations obliging cable companies to carry community channels.[3]

In Europe, several countries, among them Belgium, France, the Netherlands, and Sweden, began to look during the 1970s at the potential of video, either used in portable units or carried on cable networks, to assist in civic and social development in urban areas, particularly in newly built housing estates and towns (Beaud, 1980). In Britain, a Conservative government allowed commercial cable companies, hitherto confined to simple relay of broadcast signals, to test the popularity of locally originated programming. In several locations the stations trained volunteers to produce and present what was, in effect, community programming, though ownership and control remained for the most part in commercial hands (Halloran, 1975; Lewis, 1978). The European initiatives acknowledged the influence of U.S. and Canadian examples and followed the usage of "community" as a prefix. In Britain at least, this was in line with a general climate of decentralization and encouragement for local initiatives such as community arts, community health, and community law projects. By then a number of independent U.S. radio stations had come on air following the example of the Pacifica Foundation's KPFA (which had originally described itself as "listener-sponsored radio") and began to be known as community radio, the term used by the National Federation of Community Broadcasters (NFCB) when it formed itself in 1975. In contrast, the early phase of a similar sector of radio in Australia, which developed in the same period distinct from commercial and the ABC (Australian Broadcasting Corporation), was known as "public radio".

The explosion in the mid-1970s of local independent radio in Italy, the use of radio in Portugal's revolution, and the adoption of illegal radio by French trade unions and the Socialist Left in their opposition to a right-wing government introduced the term "free radio". "Free" connoted freedom from regulation and from the monopolies of centralized state broadcasting organizations, but in retrospect proved to be a Trojan horse for the commercial assaults on those same monopolies. As the French *radios libres* began to be taken over by commercial networks, other terminology was adopted: *radios associatives* became the official label for radios in the truly nonprofit sector, and the adjective *communautaire* signified the general type. It was perhaps no coincidence that the strong presence of French participants at AMARC's founding conference in Montreal adopted the terminology of their Quebec cousins. In Britain, Scandinavia, and the Netherlands, the pressure for local expression was to some extent pre-empted by the introduction of a local radio dimension within the public broadcasting system, as well as the experiments already mentioned with community programming on local cable networks. Access at the national level, the main feature of Dutch broadcasting, was granted minimally by BBC Television, Danish Radio, and some other national and regional networks.

In Latin America, the Colombian *Radio Sutatenza* had marked the first break from the mainstream in 1947, launching the model of the radio school. Over the next three decades the region suffered the effects of repressive regimes to which mass media were largely subservient. Only in the margins and rural areas far from the central authorities was it possible to develop, often with the support of the Roman Catholic Church, sometimes with that of foreign aid programs, a participatory approach in local media (Encalada Reyes, 1984; Peirano, 1993; Reyes Velásquez, 1993). In Bolivia, famously, miners' unions openly defied the central government with their radio (O'Connor, 2004).

Latin American Research

From the mid-1970s, Latin American communication researchers began to challenge the dominant assumptions underpinning mass media and to propose theoretical models that supported alternative communication (Huesca & Dervin, 1994). A major source of inspiration was the work of Paulo Freire, the Brazilian philosopher and adult educator whose *Pedagogy of the Oppressed* was first published in 1970.[4]

This most famous of Freire's publications drew on his experience in adult literacy training in Brazil and in Allende's Chile. Freire contrasted his method of teaching with what he called a "banking" form of education in which students are "filled" with knowledge supplied by the teacher. Students taught in such a way feel that "their ignorance justifies the teacher's existence," a relationship that "mirrors oppressive society as a whole" (Freire, 1972, p. 59). In contrast, Freire used a dialogical method in which "educators and learners all become learners assuming the same attitude as cognitive subjects discovering knowledge through one another and through the objects they try to know. It is not a situation where one knows and the others do not" (Freire 1976, p. 115, cited in Mayo, 1999, p. 65). (In his later writing Freire shows that this need not preclude a rigorous questioning of the knowledge produced, nor the need for a teacher's authority, provided it is not authoritarian, in occasionally having to "accede to the learner's demands for traditional teaching," Mayo, 1999, p. 139.) Through this process, which Freire termed *conscientization*, students learn "to perceive social, political and economic contradictions, and to take action against the oppressive elements of reality" (Freire, 1972, p. 19).

The stages of conscientization were, first, that the educator familiarizes him/herself with the way the students use language, their descriptive vocabulary; there follows a mutual search for words that have special meaning in the students' experience, thus allowing them to name their own reality; then comes a process of "codification" of these words into visual images (Freire used photographic slides for this purpose) "which stimulate people 'submerged' in the culture of silence to 'emerge' as conscious makers of their own 'culture'"; "decodification" (we might say nowadays "deconstruction") of the images by a "culture circle" is followed by "a creative new codification, this one explicitly critical and aimed at action, wherein those who were formally illiterate now begin to reject their role as mere 'objects' in nature and social history and undertake to become 'subjects' of their own destiny" (Goulet, 1973, cited in Mayo, 1999, p. 65).

Pedagogy of the Oppressed, which combines an almost biblical fervor (Freire's Catholicism was firmly in the Liberation Theology camp) with ideas drawn from Marxism, became widely influential across the world, especially after its translation into English. Notions such as dialogic education, conscientization, and the "culture of silence" resonated with the *zeitgeist* and were used selectively and sometimes out of context in contemporary campaigns. The dialogic education appealed to the de-schooling movement, and conscientization was close to the consciousness-raising technique favored by feminists. Critical as these were (and have often been since) of the sexism to be found in Freire's early writings, many in the women's movement recognized the reality of patriarchy in his discussion of the collusive relationship between oppressors and oppressed. The same relationship was suggestive for radical media activists whose campaigns for access or independent community media went hand in hand with a critique of oppressive mainstream media and the culture of silence they induced.

In Latin America, the work of scholars such as Jesus Martin Barbero, Luis Ramiro Beltran, Juan Diaz Bordenave, Fernando Reyes Matta, and Rafael Roncagliolo, to name only the most prominent, powerfully argued the case for participatory communication, but, as we have already noted, little of their work reached the Anglophone world at the time. The radical character of the region's approach was made clear at a UNESCO meeting in 1978 in Quito[5] where Latin American participants questioned the relevance to their region of UNESCO's ideas on access and self-management, notions that were in circulation since the publication by UNESCO of Berrigan's study the previous year (Berrigan, 1977). At the Quito meeting, it was pointed out that access to mass media was pointless given the latter's commercial and political goals, and that participation was only conceivable in the kind of political space not yet available in the region. Ten years later Robert White was to confirm this in his observation that "the democratization of Latin American society is more likely to begin in the marginal sectors and work towards the center" (White, 1988, p. 24, cited in Lewis, 1993, p. 22).

European Research

In Europe also, the 1970s saw the appearance of a literature concerned with community media. The Council of Europe's Council for Cultural Cooperation commissioned a series of reports on local initiatives using audiovisual media culminating in Paul Beaud's *Community media?* Beaud draws on a number of the reports in his survey and lists the whole series in his bibliography (Beaud, 1980). One report in the series, by Roberto Faenza describing the "radio phenomenon" in Italy at this time, included an early citation of Freire (Faenza, 1977, p. 4).

Access, the newsletter of *Challenge for Change/Société Nouvelle*, was read in Europe, and articles by George Stoney, director of the program from 1968 to 1970 when the important move from film to video was made, explained the *Challenge for Change* philosophy and its debt to the work of Saul Alinksy, American social organizer and civil rights activist. Stoney went on to found the Alternate Media Center in New York, which promoted the campaign for public access on cable. This pioneering work in Canada and the United States was described, along with some European initiatives, in Berrigan's *Access: Some Western Models of Community Media* published by UNESCO in 1977. Berrigan discussed public access at different levels—policy, program choice, production, and response (the right of reply). UNESCO's main preoccupation at that time was how to achieve a "free and balanced flow" of communication at the international level (see below). This was, however, linked with an interest in local initiatives to encourage access, participation, and self-management. These last three notions formed the title of a UNESCO meeting[6] in Yugoslavia in 1977, a country that was able to claim a number of examples of self-management in media, the rationale for which had been explained by two Yugoslav writers the previous year (Lekovic & Bjelica, 1976). Present at that meeting was Juan Diaz Bordenave, whose *Communication and Rural Development* was also published by UNESCO in 1977, and which was one of the first opportunities for an anglophone readership to learn of Latin American experience in participatory media for development.

The rapid spread of Freirean ideas into the anglophone world, thanks to the timely translation of *Pedagogy of the Oppressed*, has already been noted. That a gulf should exist between German and British work in media education is not surprising given the long-standing difference in education systems in the two countries. But anglophone ignorance for so many years of Habermas's seminal work on the public sphere was a serious loss to the study of community media, not to mention philosophy, and illustrates the different historical and critical contexts within which media studies developed on each side of the Channel. Published in Germany in 1962, it was not until 1989 that *The Structural Transformation of the Public Sphere* became available in its entirety in an English translation.[7] For nearly three decades his concept of the public sphere, of considerable value in discussing the place of community media within a communicative ecology, was unknown to all but a few specialists, much less its critique by Negt and Kluge, published in German in 1972. "How do certain concepts gain wider currency and when, at which juncture of academic paradigm shifts, cultural politics, and publishing trends?" asked Hansen 20 years later in her foreword to the first English-language translation of Negt and Kluge's *Public Sphere and Experience* (Negt & Kluge, 1993), a question that might well be asked of *Pedagogy of the Oppressed,* which appeared in Britain translated in the Penguin Education series only two years after its original publication.

British Media Studies

Something of an answer can be found if one traces the path of the different antecedents of British media education. One strand was nourished by Penguin's publishing policy through 1970s, especially the Penguin Education Special imprint. This brought, at an affordable paperback price, the key texts of the de-schooling movement (e.g., Goodman, Holt, Kohl, Reimer) to the attention of a wide readership. The same series introduced, as a contribution to McQuail (1972), Enzensberger's *Constituents of a Theory of the Media* with its talk of the "mobilizing power of the media [making] men . . . as free as dancers, as aware as football players, as surprising as guerrillas" (in McQuail, 1972, pp. 99-116).[8] Enzensberger's essay, together with another Penguin Education Special, Brian Groombridge's *Television and the People: A Programme for Democratic Participation* (1972), matched the radical mood of the time and marked a significant moment. It was a period of political unrest across Europe and North America, in which specific protests—for civil rights and against the Vietnam war, for more student control of university curricula, against the stockpiling of nuclear weapons—converged with the women's movement and, in Western Europe, with militant trade union response to government attempts to scale down traditional industries. These social movements were becoming increasingly aware of the power of media, especially television, to influence public opinion and set the agenda for public debate, a perception confirmed by the publication of the Glasgow University Media Group's *Bad News* study (Glasgow University Media Group, 1976), which demonstrated the systematically unfavorable representation of trades union positions, and of Todd Gitlin's

The Whole World Is Watching (Gitlin, 1980) about mass media's treatment of the New Left in the United States.

In Britain, cultural studies was an important parallel strand that fed into the study of media and influenced the development of media education. Hoggart's *The Uses of Literacy* had been published in 1957. A critique of contemporary popular culture, as well as a somewhat nostalgic celebration of working class culture, its success led to the founding in 1964 of the Centre for Contemporary Cultural Studies at the University of Birmingham under the joint leadership of Richard Hoggart and Stuart Hall, an alliance of literary criticism and sociology that is generally regarded as having laid the foundations for the subsequent development of British media studies. Raymond Williams's writings on cultural theory and history from a socialist point of view were influential in both adult education and media studies: *The Long Revolution* was published in paperback in 1965, and his *Television: Technology and Cultural Form* (1974) was to make explicit and perceptive reference to community television (Williams, 1974, p. 150). E.P. Thompson's *The Making of the English Working Class* (1963) was a landmark interpretation of history by a leading voice in the New Left, whose experience of the BBC—in 1961 his radio talk *The Segregation of Dissent* (later printed in Thompson, 1980) was censored—allied him with the groundswell of dissatisfaction among intellectuals with developments in British broadcasting.

Thus radical approaches to schooling, especially that of working class students and allied to progressive thinking in adult education, interacted with radical media practice and protest at the margins of and outside broadcasting. This mix came under, in Atton's phrase, the "multiperspectival lens of culture, sub-culture, ideology and hegemony." "Methodologically" he continues, "this [i.e. cultural studies] suggests an ethnographic approach that is able to account for the individual's and group's life practices as the cultural context in which their media practices are embedded," and he cites Morley's (1980) audience study as a key example of this approach (Atton, 2004, p. 3).

From the related field of media education one might cite also a book published in the same year, Masterman's influential *Teaching About Television* (Masterman, 1980), a lone advocate of television study at a time when film theory, imported from France, dominated media studies and threatened to make the field remote and inaccessible. Masterman's approach, an English version of the action-oriented media pedagogy discussed by Günnel in Chapter 3, drew on Freire's writing to urge a "conscientization" that would enable working-class pupils to find, through the practical work of television production, "an authentic voice." "Only when pupils value their own language, background and personalities and are not demeaned by them, will they recover their eagerness for expression" (Masterman, 1980, p. 141).

Across the rest of Europe, if barely perceptible in Britain, isolated instances of academic study of community media were encouraged and brought together by the formation of a Local Radio and Television group, founded at the 1982 Paris conference of the International Association of Media and Communication Research (IAMCR), and it was this group that supplied the material for *The People's Voice* (Jankowski, Prehn, & Stappers, 1992).

International Debate

The decade in which *Pedagogy of the Oppressed* became translated and read around the world was also the decade of NWICO, the New World Information and Communication Order, a set of proposals for more just and equitable relations at the level of international communications, which was UNESCO's main concern in this decade. Its 1976 General Conference in Nairobi had backed a proposal to set up an International Commission for the Study of Communication Problems, chaired by the Irish diplomat, Sean MacBride. The *MacBride Report*, published in 1980 (MacBride, 1980), was the culmination of a struggle by developing countries, led by the "non-aligned" group of nations, to win acceptance of their perception that global communication was unfairly organized, both in its flow (one-way) and in the distribution of hardware and infrastructures, in favor of the West. (In the midst of the Cold War, "West," "East" and "Non-aligned" were the labels then in use to describe the power blocs.) MacBride largely supported the NWICO proposals, and predictably, Western media, wedded to the idea of the "free-flow of communications," condemned the report and Western governments dismissed it as Soviet-inspired (Lewis, 1993, p. 22).

Academic attention in this period was for the most part still largely focused on these international and mainstream dimensions of communications media, and indeed had contributed the research on which *MacBride* was based. NWICO took as its premise an analysis of the existing order derived from academic studies of media imperialism and cultural imperialism. This approach argued that the developing world may have gained political independence from former colonial powers, but the economic domination of the industrialized nations ensured the continuance of a subtler form of imperialism through the cultural products and media systems poorer countries were unable to resist. The idea was close to Freire's notion of "cultural invasion" which "implies the 'superiority' of the invader and the 'inferiority' of those who are invaded, as well as the imposition of values by the former, who possess the latter *and are afraid of losing them* [emphasis added]" (Freire, 1972, p. 129). The final phrase of the quotation suggests the interrelationship between oppressor and oppressed emphasized by Freire, but overlooked by proponents of the cultural imperialism thesis. More recent versions of the theory have criticized the earlier implicit acceptance of a crude "bullet" theory of communications, an essentialist idea of culture, and the patronizing assumptions that accompanied it. Following Hall (1973), studies in the 1980s of the reception of media messages were showing that there is no guarantee that the producer's encoding of a message will be read or decoded in the same way as intended, and that audiences bring their own cultural and contextual baggage to the interpretation of messages (e.g., Morley, 1980; Radway, 1984 Ang, 1985). In any case it is mistaken to think of culture as singular or monolithic: any nation will be a mixture of cultures and traditions capable of handling incoming cultural pressures in surprisingly complex ways that often give birth to original hybrids and customizations. The historical context of NWICO, very much a reaction to the politics and ideology of the Cold War in which nation-states were perceived as the units that mattered, meant that its interpretation of cultural imperialism theory overlooked these complexities.

After the political failure of NWICO and the withdrawal from membership of UNESCO by its two major funders, the United States and the United Kingdom, in the mid-1980s, UNESCO lost some credibility at the international level, and it may be no coincidence that its interest in alternative media became more visible as the decade of the 1980s drew to a close. UNESCO had by then supported two community radio initiatives in Kenya (Heath, 1986; Lewis & Booth, 1989, p. 171) and Sri Lanka (David, 1992; Gumucio Dagron, 2001; pp. 127-132), and like most international funding agencies was interested in the question of "impact," commissioning a study of alternative media (Lewis, 1993) discussed below. Meanwhile, in the decade that followed, a series of meetings known as the MacBride Round Tables kept alive the concerns of *MacBride*. They were organized by NGOs aiming to assert their interest in democratic communication, an interest for the most part ignored in the NWICO debate (Traber & Nordenstreng, 1992). The MacBride Round Table meetings were successful in building up an alliance among NGOs that prepared the ground for the consultation at the World Summit on the Information Society (WSIS)[9] to which, for the first time in international telecommunications conferences, NGOs and representatives of civil society was admitted.

COMMUNITY AND PARTICIPATION

Moving from this historical summary to a discussion of theory, the most helpful place to begin may be with an examination of the two labels most frequently applied to the field. Each comes with a history, one that encapsulates the experience of a region or a school of thought.

The use of the concept "community" in relation to media can be traced back to sociological interest in the 1950s in the effect of modern urban living on the relationships characteristic of traditional communities, such as Young and Willmott's *Family and Kinship in East London* (Young & Willmott, 1957) or Janowitz's study of the community press in Chicago (Janowitz, 1957). In his "search for the social indicators of the symbolism and collective representations of the city and its suburbs." Janowitz remarked that the community newspaper was important in its representation of "a wide range of activities, values and aspirations present in the community which are *not* given expression in the daily press" (emphasis added, Janowitz 1957, p. 7). The mass media's coverage, he concluded, was too general to be relevant to local interests. While the two levels of media are contrasted in Janowitz's analysis, the community press is not oppositional but rather a defender of traditional values. Janowitz need not be held responsible for the nostalgic connotations which attached themselves to "community" over the next few decades, but they undoubtedly exist, and in political discourse the term is unthreatening and respectable. The canonization of "community" by, successively, the NFCB, UNESCO, and AMARC (all organizations with a need to represent a miscellany of interests and present an acceptable policy to the outside world) can be understood in the same political light even if, ostensibly, its usage was claimed to be an indicator of organizational features such as ownership and control.

With the growth of AMARC's membership in Africa and Asia, its President, Michel Delorme, speaking at AMARC-4 in Dublin in 1990, was able to summarize the movement in words much subsequently quoted:

> Our movement encompasses a wide range of practices. In Latin America we speak of popular radio, educational radio, miners' radio or peasants' radio. In Africa, we speak of local rural radio. In Europe of associative radio, free radio, of neighborhood radio and of community radio. In Asia we speak of radio for development and of community radio. In Oceania of aboriginal radio, public radio and of community radio. All these types of radio reflect a large diversity. The diversity of this participatory radio movement is large and very rich. In this we find our strength. (Delorme, 1990, p. 5)

Despite the "broad church" this rallying call suggested, AMARC has more recently projected a tighter definition of community radio that, one critic has suggested, has been influential with international funding agencies with the consequence that oppressive expectations are put upon systems that would prefer a more flexible definition. Writing of radio in

Mali, Craig Tower concludes that the "system of FM radio confounds standard thinking about radio in the West. . . . Like contemporary community media in the West, they developed and generally stand in some kind of opposition to establishment media . . . but without the hallmark structures of community media promoted by groups like AMARC" (Tower, 2005, p. 17).

AMARC-4 in Dublin was titled "The Right to Communicate." a phrase that had become a watchword after the publication of the *MacBride Report*. By the time of AMARC-Europe's first Pan-European conference in Lubljana in 1994, the right to communicate had entered the list of objectives "which community radio stations share and should strive to achieve" as proposed in The Community Radio Charter for Europe, agreed on by the Conference. In its key points the Charter spoke of the right to communicate as

- contributing to the democratic process and a pluralist society
- providing access to training
- encouraging local creative talent and fostering local traditions
- seeking to have ownership representative of local, geographically recognizable communities or of communities of interest
- [encouraging the development] of radio stations established as organizations not run with a view to profit, editorially independent of government, commercial, and religious institutions and political parties, and providing a right of access to minority and marginalized groups.

The last-mentioned independence was to prove difficult to achieve in the political conditions of some countries. Nevertheless it reappears as an aim in South African community radio and in a UNESCO manual that sums up UNESCO's experience in fostering debate and encouraging initiatives in the field (Fraser & Restrepo Estrada, 2001).

Unpacked, "community" proves to be carrying a set of prescriptions that bear witness to past struggles as well as bureaucratic accommodations. Although it is hard to disagree with Downing's unease with the term's ordinary connotations—"[it] persistently raises many more questions and dilemmas than it answers" (Downing, 2001, p. 39)—it is the term that many practitioners have used about their work, and the arrival of the internet has obliged media studies to look again at the meaning of community (see below).

Participatory communication is similar in being used by practitioners themselves. It speaks for the Latin American tradition but, interestingly, does not of itself signal its radical connotations. Servaes has noted the discontinuity between a Freirean discourse that bluntly spoke of "the oppressed" and the blander UNESCO rhetoric (Servaes, 1999, p. 85). He summarizes its characteristics as follows:

> The participatory model views ordinary people as the key agents of change or participants for development, and for this reason it focuses on their aspirations and strengths. Development is meant to liberate and emancipate people and, in so doing, enable them to meet their basic needs. Local cultures are respected . . . in essence participatory development involves the strengthening of the democratic processes at the community level and the redistribution of power. . . . As such, it directly threatens those whose position . . . depends on power and its control over others. (Servaes, 1999, p. 93)

In this reading, "participatory" carries far more militant baggage than its surface meaning of sharing or than was being proposed by, for example, Groombridge or Berrigan, and like "community," it encodes a specific historical tradition.

The concept of participation has also received attention in development studies. Here, a central concern has been with the methods and approaches needed to engage local populations in the design, monitoring and evaluation of projects involving them (Estrella & Gaventa, 1998).[10] Interestingly, there is scant reference to media in this literature and correspondingly there has been little application of participatory monitoring and evaluation (PM&E) in community media practice (Lewis, 2003).

ALTERNATIVE?

It is only recently that academic media studies have begun to examine the history and practice of these forms of media, although for a decade and more community radio has featured in English-language histories and case studies whose commentaries moved from description and categorization—a necessary first step if the record of small, local, and often ephemeral initiatives is not to be lost—towards the articulation of theory. Recognition of these media had already found a place in the 1987 edition of McQuail's *Mass Communication Theory* in a review of "normative theories of media performance". McQuail described "democratic-participant media" as small-scale, formed by "groups, organizations and local communities" as "inter-active and participative" in contrast to "large-scale, one-way, professionalized media" (McQuail, 1987, p. 123). Downing's *Radical Media* had appeared in 1984 and his case studies clearly informed McQuail's summary. Downing's 2001 edition was a substantial revision that took account of the collapse of communism and the increased salience of new social movements, but which included the admission that his earlier treatment had slipped towards a "binarism" in discussing "alternative media" and "mainstream" that had led him to ignore the latter's potential to be used in radical ways.

The 1993 UNESCO study, *Alternative Media: Linking Global and Local*, edited by the present writer, listed a number of ways in which a media project might be regarded as alternative. These might relate to motive or purpose, sources of funding, regulatory dispensation, organizational structure, "alternative in criticizing professional practices," message content, relationship with audience, composition of audience, range of diffusion, alternative nature of research methodology. Any one of these, it was suggested, might qualify the example for the description "alternative" and to that extent "binarism" could be left behind in studying a variety of forms of the phenomenon. A "temporal dynamic" was also involved: "yesterday's underground alternative may to-day be a legal best-seller and tomorrow could be taken over by an international conglomerate" (Lewis, 1993, p. 12).

"Alternative" appears to be the most favored label in the current academic discussion (see, e.g., Atton, 2002, 2004; Couldry & Curran, 2003) and, as editors of a recent issue of *Media, Culture & Society* devoted to alternative media, Atton and Couldry suggest four reasons "why alternative media might now be emerging from the margins of scholarly attention": the revival of social activism, often on a global scale and using non-mainstream media production that is linked to the Internet; the apathy towards, or commercial appropriation of, conventional democratic processes; the recent increased interest of international agencies in local empowerment within development projects. The fourth reason might be regarded as an "in-house" one: a "loss of momentum" in certain "critical traditions" within media and cultural studies (Atton & Couldry, 2003, pp. 579-580).

For present purposes, the definitional problems that beset the study of other favored labels, such as "radical" (Downing, 2001) or "citizens" (Rodriguez, 2001) each draw attention to important features of the genre, some of which will be encountered as we explore three aspects of theory that relate to the experience of the *Creating Community Voices* and *Digital Dialogues* projects.

Freirean Pedagogy

The first and most obviously relevant area of theory is that of Freire's pedagogy which Downing recognizes as "a core philosophy within which to think through the nature of the activist producer/active audience relationship" in its proposal for a "democracy of the communication process" that recognizes "the audience as joint architects with the media producers" (Downing, 2001, p. 46). In particular, the idea of conscientization underlies the whole approach in both projects. Two instances of the training discussed in Chapter 4 illustrate the process, although the accounts do not use that term. One is in the taster courses used in the Bridge project for women in Sunderland, the other at Radio Robin Hood in Turku, Finland. In both, trainees were invited to begin by "naming their own reality"; that is, to discuss the radio they listened to and the television they watched and relate it to their own lives and experience. They were encouraged to articulate what they understood all along—that the mass media reality was quite removed from their own experience. Some contextual information supplied by the trainers enabled them to question and decode the media representations, and as they reflected on their own reality they began to see ways to express it and to learn the techniques needed to encode it in the medium of radio. This is, to use Rodriguez's words, to express "dissent in the realm of the symbolic . . . where symbolic resistance can potentially take place . . . [because] pre-established social and cultural codifications of power cease to make sense" (Rodriguez, 2001, p. 151). The training in these instances took place in a (Freirean) dialogic mode and in settings designed to be "congruent with their interests, needs and life experience"—words that Günnel and her colleagues use to summarize "situated learning" at the end of Chapter 5.

Another form taken by "naming reality" is the telling of one's own story. Asylum-seekers finding the security in which to reclaim their personal histories (Chapter 6), Barbalato's informants recalling their lives in Panni (Chapter 8), and, in their own way equally expressive of their identities, the school students in Freiburg putting their musical performances on the internet platform Soundnezz (also in Chapter 8)—all were breaking the "culture of silence" and in many cases (a double empowerment) learning technical skills that opened up new social and employment horizons. A further aspect of the process is that of using a medium, be it radio or the internet, to publicly diffuse the stories told, the productions, or the performances. As Günnel comments in her conclusion to Chapter 3, creating a communication space to reach a wider audience "opens the possibility for them to participate in social discourse and contributes decisively to their empowerment."

Hegemony

This raises the question of the relationship of alternative media practice to the mainstream and brings us to a second useful theoretical area,

Gramsci's notion of hegemony. It is useful in two ways: first, as Caroline Mitchell and Susan Jones suggest in discussing the internet dimensions of community radio activity (Chapter 6), what is being used is a global, mainstream institution—the internet. There is here no sharp dichotomy between alternative and mainstream, and we can agree with Atton's suggestion that the relationship between the two exemplifies the "classic features of hegemonic practice—the notion of an unstable, non-unitary field of relations, where ideology is mobile and dynamic and where strategic compromises are continually negotiated" (Atton, 2004, p. 10). In this view, the technology and even some of the practices are not inherently mainstream or alternative: what differentiates the two types of media are the social and political settings and motives. Commercial radio competitors copied jazz formats from U.S. community radio stations when its increased popularity made it worthwhile for them to do so; conversely, in a famous scam, one of the first French *radios libres*, Radio Vert, hijacked a TV show to get nationwide publicity (Lewis & Booth, 1989, p. 148).

Secondly, perhaps more obviously, the notion of hegemony can explain manifestations of power, such as masculinity, that are inherently unstable, yet may be accepted as normal and unquestionable in any particular period. Counter-hegemony, a notion developed subsequent to Gramsci's work, is also applicable to, for example, the goals of feminist communication as stated by Riaño and cited by Mitchell and Baxter in Chapter 4, as well as those alliances of new social movements that now oppose global economic domination by wealthy states and transnational corporations.

A very clear statement of counter-hegemonic possibility, as well as of the relations between social movements and alternative media, was summed up by Mattelart and Piemme at the end of an article written in 1979, "New Means of Communication: New Questions for the Left" (Mattelart & Piemme, 1980). (The new media in question were video and *radios libres*.)

> New social relationships are not means to an end of new types of communication. Nor will new types of communication be means to an end of new social relationships. The two will develop in parallel, as the slow and lengthy effort to build a popular culture advances. Neither populist, nor unscholarly, nor anti-intellectual (all characteristics of "mass culture" as it is conventionally understood), this popular culture will be the result of multiple contributions of groups in struggle, the intersection of economic resistance, the questioning of the forms of individual or social power, artistic practices, and the practices of everyday life. (Mattelart & Piemme, 1980, p. 337)

Downing underlines the above point about artistic practices with his suggestion that "one way of describing capitalist hegemony would be in terms of *self*-censorship by mainstream media professionals . . . [and] their unquestioning acceptance of standard professional media codes" (Downing, 2001, p. 16).

Public Sphere

A third area of theory useful in the analysis of alternative media is that of the public sphere in a form that amends and updates Habermas's original concept.[11] The recent growth of interest in citizenship and the possibilities that new information and communication technologies (ICTs) hold for a renewal of democratic involvement reinforce the usefulness of public sphere theory in understanding community media.[12] The discussion in Chapter 4 of the introduction of Tandem training at *Radio Robin Hood* in Turku is a particularly good example. Eleven different organizations form the association which owns the station. The station here is providing civil society with a local public sphere[13] that on closer inspection, as we follow the account of the three organizations involved in Tandem training, can more accurately be described as the intersection of several local public spheres. For many community radio stations the reconciliation of the competing demands or differing outlooks of the different groups demanding airtime is a problem; even finding a time convenient for different groups to meet and discuss common issues is difficult. The *Radio Robin Hood* example shows the differing expectations of three groups (a local employment agency, a women's organization, and the metalworkers union) that had a long term commitment to the station and the benefits that came from finding time and space to talk through the differences. Exclusion from the public sphere of mainstream media is what a range of different groups have in common, and their commonality is further strengthened—and often their differences revealed and negotiated—by the need to agree on the division of airtime and the principles and priorities involved in the management of a radio of their own.

Often, such debates spill out onto the airwaves of community radio, becoming what Downing calls a "public conversation". An example of such a conversation occurred during a phone-in on *Radio Popolare* in May 1977, after a demonstration in which a policeman was shot dead. The group, one of whose members was responsible for the shooting, was criticized by callers-in and in turn defended the action on air. The comment of a media analyst, describing the style of program that was a natural consequence of the heightened political awareness of that period in Italy, was recorded the next day:

An interpretation of what happened takes shape from the contributions of the different people involved. Each person is asked for their political analysis. . . . So, things happen during the day on the streets and are discussed at night on the radio, and each station is able to be in touch with the other and to make links between stations. The whole thing [i.e. the use of free radio by the Left] is absolutely not as anarchic and out of control as the press and government would have us believe. It is the kind of control that comes from an action being discussed by tens of thousands of people over the air. Each person who telephones really has something to say. They don't telephone simply to give their personal opinion, but they make their call a political intervention and in this way add something to the debate. (Francesco Cavalli-Sforza, cited in Lewis, 1984, p. 144)

In altogether less turbulent settings, Free Radio Freudenstadt in the Black Forest (Chapter 7) and the regional Archive of Autobiographical Heritage where Panni's stories are lodged (Chapter 8) illustrate the local public sphere made accessible through a media project. The live broadcasting of events organized by local groups in Freudenstadt allows a wider participation and celebration of the events, and their (often regular) inclusion in the radio station's schedule over time helps to constitute a temporal version of the local public sphere. In Panni, individual autobiographical memories become part of the shared heritage of the village and the region accessible physically and on-line.

COMMUNITY AND INTERNET

Finally, it is necessary to revisit the notion of "community" to take account of the fact that growth in the use of the internet obliges us to recognize some new meanings. That one person can be a member of several communities simultaneously is a commonplace of experience, as well as of the technology of broadcast transmission. A local radio station, for example, can target a particular community of interest (e.g., devotees of a type of music, linguistic or ethnic communities, etc.) while inevitably broadcasting over a geographical area including geographic communities. The internet has added further dimensions to the individual experience—as well as to the audiences for radio. But this is not to accept some different, "virtual" status for internet relations set apart from the existing experience. As Miller and Slater urge, "we need to treat Internet media as continuous with and embedded in other social spaces . . . they happen within mundane social structures and relations that they may transform, but from which they cannot escape into a self-enclosed cyberian apartness" (Miller & Slater, 2000, p. 5).

Webcasting, or web radio, illustrated in Chapter 6, illustrates this continuity with existing practice. The growing accessibility and afford-ability of this form of transmission for local nonprofit radio stations mean that programs, including live events, can also be made available to lis-teners outside the locality where they are produced. An event streamed onto the internet in "real time" certainly transcends the geographical lim-its of the terrestrial transmission and potentially extends the communi-ties of interest. Whether webcasting in such contexts is practiced as real time programming or involves delayed availability (program material for download on demand off a server), there are implications for the way the "community" is imagined, both by the station and the listeners them-selves. In an interesting discussion of these issues, Atton (2004) takes as a case study Resonance FM, which has a community radio analogue licence in London and simultaneously webcasts. Because the station is mainly devoted to specialist/alternative music, Atton's discussion is lim-ited to the implications for music broadcast globally, and it is clear from his study that Resonance makes little concession to modify and explain the local references that, as Susan Jones points out in Chapter 7, help provide a distinctive identity and a basis for identification with regional culture and customs.

Speech items, features, and documentaries covering issues that unite dissenting communities across a globalized world are commonly shared by stations using the internet, and any contextual confusion is outweighed by the surprise, excitement, and empowerment that can occur when webcasting flows back into local broadcasting. Downloading from archive servers full of international material and rebroadcasting locally is a regular part of Radio Orange's schedule in Vienna.

A server handling daily material from Austria, Germany, and the German-speaking part of Switzerland illustrates this effect at a regional level for German-speaking local community stations. It enables them to cover more topics of national interest in the political and cultural field, resulting in new emphases (for local media) on themes such as criticism of foreign policy, or interviews and investigative reports on the treatment of refugees. Even the small Free Radio Freudenstadt in the Black Forest, in an area not noted for political awareness (see Chapter 7 for its live broadcasting experience), picks up a program called *Europa von unten* (Europe from down below), produced in southern Austria with an eye toward the Balkans and Eastern Europe and with interesting coverage on new EU member and candidate countries.

These examples illustrate the need for community broadcasters to adapt to the extended and variant communities the Internet accommo-dates. To sum up an understanding of community in the internet age, Silverstone's discussion is one of the most helpful. Community, he points out, is both descriptive and evaluative, and always involves a claim "to be part of something shareable and particular." Communities have always been symbolic as well as material; all communities are virtual communities insofar as membership of them has to be imagined (Silverstone, 1999, p. 104).

THEORY, PRACTICE, POLICY

It has been the aim of this chapter to summarize the background of experience and theory on which the CCV and DD projects drew. To single out a specific theme, the account traces a relationship between theory and practice that in an early period was undeveloped or unacknowledged in most parts of the world except Latin America. Then, for the industrialized North/West, came a period of description, classification, and documentation, much of it supported by UNESCO and the Council of Europe. More recently, a growing academic interest in theorizing alternative media has been matched by a concern on the part of international aid agencies to seek ways to reduce poverty and find methods to test what part alternative media can play in this endeavor. This convergence of interest has brought together academics, practitioners, and policymakers in an alliance called OURMedia (*www.ourmedianet.org*). The unstated antithesis—"*not theirs!*"—marks out the stance of the organization in relation to the alternative and mainstream. The important policy challenges posed by global summits such as WSIS (the World Summit on the Information Society), the World Social Forum, and the G8 meetings require as never before that connections be made between local alternative media experience and global decision making. We return to this question in Chapter 10.

NOTES

1. See http://www.amarc.org/site.php?lang=EN
2. A considerable disadvantage, not mentioned by Gumucio Dagron, is that radio using spectrum space needs a license from the regulatory authorities to function legally. Although there have been many instances in Latin America and Europe of stations operating to considerable effect outside the law, the wish to control frequencies has often been the reason why governments are reluctant to allow independent community radio to exist in the first place. Webcasting, sig-

nificantly, needs no such license, hence its importance, discussed later in this chapter and elsewhere in the book.

3. http://www.radicalsoftware.org/volume1nr4/pdf/VOLUME1NR4_art 08.pdf
4. Published and translated in London as Freire, 1972.
5. "The First Latin-American Seminar on Participation" at CIESPAL (Centro Internacional de Estudios Superiores de Comunicación para América Latina), Quito, 27 November–1 December, 1978.
6. Meeting on Self-Management, Access and Participation in Communication, Belgrade, 18-21 October, 1977.
7. Habermas (1989). A brief article by Habermas on the public sphere was included in Mattelart and Siegelaub (1979), pp. 198-201.
8. An excerpt from Hans Magnus Enzensberger's essay was reprinted in McQuail (1972) from the original, translated by Stuart Hood, in *New Left Review 64(* Nov-Dec 1970), pp. 13-36.
9. The first phase of the WSIS was held in Geneva in December 2003, and the second in Tunis, November 2005.
10. See also the website of the Institute for Development Studies at the University of Sussex: http://www.ids.ac.uk/ids/particip/index.html
11. See Downing (2001, pp. 27-33) for a summary of this debate.
12. They also justify Rodriguez's preference for the phrase "citizens' media" in her study (Rodriguez, 2001).
13. See Hollander and Stappers (1992, p. 22) for a discussion of community media and local public spheres.

REFERENCES

Ang, I. (1985). *Watching Dallas*. London: Methuen.

Atton, C. (2002). *Alternative media*. London; Thousand Oaks, CA; New Delhi: Sage.

Atton, C. (2004). *An alternative internet: Radical media, politics and creativity*. Edinburgh: Edinburgh University Press.

Atton, C., & Couldry, N. (2003). Introduction. *Media, Culture & Society, 25*(5), 579-586.

Beaud, P. (1980). *Community media?* Strasbourg: Council of Europe.

Berrigan, F. (Ed.). (1977). *Access: Some Western models of community media*. Paris: UNESCO.

Bordenave, J.D. (1977). *Communication and rural development*. Paris: UNESCO.

Couldry, N., & Curran, J. (Eds.). (2003). *Contesting media power: Alternative media in a networked world*. Lanham, MD: Rowman & Littlefield.

David, M.J.R. (1992). Mahaweli community radio. In B. Girard (Ed.), *A passion for radio* (pp. 132-140). Montreal/New York: Black Rose.

Delorme, M. (1990). AMARC: A plan for action. *AMARC 4 Report* (pp. 5-7). Dublin: 4th World Conference of Community Radio Broadcasters, "The Right to Communicate."

Downing, J. (2001). *Radical media: Rebellious communication and social movements*. London: Sage.

Encalada Reyes, M. (1984). Latin America. In P. M. Lewis (Ed.), *Media for people in cities* (pp. 159-186). Paris: UNESCO.

Estrella, M., & Gaventa, J. (1998). *Who counts reality? Participatory monitoring and evaluation: A literature review*. University of Sussex, Institute for Development Studies, Working Paper 70.

Faenza, R. (1977). *The radio phenomenon in Italy*. Strasbourg: Council of Europe, CCC/DC (76) 93-E.

Fraser, C., & Restrepo Estrada, S. (2001). *Community radio handbook*. Paris: UNESCO.

Freire, P. (1972). *The pedagogy of the oppressed*. London: Penguin.

Freire, P. (1976). Literacy and the possible dream. *Prospects, 6*(1), 68-71.

Girard, B. (1992). *A passion for radio: Radio waves and community*. Montreal / New York: Black Rose.

Gitlin, T. (1980). *The whole world is watching: Mass media in the making & unmaking of the New Left*. Berkeley, London: University of California Press.

Glasgow University Media Group (1976). *Bad news*. London: Routledge & Kegan Paul.

Groombridge, B. (1972). *Television and the people: A programme for democratic participation*. London: Penguin.

Gumucio Dagron, A. (2001). *Making waves: Stories of participatory communication for social change*. A Report to the Rockefeller Foundation, New York.

Habermas, J. (1989). *The structural transformation of the public sphere: An inquiry into a category of bourgeois society* (Trans. Thomas Burger with the assistance of Frederick Lawrence). Cambridge: Polity.

Hall, S. (1973). Encoding/decoding in television discourse. Reprinted in S. Hall et al. (Eds.), *Culture, media, language* (pp. 128-138). London: Hutchinson.

Halloran, J. (1975). *The development of cable TV in the United Kingdom: Problems and possibilities*. Strasbourg: Council of Europe, CCC/DC (75) 46.

Heath, C.W. (1986). Politics of broadcasting in Kenya—community radio suffers. *Media Development, 2,* 10-14.

Hoggart, R. (1957). *The uses of literacy*. London: Chatto & Windus.

Hollander, E., & Stappers, J. (1992). Community media and community communication. In Jankowski et al. (Eds.), *The people's voice: Local radio and television in Europe* (pp.17-27). London: John Libbey.

Huesca, R., & Dervin, B. (1994). Theory and practice in Latin American alternative communication research. *Journal of Communication, 44* (4), 53-73.

Janowitz, M. (1952/1967). *The community press in an urban setting: The social elements of urbanism*. Chicago, London: University of Chicago Press.

Jankowski, N., Prehn, O., & Stappers, J. (Eds.). (1992). *The people's voice: Local radio and television in Europe*. London: John Libbey.

Lekovic, Z., & Bjelica, M. (1976). *Communication policies in Yugoslavia*. Paris: UNESCO.

Lewis, P.M. (1977). *Different keepers: Models of structure and finance in community radio*. London: International Institute of Communications.

Lewis, P.M. (1978). *Community television and cable in Britain*. London: British Film Institute.

Lewis, P.M. (1984). Community radio: The Montreal conference and after. *Media, Culture & Society, 6*, 137-150.

Lewis, P.M. (1993). *Alternative media: Linking global and local*. Paris: UNESCO Reports and Papers in Mass Communication, Nr. 107.

Lewis, P.M. (2003). Est-ce que ca marche? L'observation et l'évaluation des radios communautaires. In J-J.Cheval (Ed.), *Audiences, publics et practiques radiophoniques* (pp. 83-94). Bordeaux: éd. Maison des Sciences de l'Homme de l'Aquitaine.

Lewis, P.M., & Booth, J. (1989). *The invisible medium: Public, commercial and community radio*. London: Macmillan.

MacBride, S. (1980). (International Commission for the Study of Communication Problems, chaired by Sean MacBride). *Many voices, one world: Communication and society today and tomorrow*. Paris: UNESCO.

Masterman, L. (1980). *Teaching about television*. London and Basingstoke: Macmillan.

Mattelart, A., & Piemme, J.M. (1980). New means of communication: New questions for the Left. *Media, Culture & Society, 2*(4), 321-338.

Mattelart, A., & Siegelaub, S. (Eds.). (1979). *Communication and class struggle: 1. Capitalism, imperialism*. New York: International General, Paris: IMMRC.

Mayo, P. (1999). *Gramsci, Freire and adult education: Possibilities for transformative action*. London, New York: Zed.

McQuail, D. (Ed.). (1972). *Sociology of mass communications*. Harmondsworth: Penguin.

McQuail, D. (1987). *Mass communication theory: An introduction*. London; Thousand Oaks, CA; New Delhi: Sage.

Miller, D., & Slater, D. (2000). *The internet: An ethnographic approach.* Oxford: Berg.

Morley, D. (1980). *The nationwide audience.* London: British Film Institute.

Negt, O., & Kluge, A. (1972). *Öffentlichkeit und Erfahrung: Zur Organisationsanalyse von bürgerlicher und proletarischer Öffentlichkeit.* Frankfurt/M.: Suhrkamp.

Negt, O., & Kluge, A. (1993). *The public sphere and experience: Toward an analysis of the bourgeois and proletarian public sphere* (Trans. P. Labanyi, J.O. Daniel, & A. Oksiloff). Minneapolis: University of Minnesota Press.

O'Connor, A. (Ed.). (2004). *Community radio in Bolivia. The miners' radio stations.* Lewiston, NY: Edwin Mellen.

Peirano, L. (1993). The villa El Salvador people's communication centre. In P. M. Lewis (Ed.), *Alternative media* (pp. 97-106). Paris: UNESCO.

Postgate, R., Lewis, P.M., & Southgate, W.A. (1979). *Low cost communication systems for educational and development purposes in Third World countries.* Paris: UNESCO with Intermediate Technology Development Group, London.

Radway, J. (1984). *Reading the romance.* Chapel Hill: University of North Carolina Press.

Reyes Velásquez, J. (1993). Alterative radio: Access participation and solidarity. In P. M. Lewis (Ed.), *Alternative media* (pp. 87-96). Paris: UNESCO.

Rodriguez, C. (2001). *Fissures in the mediascape.* Cresskill, NJ: Hampton Press.

Servaes, J. (1999). *Communication for development. One world, multiple cultures.* Cresskill, NJ: Hampton Press.

Silverstone, R. (1999). *Why study the media?* London: Sage.

Thompson, E.P. (1963). *The making of the English working class.* London: Gollancz.

Thompson, E.P. (1980). *Writing by candlelight.* Whitstable, Kent: Merlin.

Tower, C. (2005). "Arajo efemu": Local FM radio and the socio-technical system of communications in Koutiala, Mali. *The Radio Journal, 3*(1), pp. 7-20.

Traber, M., & Nordenstreng, K. (1992). *Few voices, many worlds.* London: World Association for Christian Communication.

Williams, R. (1965). *The long revolution.* London: Penguin.

Williams, R. (1974). *Television: Technology and cultural form.* Glasgow: Fontana/Collins.

Young, M., & Willmott, P. (1957). *Family and kinship in East London.* London: Routledge and Kegan Paul.

3

Action-oriented Media Pedagogy: Theory and Practice

Traudel Günnel

Since the early 1970s media—analog or digital—have become an indisputable part of modern life. They are, according to Theunert and Eggert, "integrated into social life. Fulfilling various individual and social functions, their use is imbedded in daily routine and they contribute significantly to the way people orient themselves subjectively and develop ideas about their own identities and lives" (2003, p. 3). This understanding of media is inherent in the activities that took place in the EU projects *Creating Community Voices (CCV)* and *Digital Dialogues (DD)* aimed at facilitating access to media for people of all social groups and helping them to receive and use media in different life situations, but also to create media in a self-directed way, as well as to develop a critical attitude towards media.

In terms of media education this means that the pedagogic principle underlying activities, workshops, and training was based on encouraging active and self-directed participation in media. This encouragement was aimed especially at those sections of the population who, given the tendency towards a "digital divide" within society (see Kubicek, 2002[1]; Winterhoff-Spurk, 1999), have limited access to the broad range of possibilities for media use and creativity. Here the concept of action-oriented media pedagogy[2] offers an important contribution to the formation of theory and practice in media education and it has proved relevant for most of the activities discussed in this book.

In this chapter, then, I first introduce the theory and practice of action-oriented media pedagogy and apply the ideas in contexts that are, respectively, concerned with media politics, communication theory, and theory of adult education. Next, I discuss the theory of action-oriented media pedagogy with regard to individual activities pursued within the *Creating Community Voices* and *Digital Dialogues* projects (illustrated in Chapters 4 to 8); in conclusion, I take a closer look at theory formation.

THEORETICAL BACKGROUND

Action-oriented media pedagogy (AOMP) has been established in its theoretical, methodological, and practical dimensions by, among others, Schorb (1995), Baacke (1996), and Schell (1999). It was developed as a separate discipline within media education in the context of the debate over an "emancipatory" approach in education theory during the 1970s, of which some facets and influences are taken up in this chapter. By the 1980s, according to media theorists Jürgen Hüther and Bernd Schorb, AOMP was generally recognized as an accepted approach. It is concerned with "democratizing the structure of communication, . . . as well as in using media as a means toward behavioral change and development of perceptive abilities through active and self-directed handling of media" (Hüther, Schorb, & Brehm-Klotz, 1997, p. 244). According to Baacke (1997), key concepts of AOMP include communication competence, media competence, social environment, everyday life, and conscious, competent action.[3]

This perspective on media education places the human being as a self-responsible agent or social subject at the center of its pedagogical efforts and research interests. In this respect AOMP differs from "normative" and "technological" approaches.

Normative media pedagogy, characterized also as "protective" pedagogy, concentrates on establishing standards and on developing preventive measures to shield recipients from ethically or morally objectionable media content.[4] This approach is based on the skeptical view of media taken especially in the postwar period by many educators wishing to distance themselves from the manipulative power of media under Hitler's regime (see Hüther, 2004). Even today, skepticism towards media plays a role in protective approaches, as in recent discussion on whether depictions of violence in film and television tend to reduce young people's inhibitions and encourage imitation, and on whether such media productions should be prohibited.

Technological approaches within media education are concerned mainly with the optimal use of media for teaching and learning. They mostly focus from a functionalist standpoint on economic and technological advantages, tending to structure the process of education with reference to, and assuming, the primacy of technological options. The current trend towards teaching and learning based on computer and internet use shows a certain affinity to the ideas and key concepts of the technological approach in education. At the same time, discussion on teaching and learning arrangements that support learners' self-determination has its broadly diffused theoretical anchoring in the "constructivist" theory of learning (explained below in the context of adult education) and shows a certain affinity to the principles of AOMP, encouraging self-directed learning and regarding learners as responsible subjects.

In contrast to normative and technological positions, action-oriented media pedagogy sees itself as a facet of emancipatory education (Schell, 1999). The starting point is that any individual, on the basis of his or her life experience and social relationships, is fundamentally able to act in a critical, reflective, creative, and effective way within the social context. Media being a part of this context, human beings can neither be seen as passive victims overwhelmed by them, nor ought they to adapt or surrender to the technological dictates of the media. On the contrary, action-oriented media pedagogy emphasizes the self-responsibility and sovereignty of individuals, who work actively with the media's messages and who potentially can use or create media in order to articulate their interests.

The paradigm shift that took place within media education theory with the arrival of action-oriented media pedagogy is closely connected to changes occurring simultaneously in the politics of media and within communication science and adult education, both areas relevant to action-oriented media pedagogy.

Media Politics

Media education discourse in Germany was directly or indirectly influenced in the 1970s by the political movement of alternative media that were supposed to be managed and used by those with no other access to self-determined media production, and by the debate on setting up "open channels" in the former Federal Republic (FRG).[5]

The so-called "alternative movement" fought for spaces granting more social freedom, autonomous structures and control in life and media (self-run businesses, self-determined media, independent cultural centers, etc.). In the 1970s in the FRG, apart from the radical press and free video laboratories, the first 'free radios' were founded (see Chapter 2). Despite prosecutions due to their illegality, they tried to broadcast radio programs regularly that gave special priority to information otherwise suppressed and to the authentic statements of individuals—unedited, often live, and unconstrained by journalistic interviewing conventions. Stamm (1988, p. 133f) considers one central characteristic of the alternative movement to be its "experientially oriented public production," which does not cut off individual, direct experience (see Negt & Kluge, 1972, p. 20ff and p. 57ff; 1993, p. 3ff and p. 27ff) but instead considers it a major point of reference for left-wing politics. By way of self-definition, media projects and cooperatives (newspapers, groups producing videos, free radios) saw themselves as serving a "counter" public forum (e.g., Grieger, Kollert, & Barnay, 1987; ID-Archiv, 1989; Jarren, 1983) characterized by critical public discussion carried on in autonomous media, "contrary to the public forum as it presents itself today, contrary to the media determined by capitalist or state control" (Stamm, 1988, p. 134).

Whereas the student movement at the end of the 1960s[6] had emphasized theoretical criticism of the established mass media, media criticism now became practice-oriented. The new free radio stations, for example, referred to the tradition of workers' radio clubs that, in 1925, had claimed the right to run autonomous radio stations in Germany (Dahl, 1983), to Brecht's radio theory of 1932, in which he urged that radio "should be converted from a distribution system to a communication system" (Brecht, 1983, p. 169), and to statements of Hans Magnus Enzensberger in his essay *Constituents for a Theory of Media*. Distinguishing between "repressive" and "emancipatory" use of media, Enzensberger invites the "new left" to overcome its "hostility toward media," to use the stimulating power of electronic media for its own purposes, and to develop collective forms of production (1972, p. 99-100).

Enzensberger's optimism—about media as fundamentally egalitarian in their structure and capable of circulating emancipatory or even revolutionary messages—later gave way to a more critical view, not only for Enzensberger himself.[7] Vogel (1991, p. 123) points out that, in Enzensberger's theoretical *Constituents*, the struggle over "effective possibilities of distribution" is ignored. Baudrillard (1978) and Wenzel and Treutle (1993) criticize Enzensberger's unreflective recourse to a simplifying theory of communication, based on the technical model developed by Shannon and Weaver (1949). The latter regarded the communication process as a one-way affair, with a communicator or transmitter directing a message to a recipient. In contrast, reception studies and the constructivist approach argue, as do cybernetic and system theory, that real

people in their daily contact with others have entirely different communicative habits. They experience communication as interactive relation
on various levels. More recently, communication has been represented
as a highly complex social system, characterized by reflexive structures,
selectivity of perception, and differentiations (Luhmann, 1986; Merten,
1991; Watzlawick, Beavin, & Jackson, 1990).

Quite apart from this surely legitimate criticism of Enzensberger's
Constituents, his statements at the end of the 1970s definitely contributed to the support of a developing, socially critical and autonomous
media practice. His plea for an actively creative, emancipatory use of
media stimulated sociopolitically active groups in the German-speaking
world to found independent, so-called "alternative media." From then on,
not only the FRG, as previously noted, but also many Western European
countries witnessed the appearance of an independent press, video, and
radio projects[8] organized and financed by their producers and users.
Free radios in Germany fought for their model of local, self-determined,
noncommercial, socially conscious radio. They succeeded to the point
that today part—albeit, a small part—of the radio frequency spectrum is
available to noncommercial stations (see Günnel, 2001a). Their main
interest still lies in offering a critical alternative to established media and
in providing access to broad sectors of the population, allowing them to
produce programming themselves for which they are accountable.

Open Channels: A Media Education Implant

Another development in the 1970s, arising from discussion among
media experts and politicians about the introduction of "new media" in
the FRG, was the establishment of so-called "open channels." As distinct from the free radios—the result of socially critical movements "from
below"—the open channels in the FRG were implemented "from above."
They were "important for tactical political reasons" and took place "in the
context of political and legal debate about the licensing of private radio
and television applicants" (Jarren, Grothe, & Müller, 1994, p. 10).

The official objective of those who campaigned for open channels
was to support plurality of opinion and to create a space for local communication open to populations groups normally left out of communication processes (Longolius, 1990). The idea was to adapt, for Germany,
the model of "public access" (see Chapter 2) practiced for years in the
United States—the citizen's right, guaranteed by law, to broadcast programs, free of advertising, on local networks (Winterhoff-Spurk,
Heidinger, & Schwab, 1992).

The organizational structure of open channels, as existing in several
German states, differs from that of free radios. In many cases it is linked

directly to state media authorities, or very closely associated with them. The main emphasis is on media training, granting interested individuals the opportunity to learn and apply production techniques. Often, "space available" determines the programming, rather than a collective process of decision making or an ongoing discussion of social development or journalistic standards. Of late, however, some tendencies toward more reliable and structured radio programming within a number of open channels can be observed.

Communication Theory

In parallel with these political trends and policy initiatives, German communication theory, as elsewhere, moved in a direction that gave support to action-oriented media pedagogy with its orientation towards subjects and real-life situations and its aim of supporting media competence, independence, and emancipation of individuals. Reception theory, with its emphasis on the role played by the consumer of media products in the production of meaning, provided further support for this trend (see Blumler & Katz, 1974; Günnel 2003; McCombs & Shaw, 1972; Teichert, 1973). In particular, what have been called the "extended" approaches in communication theory (Baacke, 1989; Renckstorf, 1989) were part of a move away from traditional approaches that cling to a "communicator-oriented, intentional point of view" (Kübler, 1989, p. 47) and towards a view of people's relationship with media as part of their social relations, embedded in social interaction and not to be seen independently from social constellations. Given the orientation toward individuals and real-life situations, AOMP and its objectives correspond largely to the extended approaches within communication theory. At the center of AOMP's pedagogical and scientific approach stands the human being, seen as a responsible subject, willing to express him- or herself, actively using and creating media, and in communication with his or her social surroundings.

Theory of Adult Education

In adult education, too, a number of ideas have come increasingly to the fore that show parallels to the enlarged approaches of communication research and action-oriented media pedagogy. These are the constructivist direction (Arnold & Siebert, 1999; Kösel, 1995), the project method (Frey, 1993; Gudjons, 1991) and the approaches of self-organized learning (Derichs-Kunstmann et al., 1998; Greif & Kurtz, 1996). Learning situations should respect the learners' differing needs and interpretations and should aim at self-determination and self-organization; they also should bring everyday life into the learning process (here, there are parallels to the pedagogic approach of Paulo Freire, 1977, discussed in Chapter 2). Constructivist adult education assumes that learning has to be regarded as a self-organized "construction process" carried out by the learners; not imposed by others or induced intentionally through teaching. In this view, pedagogic interventions can have diverse effects on learners, therefore educational processes are characterized by their difficulty to plan, by ambivalence, by "contingency." to use Siebert's (2000) phrase. Representatives of constructivist theory emphasize, however, that this does not suggest reducing teachers' responsibility for the learning process, but rather moving toward a new understanding of plurality (Arnold & Siebert, 1999, p. 147).

Certainly constructivist adult education has had positive aspects: it questions the certainties and fantasies of adult educators about the rightness of their interventions in the educational process and puts the focus on individual responsibility in adult learning. But it contradicts itself at the level of pedagogic practice whenever it attempts to exclude intentional and normative determinants. As Faulstich observed (1998, p. 12), new learning always challenges participants to go beyond the framework initially available to them. It is essential to recognize that learning processes occur in an active mode lying between autonomous learning and teachers' guidance. Arnold and Siebert (1999, p. 120f), themselves proponents of constructivist adult education, consider that the constructivist theory of knowledge, concentrating as it does on the cognitive and rational principle of viability, is an insufficient base on which to build didactic decisions. They refer to the danger of neglecting structural injustice and relations of power, and consider it necessary to bring into educational work an ethical orientation that reflects the morality and legality of the consequences of action; and they refer to the classical educational ideals of the enlightenment. In this they come close to approaches that are critical of the constructivist educational stance, according to Klafki (1994), whose educational aim—emancipation—is shared both at the individual and the social level by action-oriented media pedagogy.

ACTION-ORIENTED MEDIA PEDAGOGY AT WORK[9]

When planning a learning scheme, action-oriented media pedagogy depends on what I call "activating media work," which is based on the method of learning by action. The development of communicative competence can be considered an essential condition for self-responsible and independent dealing with media (Baacke, 1973; Habermas, 1971).

Referring to Baacke's statements, Theunert defines it as "the ability to engage in communication which is self-determined and reflected" (1987, p. 200). Communicative competence in this sense includes competence in speech and action. It places the individual in a position to understand communication structures and conditions, to participate in social communication, and to establish symmetrical communication.

Mead's (1934) interaction theory proposed that human learning processes arise from interaction among individuals and with their surrounding environment. From this starting point, action-oriented media pedagogy draws on the method of learning through action (Dewey, 1916). In this method, the learning process is planned so that students actively and creatively consider how to deal with their social reality, to work at the solution of problems independently and communally, and to use their knowledge in molding their environment—nowadays this includes the "virtual reality" of computers and the internet. This means that individuals acquire media competence—understood as competence in perception, reflection, usage, action, and structuring[10]—in organized and creative relations with media, characterized by Schell (1999) as action-oriented media pedagogy. In order to respect the individual as well as the collective interest of those involved and to encourage the communicative and reflexive process, active media engagement is planned as teamwork.

According to Schorb (1995), the fundamental premise of active media engagement is to incorporate the interests, experiences, and requirements of the target group and to structure the training steps in such a way that the trainees create media products autonomously and independently as part of a group process. Skills employed may require use of media for expressing their own interests and for developing their own forms of expression (see Baum, 1997; Schell, 1999). Keeping these concerns in mind, Schorb (1995) suggests the following aspects of action-oriented media pedagogy, which should be realized through active media training.

Extension of perception and reflection skills. By making their own media programs, participants work on specific topics, applying dramaturgical and technical effects, and, in communication with others, consider the different possibilities and their consequences, thus learning to understand a situation by means of the media.

Extension of production skills. In the process of making their own media products, participants discover and develop skills and knowledge regarding subject matter, and technical, creative, and structural processes.

Extension of communication skills. By creating media products, participants learn to use specific expressions and to consider their meaning and thereby broaden their ability to express themselves. At the same time, they are communicating about their media products, exchanging views, developing criteria relevant to the content and structure, and are, from this basis, in a position to critically analyze other media products.

Acquisition of self-confidence in different social situations. In the process of producing media material, participants learn how to act in different roles, such as conducting interviews with prominent personalities, and to reflect on such experiences with other members of the team.

As mentioned at the start of this chapter, the workshops and courses within *Creating Community Voices* and *Digital Dialogues* were planned to support active and self-determined participation in media, especially involving underprivileged social groups in an attempt to counter the tendency towards a "digital divide" in society. In what manner did the CCV and DD activities attempt to realize the principles of AOMP? And vice versa: was AOMP helpful and relevant for planning and conducting the projects in terms of the envisaged objectives? Here, I will compare the premises of action-oriented media pedagogy outlined above with what actually happened in the two projects, with special reference to teaching and learning aspects. This will assist a review of the projects themselves with a view to the possibility of transferring their results to future, similarly structured initiatives.

Requirements for Teaching

Teaching using the action-oriented media pedagogy approach should

- be based upon and refer to the learners' real-life situation
- take a learner-centered approach
- be structured so as to activate and involve the participants and support learning through action
- be product-oriented

These aspects, here listed separately, in reality cannot be sharply distinguished, but on the other hand do make it possible to shed light on the basic ideas of action-oriented media pedagogy. In the following paragraphs, I discuss applications of some of these principles.

Relating to the Learners' Real-life Situation

One central aim of the project activities was to address those who have limited or no access to active and self-determined use of media, and to facilitate their productive participation. A number of studies (see Fichtner, Günnel, & Weber, 2001; Günnel, 2003; Merz, 1998; Winterhoff-

Spurk, 1999) show that the existence of open-access community media is not sufficient to involve interested groups in the population. At least in those European countries where the projects took place, there is a contradiction between the aims of community media and what actually happens. Noncommercial local radio and open-access community media deal democratically with all interested citizens, regardless of their sociocultural status, gender, age, or nationality. The aim is to help them produce and broadcast radio programs by themselves, create websites and put them on the net, and generally to communicate by using media, but at the same time to assume a critical position towards media contents and structures.[11]

But up to now the reality of community media does not at all correspond to the desired aim of allowing people to participate on equal terms in radio and media productions. The relatively few empirical studies on open channels and noncommercial community radio are unanimous in showing that certain social groups, such as young people and employees without secondary education, senior citizens, male and female foreigners, and women remain underrepresented even in open-access radios (see Jarren et al., 1994; Merz, 1998; Pätzold, 1987; Rager, 1999).

On the other hand it seems overly hasty to conclude on the basis of the present user profile of community media that only a certain limited sector of the population have an interest in expressing themselves through their own productions in radio or on the internet. As shown by more recent studies (Fichtner et al., 2001; Günnel, 2003), access barriers do exist for certain population groups even in open-access media. Social and gender-specific mechanisms of selection operate also in community media and thus defeat their objectives and contradict their self-image.

The *CCV* and *DD* target groups specially addressed were those often unable to take advantage of open-access community media—women (*Project Powerful Voices*, UK), senior citizens (*Tandem Training*, Austria), young people without school exam qualifications (*Soundnezz* and *Soundcheck*, Germany), working people (Digital editing, Germany and Finland), refugees (Community Radio Training for Refugees and Asylum Seekers, UK), homeless persons (Austria), inhabitants of rural areas (Autobiography: Thought and action, Italy, and live broadcasting, Germany).

It is scarcely imaginable that under normal circumstances these target groups would have the opportunity to create radio programs or Web sites. Lacking any knowledge of the production side of media, group members are often timid or reserved. They experience mass media as structurally disconnected from themselves, the content being far removed from what really matters in their everyday lives (Günnel, 2001b).

It was, therefore, of importance for the project that individual educational courses were thematically and situationally linked to the experiences, interests, requirements, and premises of the respective target group.[12]

Each activity within *CCV* and *DD* began with the media trainers' planning, and later running, the courses and workshops deemed necessary to get close to the target group's life situations, and getting to know the trainees and their everyday lives. The *Powerful Voices* project in Sunderland UK, which trained women in community radio production, is an example of this (Baxter, 2000).

Through contact with organizations or institutions that could be possible collaborators, the trainers obtained background information for their work with the target group (women in underprivileged living conditions, female immigrants). In successive exercises a number of issues were addressed. At the outset, it was important for the trainers to understand the possible reasons for shyness or reluctance of the women to participate in their workshop. This made it possible to create a supportive atmosphere, encouraging the women to try out the unfamiliar work of media production (see Chapter 4) and overcome their perception of radio technology as strange and difficult to handle (Eble, 2002, p. 180).

Depending on the specific conditions and requirements of the course participants, "becoming involved in the life situations of the target group" can have different meanings. In the context of the *CCV* and *DD* projects, this involved, for example:

- holding the workshops at the location of a partner organization, thus enabling participants to benefit from their familiar environment (Sunderland refugees and asylum seekers project)
- treating topics the target group is attracted to (e.g., in Vienna, "young and old" or "travel"—themes that were suggested by the senior citizens)
- accommodating a group's wish to express itself: in the *Soundcheck* project in Freiburg, this meant helping them to produce and publish their own music
- collaborating closely with the target groups' self-help organizations, planning and running a training course together. Thus in Vienna, following the model of *Tandem Training* developed there[13] (see Chapter 4), radio experts cooperated with representatives of a senior citizens' organization called Senior Plus, with the city Department for Culture, and with Augustin, an organization of homeless persons. In northern England, "a lot of time was spent working in partnership with Sunderland Refugees and Asylum Seeker support Network (SRASSN) to look at the best way of working with refugees and asylum seekers" (Mitchell, Donaldson, & Baxter, 2003, p. 6).

Existing structures, habits, and preferences of potential partners differ greatly, and learning about them is the first step toward successful cooperation. In radio training at the Staudinger comprehensive school in Freiburg, the trainers reported:

> Establishing contact with schools was most successful in cases where teachers who were individually approached recognized Soundnezz (the interactive internet platform for sound) as an enrichment for their class and were prepared to modify their customary teaching schedule. The fact that this proved most successful with a sixth-grade class at Staudinger probably has to do with the relatively open curriculum of the school. The topic of radio and the production of radio clips is very well suited for instruction in schools. (Günnel & Klug, 2003, pp. 14-15)

Becoming involved with the target group's everyday experiences means to respect and take the participants' problems into account, the roles they assign themselves, and the constraints to which they are exposed (CCV, 2000, p. 26). But it also means showing the participants perspectives and possibilities that result from *not* acquiescing to these constraints, but of overcoming them at least in part and of gaining new practical and critical competencies in accordance with the aims of action-oriented media pedagogy.

A Learner-centered Approach

Action-oriented media pedagogy gives particular attention to the individual starting point, desires, and needs of participants in workshops and training courses. The trainers in the project involving mothers and daughters (see Chapter 5) describe their idea as follows:

> Our workshops in the field of media pedagogy are what we call "resource-oriented". This means that each participant's situation is taken into account—their previous background, their social and creative potential, and their individual interests determine the shape of the course. Thus the project has a broad base, it is flexible and can adapt to the experiential world of the participants. It supports them in achieving a confident and competent relationship to the media, which play such an essential role in their everyday lives. (Schumacher, Kunz, & Freund, 2003, pp. 5-6)

Perceiving trainees as autonomous subjects with their own personal strengths and weaknesses presupposes course concepts that make individual development possible, based on differentiation and giving explicit support to self-organized learning on the part of trainees. Self-organization[14] is essential because one "doesn't learn what one is 'told' to learn, but what appears relevant, meaningful, and possible to absorb" (Siebert, 2000, p. 19).

Orientation toward individuals means involving social dimensions. Thus, the focus lies on the interactive and communicative activities of the participants, in all their complexity. "Attempting to dissociate communication and subjectivity would be tantamount to ignoring their temporal and social context, and their contingency" (Kübler, 1989, p. 54). The *Tandem Training* pursued in Vienna and the media training for refugees and asylum seekers offered in Sunderland based their approaches on this insight.

Action Orientation

The insistence that media education be oriented toward practical action is based on the conviction that in creating their own media products, people develop their skills and knowledge on a technical, creative, and content level and at the same time strengthen their self-confidence and their autonomy. Moreover, what emerged as fundamental within *CCV* and *DD* was not waiting for interested people to come to radio or internet workshops on their own initiative, but rather approaching the target groups, kindling their interest, and activating them.

Within *CCV* and *DD*, action-oriented procedure as a didactic principle was applied with target groups that formerly, for various reasons, had had little opportunity for media activity. Participation in media workshops and the chance to create their own media products open up new perspectives, as observed by Klaus Lutz, director of the Parabol media center in Nürnberg, Germany.

> Particularly for young people who are at odds with the educational system, the media provide a good opportunity for self-expression. . . . Youngsters frustrated in the academic context often savor the satisfaction of successfully completing a complex creative process. For example, the production of a video film enables them to articulate thoughts, wishes and dreams in a form closely related to their life situation. (Lutz, 2003, pp. 12-13)

Lutz's remarks ring true for other media and groups addressed in *CCV* and *DD* as well. In *Soundcheck* (see Chapter 8), young bands expressed "their own independent and dynamic subculture" in and through the music they themselves produced—an activity in which "creativity, emotions, and the process of forming an identity all come togeth-

er" (Eble & Heinzel, 2003, p. 2). According to Lutz, media training is successful when it is able to stimulate the participants' motivation "to develop their own ideas and to realize them autonomously. The creative act is
manifest in the products. . . . The experience of having created something independently leaves an enduring impression" (Lutz, 2003, p. 10).
Lutz also mentions the significant fact that participants in such workshops acquire vocationally useful qualifications along the way—for
example, digital skills. That professional qualifications can result from
practical experience of media was shown by Lewis in a survey of volunteers working in community radio in different countries (1994, p. 32). For
members of disadvantaged groups involved in the *CCV* and *DD* projects,
this aspect of the pedagogical approach has proved to be of considerable importance.

At first glance, the action-oriented approach seems to be quite
straightforward and easily implemented in media training, but it should
not be misunderstood as an invitation simply to "let the participants do
what they want." As mentioned earlier, action orientation is realized within several different fields of tension: the development of the individual
(subject orientation) ever against interaction and communication among
participants; orientation towards a product attaining a certain level of
quality versus the focus on learning and the creative process; division of
labor in accord with the talents of individual participants as opposed to
the overall enhancement of experience and perceptive ability as a means
of supporting independence and emancipation.

Pöyskö and Hagen reflect on such fields of tension in their handbook
Training in Tandem as they discuss the distribution of tasks within a
group:

> Assigning production tasks: is it the aim of the project that each par-
> ticipant learn specific techniques and work steps, or is a division of
> labor possible? "Everyone goes through all work steps" serves, in
> terms of media pedagogy, to give each participant insight into the
> entire process of production. Dividing labor, on the other hand, is
> generally more efficient. If separate tasks are to be done by different
> people, personal preferences must be taken into account. This rein-
> forces their strong points, but precludes the possibility that they
> might surprise themselves—by succeeding at an activity they would
> normally not even attempt. (Pöyskö & Hagen, 2000, p. 28)

The pedagogic principle of action orientation requires trainers to support
independent work on the part of the participants while not steering or
influencing them too much. The trainers involved with mothers and
daughters getting to know the internet make these recommendations:

Participants should receive as much input as they need; however, once they have the necessary knowledge, trainers should step back and let the girls work on their own. The trainer must have the ability to support the girls in their own efforts to attain independence, often fulfilling a function as coordinator and mediator. She encourages the girls to find their own solutions and calls in other participants before becoming active herself as a problem solver. (Schumacher et al., 2003, p. 7)

Product Orientation

"If one reduces the learning dimension of a media project to the social process among participants, half of the potential of a practical media project is lost. The desire to see an end result of the project triggers motivation and interest in new areas of learning" (Lutz, 2003, p. 14). Publishing their media productions contributes in a decisive way to the empowerment of target groups who have left school early and/or are socially underprivileged. For the young musicians in the *Soundcheck* project, for example, the presentation of their own songs on a Web site and in live performance boosted their self-confidence: their first venture outside of the basement rehearsal room.

Whenever media productions created by participants in media projects or workshops are made public, they gain journalistic relevance and are no longer seen as exercises performed tentatively in a sheltered situation. The interests and opinions of the participants, the topics and content important to them, and the way they are expressed become audible/visible and thus part of public discourse—as, for example, in the case of an antiracism campaign and world music show produced by refugees and asylum seekers and broadcast on the student radio station in Sunderland.

It is not always easy to find public space, physically or on the air or the net, for productions, especially when they don't conform to mainstream norms. Community radio stations and media centers do provide the opportunity to publish outside the mainstream and in the public sphere, but are not widespread in most countries.

The idea of producing and publishing their own media products even proves stimulating and motivating for groups with little technical background. The mother and daughter project in Freiburg took advantage of this effect:

Since women and girls are more interested in content than in technical aspects and tend to see the computer as a tool, acquiring com-

> puter skills is easier for them when placed in the context of media productions . . . . The courses are planned in such a way that at the end of each course, one or more productions—e.g., audio reports, text collages and homepages—are completed and incorporated in a presentation. (Schumacher et al., 2003, p. 6)

The prospect of publishing their workshop production normally encourages participants to identify more fully with it and to work at higher levels of motivation and concentration. This contributes to a successful learning process. When publishing is a real option, the whole group has to think about the audience: who will be listening to their radio programs or visiting their Web sites? Discussing whether and for whom the chosen topics might be of interest, what priorities should apply to content, and how it should be presented to the audience—all this will encourage critical reflection on the planned project and, ultimately, a more discerning view of media products in general (see Lutz, 2003). Overall, we can conclude from the results of the *CCV* and *DD* projects that participants creating media productions for publication were able to gain confidence in their own potential, and that new possibilities and perspectives were opened up to them.

CRITICAL ASPECTS OF THEORY AND PRACTICE

Although action-oriented media pedagogy and its practical principles provided a suitable basis for the *CCV* and *DD* projects, some critical comments can be made on AOMP theory.

Involvement with Target Groups Requires Specification

Action-oriented media pedagogy claims to get involved with the life circumstances of the target group and with the group itself as a way of attracting, motivating, and involving people. What might this "getting involved with life circumstances of the target group" look like, apart from the basic readiness of the teachers involved: what kind of approach and concepts will be appropriate? There do exist descriptions of several practical projects (see Baacke, Kornblum, Lauffer, Mikos, & Thiele, 1999), but no systematic, well-founded theoretical explanations of AOMP theory. The participation of the chosen target group is often taken for granted.

Experience gathered in these European projects suggests that so-called "socially underprivileged" groups require a particular pedagogical approach if they are to be reached. Often media trainers live in a completely different context, lacking any contact with the target group, and they don't speak their "language". This can create obstacles to the development of a media project. The *Tandem Training* idea, referred to above and described in a practical context in Chapter 4, is one way to overcome such barriers.

Action Orientation in the Context of Divergent Interests

AOMP tends to neglect the relation between its own pedagogic premises and proceedings and the shifting requirements of the economy with regard to qualifications. New developments in work organization have necessitated changes in learning processes and arrangements in vocational training within companies and firms, and these refer to action orientation as an essential characteristic (Krieger, 2000). The principle of action orientation has also become a leading category of pedagogical practice in schools as well as in nonvocational training since the middle of the 1990s (Wedel, 2004).

The obvious correspondence between industrial demands for higher qualifications and the aims of learner-centered and action-oriented approaches in education suggests two different conclusions. It could be interpreted as an advantage of the education system, in school and in extracurricular activities, that it is the best preparation for future demands in work situations. On the other hand this "best" preparation risks being functionalized as ideal adaptation to the demands of the economy, omitting critical reflection on the question of who reaps the benefit of self-determination, independence, and the ability to work in a team.

The fact that AOMP is itself a social construct has not been sufficiently reflected within its theoretical position as a whole. Yet an understanding that this is the case represents an important part of the work media educations projects need to do if they are to avoid being indirectly and unintentionally instrumentalized. It follows that action-oriented media pedagogy should address, in its theory and practice, the societal conflicts of interest associated with the concept of "action orientation." This would include taking on such topics during training courses, and thus encouraging participants toward emancipation by reflecting on social mechanisms.

Media Access: A Reason to Intervene in Media Politics?

It can be observed that those applying the action-oriented approach to media education normally take a socially critical standpoint, emphasizing the influence of economic interests in the media sector, the development of media and communication structures dominated by economic interests, and the media's construction of "reality" (see Baacke, 1997; Schell, 1999; Schorb, 1995). In doing so, their objective is to impart the kind of media competence that goes beyond simple usage and includes the ability to analyze and reflect critically, and to show independence in creating and transforming media products and structures.

Nevertheless, very few published references are to be found that comment on initiatives making the political case for wide media access not contingent on established media structures; for example, noncommercial local radio in Germany. Although one of the aims of action-oriented media pedagogy is to "democratize communication structures" (Hüther et al., 1997, p. 244), although the diffusion of workshop productions made by participants opens the possibility for them to participate in social discourse and contributes to their empowerment (see Lutz, 2003, p. 14), and although publication opportunities in established media are very limited, the protagonists of action-oriented media pedagogy hardly intervene in the debates surrounding media politics and media access. There is a danger in media education to regard the presentation of workshop outcomes among friends, family, or in the school assembly as a reward in itself, thereby ignoring the need to create publishing options and communication space open to a wider audience. Only when the improvement of media access is emphasized in training is it possible for participants to grasp this political dimension and its relevance—a *sine qua non* if media criticism is to be practical and not only theoretical.

Contribution to the Further Development of Theory

From the *CCV* and *DD* media projects we can gain certain clues on how the weaknesses in the theoretical development of action-oriented media pedagogy might be overcome. Three points suggest themselves. First, the concept of *Tandem Training* supplements the theory of action-oriented media pedagogy, making up for deficits in relating to the living circumstances of participants groups and orienting teaching toward their needs. Second, by not limiting action orientation to media production in the sheltered context of courses and workshops, but always relating it to the social and cultural needs of participants in a real-life context, the projects make societal issues and contradictions a part of the educational message (issues such as gender, racism, and their consequences). Thirdly, the creation of publishing options opens the door for participation in social discourse as conveyed by media, and this is part of the idea of media projects. Publication can be achieved even against initial resistance of radio stations, encouraging communication on issues beyond the project itself—as shown (see Chapter 6) by the example of an antiracism campaign in Sunderland, UK.

NOTES

1. See also: UNESCO World Summit on the Information Society, Document WSIS/PC-3/DT/6 Rev 1-3, Geneva 14.11.2003, Draft Declaration of Principles: *Building the Information Society—a Global Challenge in the New Millennium*, and the explanations in Chapter 5.
2. Action-oriented media pedagogy, though not a phrase common in English academic discourse, is a convenient *portmanteau* that encapsulates the idea of a critical approach to media arrived at through practice, and a tradition of learning through self-directed action [Eds.].
3 Pöttinger (1997, p. 32 f.) points out that, although action-oriented approaches of media pedagogy rest on common key concepts, individual projects set their own emphasis—for example, on journalistic or aesthetic aspects, or on the life experience of participants.
4. Among the representatives of normative approaches in media education are Gerbner (1981) and, in the context of the recent discussion on media inciting young people to violence, Glogauer (1991).
5. For overall discussion of the situation in FRG, see Günnel (2003, pp. 32-42).
6. The students' standard frame of reference for debates on mass media was the book *Dialectics of Enlightenment* by Max Horkheimer and Theodor W. Adorno (1971), according to which the cultural industry is directed towards disabling, manipulating, and deceiving consumers.
7. In his later statements, as in the essay "The Total Void: The Zero-medium, or Why All the Complaints About Television are Unfounded," first published in 1988, Enzensberger departs from his ideas of 1970, according to which electronic media could be used in a productive, emancipatory way. He contends that television, a "zero-medium" lacks any capability to convey content. The idea that electronic media and especially television were destined "to transport form and content, 'programs,' [is an] illusion. . . . The audience's secret weapon—the dreaded zapping—is the death of film. . . . The spectator is totally conscious that he is not dealing with a means of communication, but a means to deny communication" (1997, p. 153 f).
8. See ID-Archiv (1989) and, on radio, Kleinsteuber (1991). Compare also the discussion of community media in Chapter 2.
9. The following passage is a revised version of "Action-Oriented Media Education" (Günnel, 2002, pp. 337-338).
10. This definition follows those of action-oriented approaches in media pedagogy based on an extended concept of competence (as

opposed, e.g., to that of Moser, 2000), regarding options to be creative and initiative as a part of "media competence."

11. The situation is different in third world countries where radio is used either in political opposition to dictatorships or for education. See also Chapter 2.

12. On situated learning see also: Mandl, Gruber, & Renkl (2002) and Chapter 5.

13. In this method, training schemes for an individual target group are initiated, planned, and carried out systematically and on a equal-rights basis by a "tandem" consisting of (at least) one media trainer and someone associated with the group in question. This ensures that the needs and interests, as well as the problems and reservations, of the group will be recognized, and that potential participants will be addressed a context familiar to them.

14. Faulstich (1998, p. 11) justifies the need for self-organization of the learning process from two different points of view: "pedagogically: persons in their own contexts and of their own initiative are likely to learn more, more effectively and more profoundly".

REFERENCES

Arnold, R., & Siebert, H. (1999). *Konstruktivistische Erwachsenenbildung* (3rd rev. ed.). Baltmannsweiler: Schneider Verlag Hohengehren.

Baacke, D. (1973). *Kommunikation und Kompetenz*. München: Juventa.

Baacke, D. (1989). Sozialökologie und Kommunikationsforschung. In D. Baacke & H.D. Kübler (Eds.), *Qualitative Medienforschung* (pp. 87-134). Tübingen: Max Niemeyer Verlag.

Baacke, D. (1996). Medienkompetenz als Netzwerk. *Medien Praktisch, 2*(78), 4-10.

Baacke, D. (1997). *Medienpädagogik*. Tübingen: Max Niemeyer Verlag.

Baacke, D., Kornblum, S., Lauffer, J., Mikos, L., & Thiele, G.A. (Eds.). (1999). *Handbuch Medien: Medienkompetenz. Modelle und Projekte*. Bonn: Bundeszentrale für politische Bildung.

Baudrillard, J. (1978). *Kool Killer oder Der Aufstand der Zeichen*. Berlin: Merve.

Baum, H. (1997). Ältere Menschen machen Fernsehen. In U. Kamp (Ed.), *Handbuch Medien: Offene Kanäle* (pp. 119-123). Bonn: Bundeszentrale für politische Bildung.

Baxter, A. (2000). *Practical ideas for involving women in radio*. Sheffield: AMARC-Europe (brochure). http://www.digital-dialogues.de.

Blumler, J.G., & Katz, E. (Eds.). (1974). *The uses of mass communication: Current perspectives on gratifications research*. London: Sage.

Brecht, B. (1983). Radio as a means of communication: A talk on the function of radio (Trans. S. L. Hood). In A. Mattelart & S. Siegelaub (Eds.), *Communication and class struggle* (Vol. 2, pp.169-171). New York & Bagnolet, France: International General, International Mass Media Research Centre.

(CCV). (2000). *Creating community voices: Community radio and new technologies for socially disadvantaged groups*. Socrates Programme for Adult Education. Final Report. Sheffield: AMARC-Europe (brochure). http://www.digital-dialogues.de.

Dahl, P. (1983). *Radio: Sozialgeschichte des Rundfunks für Sender und Empfänger*. Reinbek: Rowohlt.

Derichs-Kunstmann, K., Faulstich, P., Wittpoth, J., & Tippelt, R. (Eds.). (1998). *Selbstorganisiertes Lernen als Problem der Erwachsenenbildung*. Frankfurt/M: Deutsches Institut für Erwachsenenbildung.

Dewey, J. (1916). *Democracy and education*. New York: Macmillan.

Eble, K. (2002). Handlungsorientierte Medienarbeit mit Mädchen und Jungen. In H. Epp (Ed.), *Gender Studies und Fachwissenschaften* (pp. 179-183). Freiburg: Fillibach.

Eble, K., & Heinzel, M. (2003). *Soundcheck*. Freiburg: Wissenschaftliches Institut des Jugendhilfswerks (brochure). http://www.digital-dialogues.de.

Enzensberger, H.M. (1972). Constituents of a theory of the media (Trans. S. Hood). In D. McQuail (Ed.), *Sociology of mass communication* (pp. 99-116). London: Penguin.

Enzensberger, H.M. (1997). Das Nullmedium oder Warum alle Klagen über das Fernsehen gegenstandslos sind (1988). In P. Glotz (Ed.), *Baukasten zu einer Theorie der Medien: Kritische Diskurse zur Pressefreiheit / Hans Magnus Enzensberger* (pp. 145-157). München: Fischer.

Faulstich, P. (1998). "Selbstorganisiertes Lernen" als Impuls für die Erwachsenenbildung. In K. Derichs-Kunstmann et al. (Eds.), *Selbstorganisiertes Lernen als Problem der Erwachsenenbildung* (pp. 10-13). Frankfurt/M: Deutsches Institut für Erwachsenenbildung.

Fichtner, J., Günnel, T., & Weber, S. (2001). *Handlungsorientierte Medienpädagogik im Bürgerradio*. München: Kopaed.

Freire, P. (1977). *Pädagogik der Unterdrückten*. Reinbek: Rowohlt.

Frey, K. (1993). *Die Projektmethode*. Weinheim, Basel: Beltz.

Gerbner, G. (1981). Die "anstrengende Welt" des Vielsehers. In H. Oeller (Ed.), *Der Vielseher: Herausforderung für Fernsehforschung und Gesellschaft* (pp. 16-42). München: Saur.

Glogauer, W. (1991). *Kriminalisierung von Kindern und Jugendlichen durch Medien*. Baden-Baden: Nomos.

Greif, S., & Kurtz, H.J. (Eds.). (1996). *Handbuch selbstorganisiertes Lernen*. Göttingen: Verlag für Angewandte Psychologie.

Grieger, K., Kollert, U., & Barnay, M. (1987). *Zum Beispiel Radio Dreyeckland: Wie Freies Radio gemacht wird*. Freiburg: Dreisam.

Gudjons, H. (1991). Was ist Projektunterricht? In J. Bastian & H. Gudjons (Eds.), *Das Projektbuch* (pp. 14-27). Hamburg: Bergmann und Helbig.

Günnel, T. (2001a). Rundfunklandschaft im strukturellen Wandel. In J. Fichtner, T. Günnel, & S. Weber (Eds.), *Handlungsorientierte Medienpädagogik im Bürgerradio* (pp. 17-50). München: Kopaed.

Günnel, T. (2001b). Bedarf vorhanden: Das Interesse von ArbeitnehmerInnen an eigenen Radioproduktionen. In J. Fichtner, T. Günnel, & S. Weber (Eds.), *Handlungsorientierte Medienpädagogik im Bürgerradio* (pp. 51-67). München: Kopaed.

Günnel, T. (2002). Counteracting the gap: Strategies for teaching media competence. In N. Jankowski & O. Prehn (Eds.), *Community media in the information age: Perspectives and prospects* (pp. 333-358). Cresskill, NJ: Hampton Press.

Günnel, T. (2003). *Experiment Arbeitsweltredaktion: Bürgerradio im Kontext von Medienpolitik, Kommunikationswissenschaften und Pädagogik*. München: Kopaed.

Günnel, T., & Klug, A. (2003): *Soundnezz.de: Handbook on creating an interactive sound website and on training its users*. Freiburg: Pädagogische Hochschule (brochure). http://www.digital-dialogues.de.

Habermas, J. (1971). Vorbereitende Bemerkungen zu einer Theorie der kommunikativen Kompetenz. In J. Habermas & N. Luhmann (Eds.), *Theorie der Gesellschaft oder Soziotechnologie* (pp. 101-141). Frankfurt/M: Suhrkamp.

Horkheimer, M., & Adorno, T.W. (1971). *Dialektik der Aufklärung: Philosophische Fragmente*. Gesammelte Schriften 3. Frankfurt/M: Suhrkamp.

Hüther, J. (2004). Pioniere und Wegbereiter der Medienpädagogik. *merz, medien und erziehung: zeitschrift für medienpädagogik, 48*(1), 52-57.

Hüther, J., Schorb, B., & Brehm-Klotz, C. (Eds.). (1997). *Grundbegriffe Medienpädagogik*. München: Kopaed.

ID-Archiv. (1989). *Verzeichnis der alternativMedien*. Amsterdam: Diederich, Hoffmann, Schindowski.

Jarren, O. (Ed.). (1983). *Stadtteilzeitung und lokale Kommunikation*. München: Saur.

Jarren, O., Grothe, T., & Müller, R. (1994). *Bürgermedium offener Kanal*. Berlin: Vistas.

Klafki, W. (1994). *Neue Studien zur Bildungstheorie und Didaktik*. Weinheim, Basel: Beltz.

Kleinsteuber, H.J. (Ed.). (1991). *Radio—das unterschätzte Medium. Erfahrungen mit nichtkommerziellen Lokalstationen in 15 Staaten*. Berlin: Vistas.

Kösel, E. (1995). *Die Modellierung von Lernwelten: Ein Handbuch zur subjektiven Didaktik.* Elztal-Dallau: Laub.

Krieger, C.G. (2000). *Schritt für Schritt zur Freiarbeit: Praktische Anregungen zu Organisation und Arrangement von Lernzirkel, Lernmosaik und Freiarbeit für Einsteiger.* Baltmannsweiler: Schneider Verlag Hohengehren.

Kubicek, H. (2002). Vor einer "digitalen Spaltung"? Chancengleicher Zugang zu den Neuen Medien als gesellschafts- und wirtschaftspolitische Herausforderung. In E. Baacke, S. Frech & G. Ruprecht (Eds.), *Virtuelle (Lern)Welten: Herausforderungen für die politische Bildung* (pp. 53-65). Schwalbach/Taunus: Wochenschau.

Kübler, H.D. (1989). Medienforschung zwischen Stagnation und Innovation. In D. Baacke & H.D. Kübler (Eds.), *Qualitative Medienforschung* (pp. 7-71). Tübingen: Max Niemeyer.

Lewis, P.M. (1994). *Community radio: Employment trends and training needs. Report of a transnational survey.* Sheffield: AMARC-Europe.

Longolius, C. (1990). Offene Kanäle. Rundfunk der Dritten Art. *Journalist, 5,* 10-13.

Luhmann, N. (1984). *Soziale Systeme: Grundriss einer allgemeinen Theorie.* Frankfurt/M: Suhrkamp.

Lutz, K. (2003). Medienpädagogik auf allen Kanälen. *merz, medien und erziehung, zeitschrift für medienpädagogik, 47*(4), 9-17.

Mandl, H., Gruber, H., & Renkl, A. (2002). Situiertes Lernen in mutlimedialen Lernumgebunger. In L. J. Issing & P. Klimsa (Eds.), *Information und Lernen mit Multimedia* (pp. 139-148). Weinheim: Beltz.

McCombs, M.E., & Shaw, D.L. (1972). The agenda-setting function of mass media. *Public Opinion Quarterly, 36,* 176-187.

Mead, G.H. (1934). *Mind, self and society.* Chicago: University of Chicago.

Merten, K. (1991). Allmacht oder Ohnmacht der Medien? Erklärungsmuster der Medienwirkungsforschung. In Deutsches Institut für Fernstudien an der Universität Tübingen (Ed.), *Funkkolleg Medien und Kommunikation. Studienbrief 9* (pp. 38-73). Weinheim, Basel: Beltz.

Merz, P. (1998). Bürgerfunk zwischen Anspruch und Wirklichkeit. *Media Perspektiven, 5,* 250-258.

Mitchell, C., Donaldson, J., & Baxter, A. (2003). *Handbook on community radio training for refugees and asylum seekers.* Sunderland: University of Sunderland (brochure). http://www.digital-dialogues.de.

Moser, H. (2000). *Einführung in die Medienpädagogik: Aufwachsen im Medienzeitalter.* Opladen: Leske und Budrich.

Negt, O., & Kluge, A. (1972). *Öffentlichkeit und Erfahrung: Zur Organisationsanalyse von bürgerlicher und proletarischer Öffentlichkeit.* Frankfurt/M.: Suhrkamp.

Negt, O., & Kluge, A. (1993). *The public sphere and experience: Toward an analysis of the bourgeois and proletarian public sphere* (Trans. P. Labanyi, J.O. Daniel, & A. Oksiloff). Minneapolis: University of Minnesota.

Pätzold, U. (1987). *Der Offene Kanal im Kabelpilotprojekt Dortmund.* Begleitforschung des Landes Nordrhein-Westfalen zum Kabelpilotprojekt Dortmund, Vol. 3. Düsseldorf.

Pöttinger, I. (1997). *Lernziel Medienkompetenz. Theoretische und praktische Evaluation anhand eines Hörspielprojekts.* München: Kopaed.

Pöyskö, M., & Hagen, F. (2000): *Training in a tandem.* Sheffield: AMARC-Europe. http://www.digital-dialogues.de.

Rager, G. (1999). Rechtzeitig Erfolgskriterien benennen. In R. Behnisch, T. Muntschik, & P. Wundenberg (Eds.), *Macht—Markt—Meinungsfreiheit. Bürgerfunk als dritte Säule in der Rundfunklandschaft?* (pp. 66-77). Rehburg-Loccum: Evangelische Akademie Loccum.

Renckstorf, K. (1989). Mediennutzung als soziales Handeln. In M. Kaase & W. Schulz (Eds.), *Massenkommunikation: Theorien, Methoden, Befunde. Sonderheft 30 der Kölner Zeitschrift für Soziologie und Sozialpsychologie,* 314-336.

Schell, F. (1999). *Aktive Medienarbeit mit Jugendlichen: Theorie und Praxis.* München: Kopaed.

Schorb, B. (1995). *Medienalltag und Handeln.* Opladen: Leske und Budrich.

Schumacher, I., Kunz, C., & Freund, M. (2003). *Mothers and daughters learn about the internet.* Freiburg: Wissenschaftliches Institut des Jugendhilfswerks (brochure). http://www.digital-dialogues.de.

Shannon, C., & Weaver, W. (1949). *The mathematical theory of communication.* Urbana: University of Illinois.

Siebert, H. (2000). *Didaktisches Handeln in der Erwachsenenbildung* (2nd ed.). Neuwied: Luchterhand.

Stamm, K.H. (1988). *Alternative Öffentlichkeit. Die Erfahrungsproduktion neuer sozialer Bewegungen.* Frankfurt/M: Campus.

Teichert, W. (1973). "Fernsehen" als soziales Handeln (II). *Rundfunk und Fernsehen, 21*(4), 367-374.

Theunert, H. (1987). *Gewalt in den Medien—Gewalt in der Realität. Gesellschaftliche Zusammenhänge und pädagogisches Handeln.* Opladen: Leske und Budrich.

Theunert, H., & Eggert, S. (2003). Virtuelle Lebenswelten: Annäherung an neue Dimensionen des Medienhandelns. *merz, medien und erziehung, zeitschrift für medienpädagogik, 47*(5), 3-13.

Vogel, A. (1991). *Rundfunk für alle.* Berlin: Vistas.

Watzlawick, P., Beavin, J.H., & Jackson, D.D. (1990). *Menschliche Kommunikation.* Bern: Hans Huber.

Wedel, M. (2004). ITG in den neuen Bildungsplänen der weiterführenden allgemeinbildenden Schulen. *Landesmedienzentrum Baden-Württemberg: Analog und digital, 1,* 4-6.

Wenzel, U., & Treutle, S. (1993). *Zugangsmöglichkeiten bei einem Freien Radio. Das Gruppenradio bei Radio Dreyeckland 1989-1991.* Freiburg (unpublished paper).

Winterhoff-Spurk, P. (1999). Von der Wissenskluft zur medialen Klassengesellschaft? Möglichkeiten und Grenzen individueller Rezeptionsautonomie. In U. Bischoff (Ed.), *Mediengesellschaft— Neue "Klassengesellschaft"?* (pp. 28-43). Bielefeld: Gesellschaft für Medienpädagogik und Kommunikationskultur (GMK).

Winterhoff-Spurk, P., Heidinger, V., & Schwab, F. (1992). *Der Offene Kanal in Deutschland.* Wiesbaden: Deutscher Universitäts-Verlag.

Section II

Examples of Praxis

4

Organic Radio: The Role of Social Partnerships in Creating Community Voices

Caroline Mitchell

Ann Baxter

Format radio and fast food have much in common. Both are products of a commercially oriented world whose goal is profit. Both are partly responsive to and partly help create the appetites and lifestyle they serve. The management and production of music format radio, in particular, often automated at the "point of sale," impose precise definitions of core audiences that leave little room for innovation either in programming or in the development of new relationships between audience and station.

In contrast—to press home the metaphor—community radio is an "organic" creation, home-grown, a product of the interaction between a station and its cultural environment, the fruit of a process of cultivation and training that takes time and is not aimed at profit. Historically, community radio stations have aimed to "give a voice to the voiceless" and the last decade has seen an increased recognition of the importance of participatory radio training and teaching methods in realizing this. It is the purpose of this chapter to discuss and illustrate the importance and relevance of different radio training approaches and partnerships in the context of the development of digital media related to radio. We focus on over a decade of developments in training, in the radio medium, and in the application of relevant digital technologies and techniques since the early 1990s, and we draw in particular on our experience in working with women in this area.

There are many ways, using community-based practice, of developing partnerships among educators, community broadcasters, and groups that are underrepresented in the media. Our praxis in developing partnerships through radio has been influenced by work in progressive adult education, feminist media studies, and participatory approaches to radio training.

We will draw on case studies of training and community education work in radio stations and on community radio training courses in Austria (in conjunction with the community radio station *Orange 94.0* in Vienna), in Finland (at *Radio Robin Hood* in Turku) and in the United Kingdom in Sunderland (with the University's community education and media departments and in conjunction with the student radio station, *Utopia FM*), and in Bradford (with *Bradford Community Broadcasting*). This work has primarily been carried out with groups of older people, trade union representatives, and women—all groups that would otherwise not find their way into a radio station.

There are a number of theoretical contexts and perspectives that have influenced our work, in particular in the area of community education, participatory radio, feminist media studies, and education. We shall be making connections between perspectives that are pertinent to participatory education, community development and community media. Central to this work are issues relating to the relationship between adult education and training, power, and identity.

PARTICIPATORY EDUCATION

> Learning is best when it is participatory, proactive, communal, collaborative and given over to constructing meanings rather than receiving them. (Bruner, 1996, p. 48)

In the quotation above the word "learning" could be substituted by "community radio." There are many parallels between the participatory approach to education and the principles of community radio. As Peter Lewis states earlier in this volume, much media education and development work has been influenced by the liberation ideology and empowerment philosophies of the Brazilian educator, Paulo Freire. Freire believed in involving all participants of an educational project in decision making and planning (Freire, 1970, 1973). Kidd cites bell hooks' Freirean solution to raising consciousness and activating change: "to define and describe identity within an analysis of the concrete material reality, offering strategies of politicization and transformation" (Kidd, 1994, p. 186). However, Kidd also notes that hooks and other feminists have argued that we need to acknowledge the limitations of some of Freire's work in terms of gender, class, and race:

> . . . there was little recognition of power differences among the oppressed, particularly between women and men, and between facilitators and participants. hooks suggests that the consciousness raising that does not link individual identity to an analysis of the complex structures of domination can and has allowed white middle class feminists to participate in "misnaming," disregarding race and class, and their own privileged relationship to exploitation. (Kidd, 1994, p. 186)

Learning for Citizenship

Johnston and Coare acknowledge the broad context of citizenship and adult education initiatives.

> . . . the term adult learning is used specifically to acknowledge and reflect the proliferation and diversity of contemporary forms and sites of learning within a complex global world. This does not mean seeing learning mainly in psychological and individualistic terms, rather it reflects the need to give a wider social and cultural context to a range of adult learning opportunities. . . . The framework is about learning for citizenship. (2003, p. 185)

The rapid pace of global economic change brings with it a seemingly irrefutable argument for lifelong learning, most prominently in its role of developing human capital (Johnston, 2003, p. 4).

Barriers to Learning

Most trainees involved in the projects connected to our case studies had experienced barriers to learning and participating in traditional educational settings. Hasan and Tuijnman cite an analytical framework to explain the influences on the decisions of "under-educated adults" to participate, or not, in adult education programs. Three types of barriers are figured: situational, institutional, and dispositional:

> Situational barriers capture the influence of circumstances that include questions about the economy, culture, family structures and

technology. Behind the institutional barriers lie issues concerning the cost of education, programme availability, the availability of pathways, supply technology, marketing etc. Finally, dispositional barriers cover dispositions, values and attitudes to education and learning . . . [which] do not lie outside the realm of policy intervention . . . [and] are shaped by life experiences, by the situational and institutional factors cited above. (Hasan & Tuijnman, 1997, p. 241)

In the United Kingdom, the *Fryer Report* underlined how difficult it is to provide the conditions for adult education work in different settings with underrepresented groups and the importance of it being recognized, supported, and properly funded as part of a national strategy for "lifelong learning."

Learners from these groups typically face obstacles created by shortage of the money for course fees and related expenses, lack of confidence, lack of outreach provision, lack of tutorial support when studying, lack of personal support and courses organized at inappropriate times and inaccessible place. (Fryer, 1997, p. 22)

This importance has been recognized in the various community radio courses involved in the *Creating Community Voices* and *Digital Dialogues* projects, where expenses were allowed for travel, childcare, and living allowances. Such a strategy should provide:

a context which allows learning to begin from people's own experience, a stimulus because motivation is increased, and a focus for wider political understanding, and finally a resource in which to challenge continued social exclusion, especially that which is too often encouraged through the institutions of education themselves. (Fryer, 1997, p. 56)

Women and Adult Education

The barriers experienced by working class women and other marginalized groups have been of particular concern in our work (see NIACE, 1991). McGivney (1993, 2002) has looked at the reasons that prevent women from taking up training activities of any sort, not just those associated with radio. Time and money are often given as "socially acceptable" reasons—but these may hide a range of other reasons. Valdivielso Gomez, in her analysis of a six-country survey of adult education provision and take-up, noted how "hidden discrimination" affected women:

because they operate within the symbolic cultural world where the images of the "good mother" and "family responsibilities" are stereo-typed. . . . Many women are struggling with these contradictions, and this may explain why they tend in all countries to look for the kind of course that aims at enhancing self-confidence and autonomy, developing different patterns of social participation, and opening new ways of solving communication problems. (1997, pp. 223-224)

It is true that the feminism of the late 1960s and 1970s was the "product of a white middle-class higher-educated Western women" whose "claim to speak for 'women' was to marginalize and silence many other groups" such as black women, Third World women and working-class women (Cockburn & Ormrod, 1993, p. 5). Yet despite this, it is also true that feminist demands can take the credit for some improvement in legislation and public opinion, while an increasing range of strong female role models (amplified by media representations) has encouraged attitudes that may disown their feminist origins but are indirectly affected by them (CCV, 1999, p. 23).

PARTICIPATORY RESEARCH PRAXIS

Exploring how the research dimension of our work connects to and impacts on radio training and the trainees themselves has been considered in terms of extending the participatory aims of the media education and training through the research itself—the partnership organization may become a stakeholder in the research. Our work is not as sustained an ethnography within an adult education setting as that described by Beverly Skeggs (1994). However her work has helped us to shed light on the continuing dialogic relationship between trainers and trainees and between different partnership organizations and, importantly, among women in women's radio groups where there is discussion of a range of issues and discourses about training, the position of women as audiences for, "subjects" of, and producers of radio.

We support the aims of Participatory Action Research (PAR), which "seeks to develop action or praxis (purposeful knowledge/change) by working with groups to achieve certain aims or outcomes generally agreed by all" (O'Neill et al., 2004, p. 205). This links to how we were trying to develop a praxis of participatory radio training that raised issues, awareness and confidence as well as having particular aims relating to practical media training. O'Neill has described her work with refugees and community photography (2001, p. 188), which uses innovative ways of consulting, life-history work and partnerships within local communities to achieve specific social changes. We have aimed to use community radio to help people to create and produce their own media narratives, challenging radio "images" of themselves, countering negative stereotypes, and producing positive representations of their lives. This could also be defined as the *performative* role of women who participate in community radio. Community radio offers space where women may creatively "reconstruct, play, subvert, produce and contest themselves as gendered subjects" (Mitchell & O'Shea, 1999, p. 19).

Participatory Communication for Development

Gumucio Dagron has identified the characteristics that differentiate participatory communication from more traditional development communications strategies in furthering social changes. Again, it is useful to consider how partnerships develop within different communications paradigms and how active the partners are in defining what communication takes place. We have set these out in full, as they specifically relate to each of the case studies outlined later in this chapter:

- *Horizontal vs. Vertical.* People as dynamic actors, actively participating in the process of social change and in control of the communication tools and contents, rather than people perceived as passive receivers of information and behavioral instructions while others make decisions on their lives.
- *Process vs. Campaign.* People taking in hand their own future through a process of dialogue and democratic participation in planning communication activities, rather than expensive unsustainable top-down campaigns that help to mobilize but not to build a capacity to respond from the community level to the needs of change.
- *Long-term vs. Short-term.* Communication and development in general is conceived as a long-term process that needs time to be appropriated by the people, rather than short-term planning, which is seldom sensitive to the cultural environment and mostly concerned with showing "results" for evaluations external to the community.
- *Collective vs. Individual.* Urban or rural communities acting collectively in the interest of the majority, preventing the risk of losing power to a few, rather than people targeted individually, detached from their community and from the communal forms of decision making.
- *With vs. For.* Researching, designing, and disseminating messages with participation, rather than designing, pre-testing, launching, and evaluating messages that were conceived for the community and remain external to it.

- *Specific vs. Massive.* The communication process adapted to each community or social group in terms of content, language, culture, and media, rather than the tendency to use the same techniques, the same media, and the same messages in diverse cultural settings and for different sectors of society.
- *People's Needs vs. Donors' Musts.* Community-based dialogue and communication tools to help identify, define, and discriminate between the felt needs and the real needs, rather than donor-driven communication initiatives based on donor needs (family planning, for example).
- *Ownership vs. Access.* A communication process that is owned by the people to provide equal opportunities to the community, rather than access that is conditioned by social, political, or religious factors.
- *Consciousness vs. Persuasion.* A process of raising consciousness and deep understanding about social reality, problems, and solutions, rather than persuasion for short-term behavioral changes that are only sustainable with continuous campaigns. (Gumucio Dagron, 2001, pp. 34-35)

Feminist Approaches to Media and Radio

With powerful voices women can organize, train, take collective action and ultimately build communities and a society based on self-determination. (Stuart & Bery, 1996, p. 211)

Some of the key partnerships in community radio training work are influenced by the legacy of feminist education and media work. Changing the roles and representations of women in the media is a central aim behind feminist media theory and feminist media production projects (see Hobson, 1980; Karpf, 1980; Steiner, 1992; Tuchman, 1979). Within community radio, gender inequalities in terms of representation in paid jobs and voluntary work have persisted: an AMARC–Europe survey showed that only 22 percent of full-time paid staff were women and that only a third of the volunteers were women (Lewis, 1994). Women's radio within community radio has been surveyed by Jallov (1996) and Mitchell (1998, 2002). There are various models of women's radio activity that include women making programs in mixed-gender stations and setting up women's radio stations and news agencies.

Riaño has outlined a typology of women, participation, and communication that compares development communication, participatory communication, and alternative communication with feminist communication where women are the producers of meaning. She understands the goals of feminist communication as: "naming oppressions of race, class, gender, sexual orientation, and disability; negotiat[ing] fair representation and equity of access, construct[ing] individual and collective identities, produc[ing] alternative meanings" (Riaño, 1994, pp. 6-7).

She defines participation as developing a sense of community with collective ownership of experiences/identities, and empowerment as "coming to voice" and "breaking the silence." The overall message defines feminist communication as "exchange [in which a] network of meanings" is created (Riaño, 1994, p. 7). Mitchell describes radio training for women as "holistic":

> integrating training and programme making, and employing community development methods to reach women who might not have been aware of community radio. An essential approach was to make courses, and the whole idea of radio, accessible and welcoming to women. The demystification of technology related to programme making and confidence building were core aims of all courses. Development of a feminist ethic of communication in the context of women's radio included strategies developed by the women's movement. Parallels might be drawn between a holistic approach to training and feminist consciousness-raising. For instance, they shared the objectives of instilling confidence and re-skilling women, raising women's awareness of women's oppression; working collectively, developing women's creativity and networking. (Mitchell, 1998, p. 80)

In a recent report evaluating community radio stations in the United Kingdom, Everitt notes that community radio training within inner city regeneration projects incorporates personal development, assertiveness, anger management, and team building (Everitt, 2003, p. 12).

Courses can also be considered to be holistic in the sense that they approach an understanding of radio in its broadest sense—combining study of radio history and aspects of radio studies (for instance, academic approaches to understanding audience behavior, learning about broadcasting organizations, exploring meanings of radio texts/programs) with the acquisition of skills in the area of production and program making, IT skills, and women's studies. In some cases, courses addressed setting up and aspects of radio station management.

Mitchell has proposed defining characteristics of feminist radio practice. These can be taken into account when developing training for women (cf. Mitchell, 2002):

Training is "women-centered" so that there are specific and specialist programming, community development, and training initiatives designed with the target group of women in mind. New technology training, whether it is in word processing, internet use, or digital editing and mixing, requires particular attention. It is now fairly well established that when teaching of practical skills takes place in a mixed gender group, men can dominate the equipment and teacher's time. Even within adult education settings, radio training courses tend to ignore the many constraints on women who might be considering taking part in radio. The gender of the tutor, the timing and setting of the course, the (in)convenience for women who have childcare or family responsibilities: all need to be taken into account when setting up a radio training project for women.

Working in partnership with organizations is crucial if radio training is to reach a wide range of women from different class, social, and cultural backgrounds.

Collective action including collective forms of work as part of feminist practice has been characterized as a method favored by women in media projects in the 1970s and 1980s (Steiner, 1992). In recent women's community radio projects (e.g., *Fem FM*; see Mitchell, 2003) collectivism has remained in the spirit of women's radio projects and stations, but exigencies of time have often meant that program makers and station managers have worked in more traditional roles or hierarchies to get the job done. Collective working within women's training programs and radio projects is still an important part of making women feel empowered— although as we shall see from our case studies, not always without problems. The nature of the "midwife" role that a trainer is able to take on here is important in facilitating collective work.

Training through program making is the focus in much of community radio, where the motivation and focus of people's energies is often on-air discourse, working towards a daily, weekly or one-off radio program that might be live or prerecorded. The end product may involve a relatively small commitment, such as conducting and editing a short interview or, at the other end of the continuum, it could be a much more wide-ranging task of working in a team to produce a daily program. This "on the job" focus has many advantages: there is a high motivation factor in completing work for broadcast and getting instant feedback. There are also disadvantages, especially where the trainees lack confidence in themselves and their skills. They may need more time to practice and make mistakes without the pressures of live radio work and deadlines.

Program content based on women's lives helps to motivate and empower participants. Feminist radio practice values the experience of women's lives as a starting point for the program content, "embedded in the local and the 'everyday'" (Mitchell, 2003, p. 100). This can also be the focus of discussion about program content for women's stations and as a starting point for the content of training exercises, that is, when students are learning how to do interviews with one another. There is often a discussion about what is "public" and what is "private"—what is suitable for mass consumption, albeit for an audience who may be expecting a women's perspective on programming. Margaretta D'Arcy, organizer of Radio Pirate Woman in Galway, Ireland, remarks on women's radio discourse that while "each of us remains private, we are public at the same time" (D'Arcy, 1996, p. 3).

Whether or not a station's programs or its radio training courses for women come from a feminist perspective is often a discussion point in itself:

> Women were sensitive to what others would think of their pro-grammes and what was "acceptable" and thereby defining their pro-gramme content through how others will see them. . . . [One station co-ordinator said:] "I think it's a feminist statement—a feminist proj-ect—but then, I don't mind calling myself a feminist. I wouldn't nec-essarily use that word in publicity or talking to groups because of what's happening to the word feminist . . . . They may shy away from the 'f' word because of the ridicule it has attracted, and would see it as being a middle class station." (Mitchell, 2002, p. 99)

CASE STUDIES: COMMUNITY-BASED RADIO COURSES WITH WOMEN

Community based radio courses took place over two periods between 1998-2003, coinciding with the two Socrates-funded projects *Creating Community Voices* and *Digital Dialogues*. In the United Kingdom, fund-ing also came from the European Social Fund for a project called *Permanent Waves*. The overall aim was to involve underrepresented communities in community radio on their own terms. Each case study takes up different aspects of the training partnerships that were devel-oped, including student-centered training and evaluation methods, the importance of program-making as a training tool for community radio, and the setting up of a women's radio station as motivators and foci for women's training. A further example of media work with women and their daughters is described in Chapter 5.

Sunderland, England

The City of Sunderland is located on the banks of the river Wear on the northeast coast of England. Its economic and industrial base has changed enormously over the past quarter century; previously it was the largest shipbuilding town in the world and was also one of the coal min-ing centers in the region. It was devastated by the decline of such indus-tries and still has some of the highest unemployment figures in the country. It has attracted government-backed job creation schemes and foreign investment, particularly in the automotive and call-center industries.

The University of Sunderland has been a partner in a number of local and regional development initiatives that promote regeneration and social inclusion. Particularly relevant to this chapter are joint initiatives between

---

SUNDERLAND, ENGLAND

Partners
Bridge Women's Education and Training Centre and two university departments at the University of Sunderland (School of Arts, Design and Media; Centre for Independent and Combined Programmes)

Focus
Course 1: training women in radio program-making and facilitating their participation in "Women on Wearside," a daily 30-minute women's radio program on the student/community radio station
Course 2: two "taster days" run by women from Course 1, followed by part-time course training women in radio production, live radio skills, IT for radio, creative writing for radio, and station management, leading to setting up a 1-week women's radio station, *Bridge FM*

Participants
Course 1: 12-15 women from a wide range of social backgrounds in Sunderland
Course 2: 15-20 women from Bridge project

Trainers / Tutors
Members of University radio lecturing staff, continuing education development worker, community-based tutors (including students from course 1), specialist tutors for IT

Timing
Course 1: 2-3 days a week for 4 months
Course 2: 2 days a week for 6 months

Locations
University of Sunderland Media Department and Bridge Women's Training Centre

Access / Support
Both sites had facilities on ground floor with wheelchair access, free child care facilities (crèche at Bridge, nursery at University), and transportation. Students received an allowance for expenses. Both sites had radio production and broadcasting facilities.

the Schools of Arts, Design and Media and the Centre for Independent and Combined Programmes (now the School of Education and Lifelong Learning). From 1989-93, the University was a partner in *Wear FM*, a community radio station set up as part of a short-lived nationwide experiment in community radio (see Gray & Lewis, 1992) but taken over by a local commercial station. The radio department at the University has set up a number of initiatives[1] involving projects between broadcasting students and local communities, including unemployed people, school children, women, refugees, and asylum seekers, and has run several short-term student/community licenses since the demise of *Wear FM*.

Overview of Training Approaches

The partnership between the tutors at the University of Sunderland and the Bridge Centre, which has over 20 years' experience in running community-based courses for women, has developed a wide range of approaches to working with women and radio. From the early stages of running radio "taster courses" in different community settings where women meet, to the ambitious project of women at the Bridge Centre running their own radio station, *107—the Bridge*, the team developed a number of approaches that are discussed in the following sections.[2]

"Gender proofing" and the Training Ethos of "Female Friendly" Courses

As outlined in the introductory sections of this chapter, there is now a well-documented body of material about running courses for women in community-based settings and ensuring that they are not alienated from the educational setting and process. This includes making sure that the course is held at a time when the target group of women is available, arranging affordable childcare, locating it in a place that women can get to easily and feel comfortable in, leaving time for informal discussion, and taking a flexible women-centered approach, perhaps including learner-led sessions. At Sunderland, taster courses were first held in women's centers in the area and at Sunderland FC. A football club may not at first seem a "women-friendly space", but it was very popular, due to the strong following Sunderland FC has particularly with younger local women. A tour of the stadium was offered as part of the course.

The course evaluator commented that locating the training day in the Bridge Centre itself meant that the participants were already in a supportive and familiar environment. It ensured ease of transport and access for the local women and also provided a stepping stone: she believed that, having been introduced to the type of training and having experienced the project's approach to learning, the women were more likely to attend the second taster day to be held in the university (CCV, 1999, p. 29).

Holding courses at the university radio workshop and adult computer center was seen as positive in encouraging women to think about the university. One said:

> When I went through the doors of the University for the first time, I felt a combination of adventure and anticipation. For a few years now I have wanted to go into the University to find out what goes on. . . . Being able to tell my friends and family I was involved in a radio station and attending University was sensational. (Bridge Project, 2000, p. 14)

Holistic Approaches to Radio Training

Developing the course in partnership with different university departments and with workers at the Bridge project led to the development of a multifaceted approach to content. There may be a tendency to see radio training as focused mainly on technical and practical skills. These courses, however, combined confidence- and team-building, practical radio and IT skills, program making, media studies, women's studies, and sometimes individual support in literacy, personal problem solving, and career advice. In the later courses, which involved working towards setting up the radio station, a wide range of skills and resources were needed, as this report about the radio station management module shows:

> This was not a formal course—it was more of a meeting, the aim of which was to oversee all practical and logistical arrangements of setting up a radio station. A typical meeting would have included the following topics: What shall we call the station? Who are we broadcasting for? Will we need planning permission for the transmitter? How will we publicize the station? Who is going to inflate the balloons for the station launch? What if it all went wrong? Going through all of these issues could be frustrating, boring, and hilarious but most of all gave the women valuable experience of managing and running their own show. (Baxter & Mitchell, 2002, p. 28)

Approaches to learning digital media production skills are discussed more closely in Chapters 5 and 6. It is, however, worth explaining here how the holistic approach, and particularly the way that confidence was developed in different course components, furthered learning of production skills. A gradual and careful approach was taken when introducing "first-timers" to technical equipment, studios, and broadcasting techniques. One technique, in fact, developed by women who themselves had only recently learned about interviewing, was observed by the external evaluator:

> The use of a microphone but no tape recorder is very interesting, and the decision to do the training in this way was obviously taken after a lot of discussion. It shows great sensitivity and understanding of the anxieties that most people feel about speaking into a microphone, hearing their voice for the first time or being recorded. It is also a reflection of the understanding which the Year 1 women have for the need to pace training and to gradually introduce each new element. (CCV, 1999, p. 30)

Underlying the way many women talked about their experiences in the courses was the importance they felt that confidence played in all parts of their learning, and how this then transferred to other parts of their lives. Instilling this is a part of the work of the Bridge project, and this was also emphasized in the partnership with the Sunderland tutors. This comment came from one of the older women (who was 70), talking about going out live "on air": "I am very proud to have taken part. It was wonderful for me, all the women included me in everything. . . . This course has done a lot for me, giving me so much confidence. I can now join in discussions, instead of just sitting and listening, and I have made some wonderful friends" (Baxter & Mitchell, 2002, p. 28).

The Role of Taster Courses and Community Based Tutors

The taster day was used at several points in the project—tailor-made courses served as a first step for women to try out radio before committing themselves to a longer course and involvement in programming or participation in a women's station. The external evaluator commented:

> The fact that the project used a taster day points to its acknowledgement of the difficulties which exist for many people and particularly women in returning to education after a long absence. It also acknowledges that adults learn through action and reflection, and the structure of the day allowed time for both of these activities by imparting skills, but also by creating a forum for discussion. . . . The sharing of their personal experience by the Year 1 women had many

functions in that it served to encourage the other women, while acknowledging any fears and anxieties which the participants may have around undertaking radio training and the running of a radio station. (CCV, 1999, p. 30)

Enabling women who had some experience of radio from the first radio course in Sunderland to become role models for newcomers was an idea developed as a means of building capacity in the community. As they had been novices themselves until fairly recently, this meant that they could remember their own nervousness about approaching new people and learning experiences. They were involved in designing and running the taster sessions at the Bridge project and became, in effect, community-based tutors working alongside more experienced tutors:

By centrally involving the Year 1 women in the planning and delivery of the training, this in its own way served to demystify "working in radio" which very often is seen as an area of working which is beyond the scope of "ordinary people." In that the Year 1 women are themselves members of the Bridge project, their participation emphasizes the possibility and potential for other members to become involved . . . ; they had a central role in both the planning and delivery of the training. This was further highlighted by the fact that it is the Year 1 women who facilitate the small groups, while the Sunderland staff stand back during this part of the day. (CCV, 1999, p. 29)

The process of being involved in the taster day in itself becomes a reflective experience for the community tutor, helping her to think about her own skills and progress in radio and education. It is generally acknowledged that community tutors do need a great deal of support, for example, in form of team-teaching approaches, mentoring, peer supervision, co-teaching, and formative feedback to inexperienced train-ers—all of which may affect staffing.

Likewise, treating evaluation as participatory and incremental, inte-grated at all stages of courses, is important to being adaptable, flexible, and learner-centered. We pursued this at various stages, informally through discussion between learners and facilitators, and at the end of individual stages through questionnaires.

Training Through Program-making

Starting from and using women's experiences is a powerful teaching tool, as well as a good source of relevant program material. The following analysis from the external observer of one of the sessions underlines this: "Participants draw on their own experience as potential material for programs, and it is an opportunity to encourage them to realize the relevancy and validity of this experience as program material" (CCV, 1999, p. 29).

In the first year of the course, the participants contributed five half-hour live magazine programs, called *Women on Wearside*, which were broadcast as part of a student-run community RSL.[3] In the second year, the course had two groups—more experienced women working on setting up the radio station and newcomers learning about and contributing to programs. Turning ideas into programs for a radio station and setting up a radio station from scratch involves a huge leap in terms of training, and it brings pressure to bear on students, tutors, community center staff, and people involved as volunteers at the radio station. For students accustomed to straightforward practical exercises, this is, arguably, too great a leap. They must adjust to working with real interviewees, meeting tight deadlines, and having to think about the many other tasks involved in putting together a live program, as well as organizing a whole station and its schedules. Women need to find time to work on interviews, edit packages, make jingles, take on technical and editorial responsibility for putting out each program, and deciding on running orders. It takes the course out of the classroom and into the real world. This requires a high level of planning, and the partnerships here need to work smoothly and employ a number of support mechanisms.

Bradford, England

Bradford in the northwest of England is the fourth largest metropolitan area in the United Kingdom and a former center for the wool trade. Like Sunderland, it suffered a significant decline in employment during the last quarter of the 20th century. *Bradford Community Broadcasting* (BCB) has been broadcasting RSLs annually for four-week periods since 1992. Currently, they broadcast with a full-time community radio license, one of the first stations in the country to operate with this status (see Everitt, 2003). The station aims to represent all sectors of the city's population, whose different ethnic communities include Bangladeshi, Punjabi, Afro-Caribbean, Irish, Arabic, Ukrainian, and Italian groups. Recently it has worked with refugee communities, broadcasting programs in minority languages such as Russian and Farsi. As part of an initiative to increase women's representation in the station, particularly in terms of programming, the female manager of the station set up Radio Venus, a women's radio station run by and for women that broadcasts every year around International Women's Day. BCB had already been involved in women's training projects such as *Permanent Waves*[4] and

Women on Line.[5] One of the female volunteers, an Asian health worker, had originally been involved in Radio Venus. She then made links with the Karmand Centre, a large Asian community center, about setting up training for future broadcasts.

The course aimed to involve more Asian women in the station, particularly working in partnership with development and community workers as a way of reaching the wider community. Setting up the course though community workers and basing it at the Karmand Centre (which has childcare facilities and a number of courses for women and girls) was seen as a strategy to help participants. Recruitment efforts, mainly by word-of-mouth, were directed deliberately toward Asian community/ development workers and neighborhood women. However, despite good liaison work by the Asian radio volunteer, turning "contacts" into course participants took much longer than expected. There was also pressure that the course lead to the production of program elements for

---

BRADFORD, ENGLAND

Partners
Karmand Centre and Bradford Community Broadcasting (BCB)

Participants
Two Asian development workers (age 40+), three Asian women in their early 20s who attend the Karmand Centre, a multi-use center for Asian people in a neighborhood of Bradford

Tutor
Female Asian radio volunteer with experience in radio broadcasting and training in a community radio setting

Timing
5 one-and-a-half-hour sessions, followed by studio and production time, held over 5 weeks leading up to 4 one-hour live broadcasts. The course was held in the early afternoon to suit participants with childcare responsibilities.

Location
Split between the Karmand Centre and the studios of Bradford Community Broadcasting

Access /Support
Ground floor access to the centre and to the radio studio. Transport to the studio was arranged for participants if necessary. Childcare on the premises, and the tutor's childcare costs were also funded. One woman spoke limited English and, where necessary, the community worker translated.

broadcast during the next RSL (which took place several months after the course started).

Course Aims and Outline

The explicit intention was to establish regular program input into Radio Venus/BCB, produced by Asian women who were encouraged to build radio skills and broadcasting confidence. Developing an on-air voice, it was hoped, would also make them more confident to participate in education, training, and community activities. The course was outlined in six stages:

- Introduction to radio and different types of programming
- Introduction to interviewing and different topics for the program
- Organizing programs, writing for radio (cue sheets and running orders)
- Introduction to the studio (at BCB)
- Program run-through (additional session seen as necessary after initial planning)
- Broadcast of program on BCB.

Activities and Outcomes

This course started off with an ambitious goal: for an experienced radio trainer/producer to work with a group of young women and community workers over a relatively short time span in order to plan, produce, and broadcast four live radio programs. It is often very difficult to balance enthusiastic aims with the reality of producing a program that meets broadcasting standards (although community radio audiences may not expect the same professional standards applied to mainstream programming). The observer of this course[6] noted the importance for first-time program makers setting modest goals: "Leave plenty of time for planning. It is easy to underestimate the amount of time needed to set up the outreach/development and training that leads to program making. Also, more preparatory time should be allowed before first-time program-makers go on air" (CCV, 1999, p. 33).

In line with a student-focused approach to training and radio program development, the trainers found it important to start with the topics that came from the students and their own interests and perspectives: "The topics discussed as possible content for the program seemed to lie in fairly traditional notions of femininity—dieting, beauty tips and cookery. In the observed session, the development worker tried to steer the conversation about dieting to a 'healthy eating' agenda . . . ; time constraints limited the amount of discussion about broader issues" (CCV, 1999, p. 33).

Evaluating Support for Trainers and Trainees

> The women felt excited by the programs that went well. They were proud of their own individual pieces, but frustrated, even demoralized on the occasions when they were let down by a contributor, and by one of their own number, a development worker who had taken a great deal of control over the content and then not turned up for the program. They took readily to the challenge of live broadcasting: two women "drove" the program after only one session of training, and with some support from the trainer. (CCV, 1999, pp. 31-32)

If one judges by Utreras's definition of three levels of participation—production level, decision-making level, planning level (cited by Peruzzo, 1996, p. 173)—the women were not yet able or willing to take full responsibility at these levels. The Bradford course experience exposed particular areas in which support for trainees and trainees working within the partnership was necessary. In this situation, the trainer was the bridge between the community broadcaster and the community organization (she had experience with both groups' cultural and work agendas). In many ways she was the person on whom the success of the partnership rested. Thus, support needed to be heavily focused on this person, and she received it from several sources—the radio, through the radio station manager, who adopted a team teaching approach, and also from the project evaluator though oral and written feedback. Her potential support from the Karmand Centre was located within the training group itself, and this caused some conflict of interest, as these were active participants in the training and had many other demands on their time. This was also the case for all the women in the group. As the CCV report notes:

> They had not realized till they became involved how much time and commitment research and production required; in many cases this clashed with domestic responsibilities their communities expected them to fulfill. A related point about the status and role of women concerns the development worker whose managers were not supportive of her taking time to contribute to the program and whose absence caused a problem for the others. The trainer commented that the managers might have been more supportive if men had been involved in the broadcast, making the whole project more credible. The women enjoyed the course but felt the trainer should have been more formal, even "bullied" them more. (CCV, 1999, p. 32)

This last comment about the role of the training sums up the precarious balancing act trainers working through and within partnerships experience and underlines how important it is for trainers to be supported through team teaching and/or for them to reserve enough time for regular peer-support sessions. Trainees, particularly first-time broadcasters, need to have achievable goals set for them, and there should be a "safety net" (i.e., support from experienced technicians/producers) when they attempt live broadcasting for the first time.

One of the outcomes of this part of the project, relating directly to digital production, was increased awareness of how greatly working in partnership depends on digital resources being available to participants. So often resources for radio are centralized at the radio station, which is not necessarily easily accessible to all sectors of the community. Although BCB does have satellite studios for work they do in some outlying communities, at the time of the course in the Karmand Centre, portable equipment was taken to the center for the course sessions, and women traveled to the main studios for studio training and broadcasts. Women, and increasingly men, seek a balance between their commitments to domestic responsibilities and the exigencies of the radio station. If, for example, laptops with digital editing software are available, women may be able to work from home at times that suit them better.

The development of this course and the way that BCB is working with Asian trainers, organizations and development workers is evidence of a desire to build a long-term relationship with women in the Asian community on their own terms.

CASE STUDIES: TANDEM TRAINING

The following section describes the development of *Training in a Tandem*, a model based on partnership. The development of the model at an Austrian community radio station is described, as are the advantages and disadvantages of using such a method. This model also has been tested by a community radio in Turku, Finland; the outcomes of this experiment are outlined.

Vienna, Austria

The community radio station *Orange 94.0* is located in Vienna[7] and has been broadcasting since 1988. Over 400 volunteers are involved in programming. With such a large pool of volunteers, training is an important element of the station's work. In 1998, *Orange 94.0* joined the Socrates-funded *Creating Community Voices* project with the aim of developing and testing new radio production training methods.

Anu Pöyskö and Frank Hagen devised an approach that they termed "Training in a Tandem." It describes a training partnership in which radio trainers work hand in hand with trainers from other organizations. Pöyskö and Hagen had observed that although many community radio stations had workshops and training programs for volunteers, these were not always the best solution when trying to increase the diversity of their volunteer cohorts. They decided that they wanted to experiment with new partnership-based approaches to their training methods, incorporating principles of good practice from adult and community education: collective development and sharing of responsibilities; equality in partnership; valuing everyone's experience.

Their idea was to work hand-in-hand with staff from various community-based organizations. Different partners bring different skills and knowledge: the radio workers bring expert knowledge about radio, and

---

VIENNA, AUSTRIA

Partners
Radio Orange 94.0 and three community organizations: Senior Plus, a social network for older people; Büro für Kulturvermittlung, which engages young working class apprentices in a variety of cultural activities; and Augustin, an organization working for and with homeless people

Focus
Course 1: training trainers from the Partner organizations
Courses 2-4: workshops on program making for members of the partner organizations

Participants
Course 1: radio staff and representatives of partner organizations
Courses 2-4: older people; young apprentices; homeless people

Tutors
Staff/volunteers from *Radio Orange 94.0* and from partner organizations

Timing
Varied according to the needs of each partner group: as an example, the Senior Plus cooperation included an initial 2-day workshop for training the trainers, followed by a series of 5 half-day workshops over the course of one month for the older people

Location
Radio Orange 94.0, Senior Plus, Büro für Kulturvermittlung, Augustin

the community partners bring valuable knowledge about issues and needs faced by their particular groups.

> Basically, the tandem concept involves fusing the expertise within the community radio and community organization together into a single unit responsible for the training of target groups in radio program development. The term tandem also implies a dynamic, collective process, which is less pronounced in other terms such as partnership and alliance. (CCV, 1999, p. 7)

In terms of communication, it was important that both parties had background information about one another. For the planning phase it was of critical importance that both partners were fully involved and that the training was seen as a joint project right from the outset.

Central to the whole notion of the tandem model is that radio trainers don't necessarily know all about the needs of different groups. A major innovation was that in the first instance the radio trainers set aside all notions about radio and program making and instead concentrated their efforts on the needs, issues, and aspirations of the group of people with which they were trying to engage. This is very much in the tradition of adult education—starting with the situation and experience of the participant.

Work Stages

The *Tandem Training* model has five distinct phases:

- recruitment of groups
- workshops for trainers
- radio workshops for participants from groups
- reflection by trainers
- documentation of project

Orange 94.0 encountered some difficulties with finding groups who were both willing to plan the project collectively and interested in being actively involved during the radio training workshop. Eventually, three organizations agreed to participate: Senior Plus, a social network for older people; Büro für Kulturvermittlung (Agency for Cultural Coordination), which engages young working-class apprentices in a variety of cultural activities; and Augustin, an organization working for and with homeless people in Vienna. All three organizations were able to commit one of their workers to the whole tandem process—from initial planning, through delivery of training, to final evaluation.

The second stage in the tandem process was "training the trainers." In a 2-day workshop, staff from *Orange 94.0* and from the participating organizations worked together to organize and plan the future shape of the projects. Anu Pöyskö, one of the *Orange 94.0* trainers, observed:

> What you as a trainer think a group needs may not be what is needed at all. Radio trainers, in fact, know the needs of a group even less than others. In such situations it is valuable to be able to work in a team with equal partners, because no matter how much I know about radio, I don't know about the codes and history of a group. (CCV, 1999, p. 7)

An important aim of the workshop was that everyone understand what was expected in terms of roles and responsibilities. Pöyskö noted:

> What we tried to do was to instruct the trainers in the value and purpose of tandem teaching. We also talked about their motivation and our motivation to offer radio for underprivileged target groups. We explained what we think radio training provides participants and why others might want to be involved in this experience. (CCV, 1999, p. 8)

By the end of the workshop each of the tandem's teams had compiled a comprehensive schedule of activities. The third phase of the tandem model was the training sessions for the participants. Each of the three tandems had its own workshop program tailored to its specific needs and interests. After the workshops the tandem trainers team spent time reflecting and evaluating the experience. The final phase of the tandem model was to document the workshop activities and the lessons learned in the overall process.

Evaluation and Recommendations

Pöyskö noted that one of her normal expectations was that the end product of a radio workshop should be a program. This expectation generates tension between the learning process and the goal of producing broadcasting material. Removing the expectation that a program will be the end result helps dissipate that tension.

One of the disadvantages noted was that if one half of the tandem is absent, then the workshop cannot go ahead. As a result of the preparatory workshop and planning, the radio staff began to develop an understanding of each group's characteristics and how to adapt accordingly. For example, the senior citizens group valued the opportunity to socialize and wanted to work at a pace slower than that usual at the radio station. As a consequence, the production schedule was altered to accommodate them.

The important point is to avoid generalizations along lines such as: all groups of older people will be the same, so that in designing radio training for older people it is always necessary to deliver the training at a slower pace. What is essential is to establish a rapport with each individual group and its specific interests, and then negotiate a program that is responsive to its particular situation.

Pöyskö and Hagen made the following general recommendations based on their experience.[8]

- Plan thoroughly. The more difficult the group, the more important it is to plan the overall workshop and the specific activities in as much detail as possible.
- Be selective. Choose tandem partners carefully. Find out things like how much time they have and what other commitments are they bound to.
- Limit workshop size. Teaching in tandem works better when the workshop groups are small. The ratio of trainer/trainee was 1:3. Although this is costly in terms of resources, the results were worth it.
- Remain flexible. It is not necessary to remain committed to producing a program by the end of a workshop. It may be sufficient, for example, simply to explore aspects of program making.
- Be aware of the needs of the group. Always keep in mind the expectations of the group during the training program.

Radio Orange in Vienna found the *Tandem Training* useful, but how translatable are these ideas in practice? As part of the *Creating Community Voices* project another partner, *Radio Robin Hood* in Finland, tested the guidelines developed by the trainers at *Radio Orange*.

Turku, Finland

The community station *Radio Robin Hood*, which began broadcasting in 1990, is based in Turku in southwest Finland. The station is supported by an association of eleven member organizations, one of which is a trade union called Metalli 49. Like *Radio Orange 94.0*, *Radio Robin Hood* has strong links with community groups but wanted to develop these further. "In general, the responsibility for the radio activities of the organizations has rested upon a few individuals. And if they stop, the regular radio broadcasts will also stop"; this is estimation of the trainer in Turku, Riitta Haapakoski (CCV, 2000, p. 63).

The *Radio Robin Hood* staff wanted to apply the *Tandem Training* method with partner organizations, specifically to help increase the involvement of women and migrants at the station. They were also eager to encourage and support individuals from of one of their member organizations, Metalli 49, to play a more active role at the radio station. The three representatives from the target groups came with different prior experiences of *Radio Robin Hood*. One was completely new; another had had some contact; the trade union representative had over ten years' knowledge of the station.

These differences were reflected by the varying expectations of the cooperation partners. The trade unionist's objectives were that the members should feel that the community radio station was a part of their movement, that they should be more involved in maintaining, supporting and running the station and understand that it was likely to have a greater social impact as a result of the increased trade union involve-

---

TURKU, FINLAND

Partners
Radio Robin Hood; Metalli 49, a Finnish Metal Workers' Union; Turku Municipal Employment Agency; Femina Baltica, Baltic-Nordic Women's Network, included nongovernmental organizations, researchers, and decision makers

Course focus
Course 1: training trainers from the partner organizations
Courses 2-4: workshops on program making for members of the partner organizations.

Participants
Course 1: radio trainers and representatives of partner organizations
Courses 2-4: trade union members; migrants; women.

Tutors
Staff/volunteers from Radio Robin Hood and from partner organizations

Timing
Course 1: 2-day workshop
Courses 2-4: 6 hours each

Location
Radio Robin Hood

ment. A women's organization entering the cooperation had other priorities: making community radio more accessible to women's organizations, building women's self-confidence, arranging for more women to be involved in all aspects of community radio, and creating more opportunities for women to influence programming. The third partner, representing the local Employment Agency, had other reasons for getting involved. He wanted to assess what training opportunities there might be for unemployed people interning at the station and to learn about how the radio could be used as a communication tool.

The participants reported that the workshop had involved considerable discussion during which they had gained new information about one another, about their colleagues, about the target groups, and the radio station. The *Tandem Training* package was followed as far as possible, but instances arose where it was modified to fit in with the working practices of *Radio Robin Hood*. The trainer noted:

> First of all we talked about problems and difficulties we had been facing in our work with refugees and immigrants, then we talked about alternatives and solutions . . . fresh ideas from participants really enriched my skills and the way we planned the training course. . . . We spent six hours working and many important contacts arose . . . the main activities were that we followed the (Tandem) package but adapted it to our way of working. (CCV, 2000, p. 76)

Comments from workshop participants included:

> When we exchanged about the problems and then discussed alternatives—it's been very positive. I was with someone from the Employment Office who is dealing on a daily basis with immigrants. It was very interesting to hear from him about his experience with that group.

> . . . you saw the possibilities of this kind of radio—really realized the huge potential that this kind of radio station has. . . . We can really do programs we want, and especially for women.

> I've learned new ways to make radio programs . . . and a thousand new ideas of what I'm going to use in the future.

> . . . discussing the principles of community radio, how it works as a way of communication—not just for any one group or for money— and for the possibility it gives for other trade unions and other groups to have a dialogue together and with the rest of the community. (CCV, 2000, p. 76)

Recommendations

The main improvement suggested was that the training materials could be adapted to reflect *Robin Hood*'s style of working. Another comment was that it would have been beneficial to extend the length of the course to allow more time to get though all of the *Tandem Training* materials. The practical outcome of the workshop for all three tandem pairings was that a course for each target group was planned for the near future.

> I have written down some good fresh ideas which will be very helpful for our training course next week, and definitely it will be important to discuss the motivation of participants and to the problems they are facing in their daily life. . . . I have always tried to get people involved but this is the first time I have had a model of how to do it. (CCV, 2000, p. 76)

From the "training for trainers" workshop, a number of positive outcomes were noted. There was a heightened awareness of *Radio Robin Hood* and its aims and objectives; new ideas were generated on how to work with hard-to-reach groups; three further courses, for young women, migrants, and trade union members, were planned; there was an offer of financial support from the Employment Department for work with migrants. There was evidence of a "multiplier" effect among *Robin Hood* people, trade unions, women's organizations, and immigrants. Links and connections were made that simply would not have occurred so quickly without the tandem training project. It was apparent that the participants were not just learning about their tandem partner, but about the needs of other groups with which they come into contact. Finally, *Radio Robin Hood* workers found that using the tandem method gave renewed life to training approaches they had already used.

CONCLUSIONS

The importance of the continuing relationships of dialogue between all parties in social partnerships—the radio stations, radio trainers, community workers, the community or voluntary organizations, and people involved in such projects—is crucial if the full benefits of such partnerships are to be realized. Examining the experiences of *Radio Orange, Radio Robin Hood, Bradford Community Broadcasting,* and women's radio projects collaborating with the University of Sunderland, we conclude that people's relationships with radio as a tool of development, expression, and creativity can be informed by radical developments in adult education and feminist educational praxis. If community radio wishes to reach a wider range of groups that have been underrepresented or even silenced by mainstream media, then training needs to be planned in such a way that people are not constrained by oppressive time frames imposed by broadcasters or by the lack of technical and financial resources that have helped exclude them from the airwaves in the first place. The boundaries between the traditional roles of tutors and pupils, program-makers and audiences should be treated flexibly. All participants must be able to use their own experience as a starting point for learning and broadcasting.

To return to the metaphor of organic versus "fast food," organic radio takes longer to develop because it entails working up from grassroots up with no quick fixes. The result is ultimately more nutritious and causes less harm to the individual and the environment. Like the organic practice of companion planting, where one plant wards off pests from another and fertilizes the soil naturally, so working in social partnership, where each partner's experience, expertise, and cultural differences are valued, results in more sustainable and diverse radio.

Above all, the experience described here makes it clear that participatory praxis has to be nurtured in developing partnerships. Appropriate community radio training courses have to be designed and programming developed that offer people a chance to realize their identities through radio. Those structuring community radio courses need time to build up trust, confidence, skills, and experience; time, also, to develop support for diverse partners, for the skill bases and resources within specific communities.

Planning time means taking what we call an incremental approach to community radio training, designing gradual steps towards participatory radio. Perhaps several different types of courses taking place through social partnerships over a period of time are better than just one type: taster days, partnership/tandem development courses, feminist-inspired "holistic" approaches to radio and self development, technical and production training, one-to-one support, and courses that train community tutors in order to developing longer-term capacity. The process of training and program making may at times be more important than the end product to be heard over the air.

Taking time to evaluate different aspects of participatory training from a range of perspectives at various stages is also integral to this practice, which values building on experience—even if that experience is, at times, difficult or fractured. In building social partnerships, there are opportunities for breaking down barriers and developing cultural awareness. There seems to be a directly proportional relationship between the extent to which a group is marginalized and the amount of work required to assist that group in making its voice heard. We would like to see more projects using participatory action research techniques, so that the documentation and dissemination of ideas and materials will increase.

In both community radio and adult education, working in partnerships is an established way of reaching groups of individuals who otherwise might not consider participating. Partnerships are important to establish a lasting sense of "ownership" of radio programs and stations, and ultimately a greater sense of individual and collective responsibility for developing community radio from the grassroots up.

NOTES

1. The two authors of this chapter were course developers and tutors for the Sunderland courses.
2. Much of this material is available as a handbook, see Baxter, 2000.
3. An RSL (Restricted Service License) is short-term radio station granted broadcasting rights by the U.K. regulatory authority—for example, for a term of four weeks. Long-term licenses, as available to community/noncommercial radio in most of Europe, are extremely rare in the U.K.
4. A European Social Fund (ESF) program of training and production with partners across Europe including Bradford Community Broadcasting and University of Sunderland (http://amarc.org/pw/).
5. An earlier ESF project aiming to train women in digital production skills.
6. One of the authors of this chapter. For a fuller account see CCV, 1999.
7. The station has a live stream, accessible via its Web Site at http://www.orange.or.at.
8. Much of this material is available as a handbook; see Pöyskö and Hagen, 2000.

REFERENCES

Baxter, A. (2000). *Practical ideas for involving women in radio*. Sheffield: AMARC-Europe (brochure). http://www.digital-dialogues.de.
Baxter, A., & Mitchell, C. (2002). Creating community voices: Using community radio as a means of widening participation. In University of Teeside, *Widening participation through community learning*. Publications of the Centre for Lifelong Learning, No. 3 (pp. 25-29). Middlesborough: University of Teesside.

Bridge Project. (2000). *Women's voices on the airwaves: A report on "107—the Bridge" community radio project*. Washington, Tyne and Wear: Bridge Women's Support Centre.

Bruner, J. (1996). *The culture of education*. Cambridge, MA: Harvard University Press.

CCV. (1999). *Creating community voices: Community radio and new technologies for socially disadvantaged groups*. Socrates Programme for Adult Education, Year 1 Report. Sheffield: AMARC-Europe (brochure). http://www.digital-dialogues.de.

CCV. (2000). *Creating community voices: Community radio and new technologies for socially disadvantaged groups*. Socrates Programme for Adult Education. Final Report. Sheffield: AMARC-Europe (brochure). http://www.digital-dialogues.de.

Cockburn, C., & Ormrod, S. (1993). *Gender and technology in the making*. London: Sage.

D'Arcy, M. (1996). *Galway's pirate women: A global trawl*. Galway: Pirate Press.

Everitt, A. (2003). *New voices: An evaluation of 15 access radio projects*. London: Radio Authority.

Freire, P. (1970). *Pedagogy of the oppressed*. New York: Continuum.

Freire, P. (1973). *Education for critical consciousness*. New York: Seabury.

Fryer, R. H. (1997*). Learning for the twenty-first century. First report of the National Advisory Group for Continuing Education and Lifelong Learning*. London: DFEE.

Gray, P., & Lewis, P. M. (1992). Great Britain: Community broadcasting revisited. In N. Jankowski, O. Prehn, & J. Stappers (Eds.), *The people's voice: Local radio and television in Europe* (pp. 156-169). London: John Libby.

Gumucio Dagron, A. (2001). *Making waves: Stories of participatory communication for social change*. New York: Rockefeller Foundation.

Hasan, A., & Tuijnman, A. (1997). Adult education: A policy overview. In P. Bélanger & A. Tuijnman (Eds.), *New patterns of adult learning: A six-country comparative study* (pp. 229-247). Oxford: Pergamon and UNESCO Institute for Education.

Hobson, D. (1980). Housewives and the mass media. In S. Hall, D. Hobson, A. Lowe, & P. Willis (Eds.), *Culture, media, language* (pp. 105-114). London: Hutchinson.

Jallov, B. (1996). *Women's voices crossing frontiers: European directory of women's community radio stations and women's production collectives*. Sheffield: AMARC-Europe Women's Network.

Johnston, R. (2003). Adult learning and citizenship: Clearing the ground. In P. Coare & R. Johnston (Eds.), *Adult learning, citizenship and community voices* (pp. 3-21). Leicester: NIACE.

Johnston, R., & Coare, P. (2003). Reviewing the framework. In P. Coare & R. Johnston (Eds.), *Adult learning, citizenship and community voices* (pp. 185-191). Leicester: National Institute for Adult and Continuing Education.

Karpf, A. (1980). Women and radio. *Women's Studies International Quarterly, 3*, 41-54.

Kidd, D. (1994). Shards of remembrance: One woman's archaeology of community video. In P. Riaño (Ed.), *Women in grassroots communication: Furthering social change.* London: Sage.

Lewis, P. M. (1994). *Community radio: Employment trends and training needs. Report of transnational survey.* Sheffield: AMARC-Europe

McGivney, V. (1993). *Women, education and training: Barriers to access, informal starting points and progression routes.* Leicester: National Institute for Adult and Continuing Education.

McGivney, V. (2002). *Spreading the word: Reaching out to new learners.* National Institute of Adult Continuing Education, Lifelines in Adult Learning Series. Leicester: National Institute for Adult and Continuing Education.

Mitchell, C. (1998). Women's community radio as a feminist public sphere. *Javnost, 5*(2), 73-85.

Mitchell, C. (2002). On air/Off air: Defining women's radio space in European women's community radio. In N. Jankowski & O. Prehn (Eds.), *Community media in the information age: Perspectives and prospects* (pp. 85-105). Cresskill, NJ: Hampton Press.

Mitchell, C., & O'Shea, T. (1999, July). Gendered practices in radio broadcasting: A critical study of cultures of management and production. Paper presented at the Critical Management Conference, UMIST.

NIACE REPLAN. (1991). *Women learning: Ideas, approaches and practical support.* Leicester: National Institute for Adult and Continuing Education.

O'Neill, M. (2001). Global refugees: (Human) rights, citizenship and imagining communities. In S. Cheng (Ed.), *Law, justice and power* (pp. 187-216). Palo Alto: Stanford University Press.

O'Neill, M., Campbell, R., James, A., Webster, M., Green, K., Patel, J., Akhtar, N., & Saleem, W. (2004). Red lights and safety zones. In D. Bell & M. Jayne (Eds.), *City of quarters* (pp. 206-224). Aldershot: Ashgate.

Peruzzo, M.K. (1996). Participation in community communication. In J. Servaes, T. Jacobson, & S.A. White (Eds.), *Participatory action for social change* (pp. 162-179). London: Sage.

Pöyskö, M., & Hagen, F. (2000). *Training in a tandem: A planning guide for radio workshops with special target groups.* Sheffield: AMARC-Europe (brochure). http://www.digital-dialogues.de.

Riaño, P. (Ed.). (1994*). Women in grassroots communication: Furthering social change.* London: Sage.

Skeggs, B. (1994). Situating the production of feminist ethnography. In M. Maynard & J. Purvis (Eds.), *Researching women's lives from a feminist perspective* (pp. 72-92). London: Taylor and Francis.

Steiner, L. (1992). The history and structure of women's alternative media. In L. Rakow (Ed.), *Women making meaning: New feminist directions in communications* (pp. 121-143). London: Routledge.

Stuart, S., & Bery, R. (1996). Powerful grassroots woman communicators: Participatory video in Bangladesh. In J. Servaes, T. Jacobson, & S.A. White (Eds.), *Participatory communication for social change* (pp. 197-212). London: Sage.

Tuchman, G. (1979). Woman's depiction by the mass media. *Signs: Journal of Women in Culture and Society, 3*, 528-542.

Valdivielso Gomez, S. (1997). Beyond the walls of the household: Gender and adult education participation. In P. Bélanger & A. Tuijnman (Eds.), *New patterns of adult learning: A six-country comparative study* (pp. 209-227). Oxford: Pergamon and UNESCO Institute for Education.

5

Digital Skills
and Networking

Karin Eble
Traudel Günnel

Today, digital skills and networking via internet and online services are regarded as essential in almost all nonvocational and vocational fields within postindustrial society, characterized by Castells (1999, pp. 55-56) as a "network society" in which the processing and analysis of information constitute the essential productive activity (Hall, 1999). "Every procedural stage in the production, handling, distribution, and application of knowledge and information now depends so heavily on the support of information technology that it would seem impossible to do without it" (Kuhlen, 1995, quoted by Röll, 2003, p. 30). Referring to their longitudinal research on how young people in Germany use the media, Feierabend and Klingler (2003, p. 450) emphasize: "Unlike any previous generation, 12- to 19-year-olds today grow up in a world largely defined by the media. This pertains particularly to the so-called 'new media'—computer, internet, and online services." Some proponents regard "alphanumeric knowledge, the ability to use the computer and the internet competently as the fourth key cultural skill, alongside reading, arithmetic and writing" (functionalist approach as critically summarized by Röll, 2003, p. 40).

But is it merely alphanumeric knowledge that is meant by the term "digital skills"? Is it the ability to write and format a letter with Microsoft's ubiquitous software, or to check a railway timetable on the internet? Is it prowess at computer games, allowing a player to kill an enormous number of "enemies" within a short time? Drawing on the experience of over four years' cooperation in media education within projects funded by the EU, this chapter discusses digital skills and networking in a broader context and describes three different practical initiatives.

In accord with Röll (2003), Moser (2000), and Baacke (1997), it seems unsatisfactory to discuss media competence and digital skills as if they were purely technical matters. We think it necessary to seek a broader understanding of the factors determining media literacy, examining how digital skills figure within the totality of an individual's skills, how they relate to life's circumstances and everyday realities—of which the media and the reality they transport are a part—and how life experience and general knowledge affect one's interaction with the media. Baacke (1997), Schorb (1995), and Schulz-Zander (1998), the latter concentrating on digitalized media and internet competence, define media literacy as the ability

- to choose among and make active use of the media (including interactive communication)
- to digest, understand, and assess the content of media
- to create, produce, and publish media material (including cooperation via internet)
- to analyze and critically review the media, judging to what extent they represent certain interests groups within society, and forming an opinion on their design and their aesthetics.

THE DIGITAL DIVIDE

Due to the growing significance of information and communication technologies in postindustrial societies, it might be taken for granted that media competence and media literacy are equally distributed among the members of such societies. But, as a notable number of investigations have shown, that is not the case. Although information and communication technologies are expanding globally, there is not only a widening "digital divide" between the postindustrial areas and the developing countries (Nadarajah, 2003), but also within postindustrial societies themselves, in North America and Western Europe. Among others, Harrison, Zappen, and Prell (2002), Kubicek (2002), and Rötzer (2003) have pointed out the tendency of disparities in computer and internet use to become more severe, rather than being overcome, and have correlated these trends to factors such as income, level of education, ethnicity, gender, and geographic region. Referring to the situation in the United States, their investigation shows that

> households with incomes of $75,000 and higher are more than twenty times more likely to have access to the internet and more than nine times as likely to have a computer at home than those at the lowest income levels. Further, whites are more likely to have access to the internet from home than blacks or Hispanics have from any location (including school, work, or community access centers). (Harrison et al., 2002, p. 253)

Kubicek (2002, p. 55) strictly opposes the hypothesis that the digital divide is a passing phenomenon caused by a "time lag" in the diffusion of new technology. He argues that the gap between groups at higher and lower educational levels has not narrowed in recent years—a fact corroborated by longitudinal surveys on the media usage of young people in Germany, conducted annually since 1998 by the Medienpädagogischer Forschungsverbund Südwest (Media Education Research Group Southwest). The findings show that although the use of computers and the internet has spread continually among young people, those attending academic high schools are at a distinct—and growing—advantage. "In the last five years, students at vocational and middle schools have increased their PC access less significantly (17 and 18%) than those on an academic track (26%), although the starting point [of the first group, ed.] was weaker to begin with" (Feierabend & Klingler, 2003, p. 454).

The digital divide seems to be a structural problem that deepens existing social clefts related to handling media and information. This effect was observed long before the digital revolution and described in the "knowledge gap hypothesis" (Tichenor, Donohue, & Olien, 1970), which postulates that differences in the use of mass media tend to exacerbate differences in the level of knowledge attained by members of different social strata. Based on his surveys more than twenty years later, Winterhoff-Spurk (1999) confirmed these findings, focusing on users of online services.

JUMPING THE GAP

Helping to bridge this digital gap was one major objective of the actions developed and run within the two EU-funded projects described in this book. *Creating Community Voices* and *Digital Dialogues* addressed learners from socially disadvantaged groups, aiming to improve their communicative skills and media literacy by encouraging involvement with new technology, community media, and broadcasting. This chapter concentrates on three examples of activities within these projects, tackling the question of how digital skills and media competence, as defined above, can be taught and learned, and how they can be employed for communication and cooperation on an interactive web platform. All three initiatives were pursued in Freiburg in southwestern Germany.

The first example focuses on computer-based training. Instructional software for digital audio editing was developed and published as a CD-ROM. This facilitates learning digital audio editing outside of community radio studios or community media centers, whose computer facilities are usually in great demand. One of the main objectives was to involve individuals with limited access to the media and to digital technique who were, however, interested in participating in community radio or other community media. Digital audio editing is now standard practice in radio production, and its application requires computer skills at a high level. The instructional software aimed, on the one hand, at supporting individual learning and self-teaching. On the other hand, it was intended that the CD-ROM be usable for teaching and learning within seminar and workshop groups. We will describe and discuss the process of creating the software in terms of its content, outreach to the envisaged target groups, and application in workshop or self-teaching contexts. In addition, evaluation results on work with the CD-ROM will be presented.

This project was followed up by other efforts extending the original initiative in two directions: in one case, toward identifying social groups that could benefit from improved digital and web skills, and in the other, fostering networking, communication, and cooperation by creating a regional web platform on which audio material could be presented.

The first of these additional cases takes up another aspect of gaining digital skills: the opportunities presented by the task of creating a homepage for arranging communicative and cooperative teaching and learning situations with specific groups. Concentrating, in this case, on mothers and daughters, workshops were organized to support them in overcoming generation and gender gaps and to help them discover ways of using the internet independently and responsibly. Together, mothers and daughters were to plan and produce a homepage and upload it onto the internet. This part of the chapter deals with the orientation of teaching and learning environments toward a target group, in the context of an approach based on action-oriented media education (see Baacke, 1997; Günnel, 2002, 2003; Schorb, 1995; Schulz-Zander, 1998). It examines the process of communication, mutual understanding, and cooperation, and the impact on the participating persons as they described it after having taken the course and published their homepage together.

As a last example, we will present a noncommercial interactive web platform for sound material that is directed mainly at two target groups: young people and media educators. Four organizations collaborated on the design and implementation. Launched under *www.soundnezz.de*, it aims to encourage publication and webcasting opportunities for children, young people, and students. A database provides training materials for teachers, and the platform has served as a focus and stimulus for children's radio and audio projects in the region, as well as an incentive to develop new ways of presenting and distributing audio productions. The decision to create a web platform promoting sound was influenced by the fact that, although the visualization of images enjoys great emphasis in general culture, the importance of sound is widely neglected—although it is essential for communication and for all genres of media production. Directing the activities to certain target groups was based on the idea that potential users belonging to culturally or socially defined communities might have similar interests and thus be more likely to communicate and cooperate with one other over and above their virtual contacts on the web.

Our description concentrates on aspects of interactive networking, publishing, and communication: how an interactive web site can be structured in order to enable cooperation within and among target groups, and how to encourage these groups to use the site regularly for exchange and presentation of their productions. The organizational problems of providing access to the internet while ensuring accountability and responsibility will be discussed. *Soundnezz* represents a relatively new format within the field of community media. Reflection on the definition of community in the context of this interactive web platform is another aspect treated here, referring to an ongoing debate that arose with the growing number of non-locally defined communities linked by the web (see Chapters 2 and 6, also Hollander, 2002; Malina & Jankowski, 2002).

The three examples juxtaposed in this chapter cover differing topics and various aspects of the overall theme 'digital skills and networking'. But, for all their diversity, they also have important aspects in common:

- an orientation towards socially disadvantaged target groups;
- interest in the question of how to organize teaching and learning environments based on the approach of action-oriented media pedagogy;
- the intention to embed instructional software and internet applications into these teaching and learning arrangements;

- attention to the importance and linkage of processes of self-teaching, distance learning, and face-to-face instruction or interaction (blended learning).

These issues are congruent with important topics of current discussion within the academic community of educators and psychologists concerned with the theory and experience of electronic (e-)learning (Issing, 2002; Kerres, 2001; Lenning & Ebbers, 1999; Mandl, Gruber, & Renkl, 2002; Röll, 2003). When learning is no longer understood as a mere transfer of information from teacher to pupil, but as an active process of constructing knowledge (see Chapter 2, also Röll, 2003, p. 108), the individual learner is regarded as a subject and learning as an autonomous process. Learning, as findings of several studies show, is most successful when self-directed. Multimedia[1] learning environments therefore should support complex problem-orientation and self-teaching activities (Tergan, 2002). By offering a variety of possibilities for individual learning approaches, multimedia environments can enhance autonomous learning.

SITUATIONAL FACTORS

Electronic learning in itself, however, should not be regarded as a guarantee for a successful learner-centered approach. "It is not the content itself, nor the involvement of certain media, that determines the success of learning, but rather the learning environment. New media do not, simply by virtue of their structure, proffer good opportunities for the assimilation of new knowledge or new experience" (Röll, 2003, p. 140). Thus, the situation in which learning takes place must be regarded as essential for the learning process. "What has been learned can never be separated from the act of learning and from the situation in which learning takes place" (Mandl et al., 2002, p. 140).

A central issue emerging from this insight is the need to arrange forms of "situated learning", designing learning situations that are oriented toward problem solving and are akin to later application contexts (see Chapter 3). This stimulates the transfer of knowledge, while taking the personal interests and previous background of the learners into account and allowing for multiple perspectives and critical reflection, as well as social exchange (see Mandl et al., 2002).

Although electronic learning features an attractive mode for learning, with new structures and advantages, it may present problems due to a lack of the face-to-face communication familiar from more traditional instruction. Compared to direct interaction, computer or web-based learning relies on different ways of absorbing and dealing with information. The learners are in distinct locations and environments. Non-verbal communication and contextual references are lacking. "E-learning usually confronts the user with hypertextual learning. A person unskilled in dealing with a multidimensional learning environment is likely to feel disoriented" (Röll, 2003, p. 328).

In addition to problems of disorientation ("lost in cyberspace") and clumsiness in navigation, Tergan (2002) stresses the possibility of cognitive overload. As a means of counteracting these difficulties, Röll refers to learning environments that have been described as "situated learning" by Mandl et al. (2002). Röll (2003, p. 328) suggests strengthening tutorial support, cooperative and collaborative forms of learning, and "goal-oriented scenarios". On the latter, he recommends having "some common interest as a starting point, and a project which results in a tangible outcome" (Röll, 2003, p. 87). In accordance with Mandl et al., he finds it necessary that trainers and teachers have access to information about the participating group. In order to realize these goals, it is considered essential to alternate face-to-face interaction—allowing development of "soft skills" such as social and communicative competence, emotional learning, or teamwork—with periods of self-teaching, simultaneous communication and messaging (blended learning). In Röll's view, blended learning thus permits a combination of e-learning with various approaches of traditional learning, providing the advantages of both.

PRACTICAL EXAMPLES

The extent to which these theoretical reflections led to practical realization within the European projects *Creating Community Voices* and *Digital Dialogues* is discussed in the following descriptions of three activities involving digital technique.

Instructional Software on Digital Audio Editing

The aim of this project led by the University of Education in Freiburg, Germany, was to develop software for instructing digital audio editing techniques at public access radio stations, for noncommercial community broadcasters, and for use in community media centers and media access projects. These techniques are increasingly important: the days of tape recording are bygone; audio editing is now based on digital technology. There are public access channels and noncommercial stations working exclusively with digital equipment. Training more people to use it is congruent with the goals of public access radio—enabling as many social groups as possible to broadcast freely. The editing package (software) referred to here, *Cutmaster*, was frequently employed in radio production at community stations and media centers in Germany.

Initial workshops on digital audio editing demonstrated the difficulty of integrating persons with little or no previous experience in using computers. At the same time, the importance of adjustment to an individual participant's needs became immediately apparent. In most cases, community radios, media projects, or schools have limited technical capacities, and typically there is a shortage of editing equipment that can be used for extensive practice. To alleviate this situation, a CD-ROM for training in digital audio editing seemed like a sensible idea. By offering a multimedia learning environment, work steps, and practical exercises in digital audio editing, it could be suited to the individual learner and be run on computers in or outside of radio studios, media centers, universities, and schools.

Adjusting to the Needs of the Target Group

Software serving the purposes described above should fulfill four criteria:

- enable flexible use in different settings (e.g., Kerres, 2001; Tergan, 2002), being applicable in face-to-face training sessions (workshops and seminars), as well as for individual learning in various contexts, including home computers;
- allow for self-directed and autonomous learning by individuals (Tergan, 2002; Röll, 2003) and accessibility at different levels suited to the previous experience of the individual user;
- match the demands of situated learning and transfer knowledge effectively (Mandl et al., 2002), presenting practical exercises on various learning levels that should be more or less identical to the techniques required for digital editing of audio productions at community radio stations and media centers
- correspond to the previous knowledge, interests, and objectives of the learners through target group orientation (Röll, 2003).

To develop such instructional software for digital audio editing, several work phases were designed and carried out, using the existing situation as a starting point—the typical difficulties encountered within community radio in enabling access to this technology for various target groups. A central element in the development of the instructional software was the evaluation at several stages of the teaching and learning process (described in greater detail in CCV, 1999, p. 19-21).

Observation and Evaluation Flowing into Software Design

At the planning stage, the intention was to incorporate practical observation gathered in various learning situations into the digital audio editing software. These observations were meant to feed into the development of the instructional software, thus allowing for optimal adjustment to the needs of future users. The first step involved designing, setting up, and evaluating a seminar that could be realized without instructional software as a teaching aid. The design of the seminar was based on the theory of action-oriented media pedagogy (see Baacke, 1997; Günnel, 2003; Schorb, 1995; Schulz-Zander, 1998, and Chapter 3) and included the following features:

- alternating phases of learning: straightforward instruction interspersed with practical exercises geared to progressive comprehension of the software;
- oral instruction complemented by audiovisual elements such as overhead projection of illustrations, beamer connected to a computer for demonstrating work steps, and audio recordings as listening examples;
- low threshold entry levels allowing the participation of persons new to computers and radio, hands-on introduction to computer parts (hardware), with audio material for illustration;
- cooperative learning: two participants working together at each computer, with the more inexperienced person handling the mouse.

The concept proved to be viable on an overall basis. In the course of the seminars, suggestions made by the participants were integrated into a redefined concept—suggestions that were important for the software design. One of the important evaluation findings was that what initially seemed plausible and logical at the planning stage did not always correspond to the learning experience of individuals. For this reason, more flexibility was introduced into the teaching concept. It was revised to ensure that, at the outset, more emphasis would be placed on explanations, including the use of *Windows* with its various screens and its system for handling files in directories. Thus, the input was divided into two parts, the first section covering this background and the second directed toward encouraging participants to enjoy working on digitalized audio material.

The seminar concept was applied in various parts of Germany at training courses that were observed by mentors and evaluated by the participants using specially designed questionnaires. Parallel to these seminars, the development of the instructional software was initiated, and the evaluation results from the seminars were incorporated into this process.

Typical Difficulties Encountered by Users

Two main aspects were noted in the participants' replies to questions about learning digital editing techniques. The feedback related, on one hand, to computer use and, on the other, to radio production—with the two aspects frequently intermingled. Typical difficulties in computer handling included: moving through the hierarchy of screens and distinguishing different work levels, saving, organizing folders, and using the mouse or icon symbols. In terms of radio production, participants mentioned problems in deleting segments of audio material and hesitation on where and why (not only how) to set a cut or a fade. Also listed among the problems were: applying what was learned, lack of previous computer background, and difficulty in maintaining an overview. In general, the participants had more trouble with the second phase of the seminar—the stage during which they had to perform the editing steps themselves.

One assumption was confirmed regarding the connection between specific difficulties and the preseminar proficiency levels of participants: Handling the digital editing program was clearly more difficult for those without previous computer know-how, whereas more experienced participants stated that everything seemed quite simple. Notably, however, even participants with previous experience encountered problems in differentiating between the work levels within the editing program and in loading the program. On the didactical approach—mixing instructional phases with practical exercises—the majority of those questioned were satisfied with the balance between the two methods and the rhythm of alternation.

Content and Organization of the Instructional Software

This feedback made it clear that the CD-ROM must accommodate individual levels of proficiency. Users facing a challenge too great (or too small) might lose motivation, so the software should be designed to respond to the abilities demonstrated by the participant. The teaching program would have to allow for straightforward learning—being more linear in its organization than the medium itself would actually require. Linearity simplifies learning by presenting progressive steps toward grasping the complexity of digital editing, and the linear progress of instruction as a basis for seminars has proven essential. "Intuitive" surfing through various regions of the editing program would be too exhausting and frustrating for many of those using the CD-ROM.

However, the instructional software would also have to make provisions for learners with previous experience so that they could approach learning steps individually without being forced to follow a predetermined linear course. Enabling nonlinear handling of the software was also important with respect to its envisaged use as a teaching and illustrative aid during instruction phases of seminars and workshops. Entire study units can be omitted, or, as is more frequently the case—individual sequences presented in a form suited to the individual's needs.

In order to create arrangements involving situated learning (as postulated by Mandl et al., 1997) and to organize learning as a goal-oriented scenario (recommended by Röll, 2003), the program also had to offer a wide array of interactive elements with practical exercises for persons with varying needs and interests. Actual editing situations had to be simulated visually, so that users could gather practical experience. Thus, problems in transition from the teaching software to the actual editing package could be reduced.

Two conclusions emerged here relating to the propaedeutic approach of the software. Firstly, the program would have to transmit basic knowledge about handling the computer, as well as certain fundamentals of radio work, and secondly, the teaching software should be able to "adjust" to the individual user. These stipulations heightened the profile of programming requirements considerably, because they extend far beyond the more modest aspirations of a teaching program covering (only) digital audio editing. Clearly, however, fulfilling them would enhance the accessibility of the software and the individual success of those learning.

Because participants must receive support for their subjective approach to this method of learning, the program invites them to request a personal learning plan and supplies it on demand. The sequence of study units spools itself down according to this individual plan. The plan is also provided on paper, giving participants the reassurance that the learning program is suited to their specific needs and enabling them to observe their own progress.

To make this "tailoring" possible, the teaching program begins with an interactive game that serves to establish an individual's proficiency level. Users are asked to complete typical work steps within *Windows* and to respond to some situations frequently encountered in radio work. Participants are not explicitly asked about their level of experience, because their judgment has often proved unreliable on this point. The software responds by creating, for each individual user, a grid matrix that will then monitor this user's course of learning.

In the following section on basics, each participant runs through selected program sequences that fill his or her proficiency gaps. After this highly individual introduction in the first module, the learner proceeds to modules addressing the software itself—the digital audio editing program. Although the personal learning plan makes recommendations on how to proceed, the software nonetheless permits the user, in any learning sequence, to decide on what learning area will be approached next and determine when a unit should be omitted or repeated. To give an overall view of content, all modules and topics of the instructional software are also shown in a tree structure. From here, links enable the user to move directly to an area of choice.

Testing and Evaluation

Further evaluation confirmed that the alternation between theory and practice sessions and the inclusion of audiovisual presentation forms enabled trainees to enjoy learning.

Particularly those with little or no previous computer experience had to learn to navigate within this nonlinear medium. For this reason, the teaching program presented various navigation aids, which met general approval. One improvement introduced after test evaluation was information on suitable points to take a work break—an animated image of a mug with steam rising, appearing at the end of each study unit.

The practical exercises proved essential for comprehension and retention of the material, but also helped participants maintain their interest. Practice sessions were rarely omitted—and when so, then with the comment that the work step in question had been understood. About half of the test persons who were asked thought it advantageous to use the teaching software in combination with traditional seminar forms.

Practical Application in a Course Context

Since the publication of the CD-ROM in 2000, it has been widely used as a teaching aid in seminars and workshops on digital audio editing and also for individual learning. In seminars and workshops, trainers use it mainly for demonstration and visualization during explanatory, teacher-centered instructional phases. Evaluation findings indicate that the best results are achieved by a combination of face-to-face learning in a seminar context and individual self-teaching phases with optional tutorial support—a successful example of blended learning as described in the introduction to this chapter.

Also, the goal-based scenario seems to boost motivation: The objective of such courses is that participants learn to work with audio editing software and complete at least one audio production by the end of the overall course. The learning arrangement normally begins with a face-to-face workshop structured in various units as described above. Participants are introduced to digital audio editing, which is quite complex, and become familiar with its basics. Phases of instruction by the trainer are interspersed with exercises in which participants work individually or in small groups. There are also group discussions. At the end of this initial workshop, participants receive a copy of the instructional software on a CD-ROM and can continue learning individually at home, following the personal learning plan devised interactively by the software on the basis of their proficiency.

As the exercises given in the instructional software simulate actual editing situations closely, the transition from the software to the actual editing package is not difficult. As soon as participants see fit, they can start working on a radio production using the software at their community radio, media center, university, or wherever they took part in the workshop. They can choose to work individually or in small groups. If necessary, tutorial support is provided.

The overall course finishes with a group meeting during which participants' productions are presented and discussed. Questions can be answered, future perspectives introduced, and contacts exchanged. The course ends with an evaluation session. Again, evaluation findings show that using instructional software in this fashion leads to positive learning effects.

Ramifications for the Design of Teaching Software

For the development of such instructional software, it seems highly recommendable—however time-consuming—to couple the design phase with practical teaching and learning applications, as was done in the case of this CD-ROM. Linking development to direct experience gathered in seminars or workshops with the envisaged target group facilitates evaluation and helps ensure that appropriate conclusions will be drawn for the design and structure of the planned software. Testing and evaluation of modules or pilot versions of the instructional program are indispensable during development if the software is to meet the needs of its potential users.

114 Eble & Günnel

Mothers and Daughters Discover the Internet

The "digital divide" is, among other things, a gender gap. The ability to handle a computer in a sophisticated fashion or use the internet to one's personal or professional advantage is still considered by many to be a male domain. Despite an significant shift among the younger generation, this gap is documented in the longitudinal study on German teenagers' media activity that was cited in the introduction to this chapter. It shows that the percentage of 12- to 19-year-old girls using computers in their free time nearly doubled from 1998 (33%) to 2002 (62%). But even this enormous increase did not bring the teenage girls up to the starting level of their male counterparts at the outset of the same study: 63 percent in 1998, rising to 77 percent by 2002 (Feierabend & Klingler, 2003, p. 453). Young people's computer activities, or lack thereof, may also be linked to interactive problems—for example, in families where parents lacking digital skills cannot support or partake in this facet of their children's lives, or where a home PC is used almost exclusively by male family members. For the Media Center in the Scientific Advisory Group of the Youth Welfare Organization in Freiburg, Germany, these were reasons enough to organize a series of workshops encouraging mothers and daughters to explore the internet together and to experiment at using it independently and responsibly.

The Media Center and Gender-Specific Activities

With its courses and projects for children, teens, and young adults, the Scientific Advisory Institute of the Youth Welfare Organization in Freiburg (WI) promotes activities in media, involving video, photography, sound studios, radio, computer, and the internet, offering introductory access to new media and technical skills. The WI has set itself the goal of giving young people in the area, especially those from socially disadvantaged backgrounds, a chance to participate in the information society. Toward this end, numerous media projects are carried out. Through active determination of their own media productions, including film, radio, computer, and multimedia projects, young people are encouraged to communicate and articulate their own thoughts and desires. One focal point in this media education work of the past years has been gender-specific activity with girls and young women.

Changes in communication and information technology have produced new forms of social exclusion. Social discrimination has been extended by an additional parameter: access to a computer and the internet. Of interest here is the significant percentage of people who are forced to "abstain involuntarily" from computer use—that is, who have no access to a PC and receive no encouragement from family or friends to seek it. For girls and women there are, in addition, gender-specific prejudices about whether it is fitting for them to demonstrate competence and interest in technical matters. This is often an obstacle in attempting to promote computer skills, a pattern of behavior frequently found in families where parents do not use computers themselves.

The Course Concept and Those It Attracted

This was the starting point of the workshop project "Mother and Daughter Learn About the Internet." The overall aim was to clear the way for mothers and daughters to gain access to new media and acquire some skill at practical work with these media. The goal of the media education efforts was the advancement of media-specific qualifications, accompanied by attention to aspects of personality development associated with self-expression. Previous projects in Freiburg and elsewhere had shown that recreational projects in media education, directed toward girls and young women with their broad spectrum of interests, can indeed contribute to overcoming gender-specific barriers (Eble & Schumacher, 2003). As diverse as the motivations for involvement with computer and information technology may be, the proper introduction will make it more likely that girls will grasp technical matters with relative ease and will begin handling them confidently. Regardless of the initial content—which may emphasize creative topics such as working with graphic images or inventing fantastic stories—the young women will acquire skills and begin to master digital techniques.

In this sequential project, two trainers worked with a group of four mothers and their six daughters over a period of three months. The workshop covered four weekends and eight weekly meetings of three hours each. To promote positive reinforcement effects in terms of role models, the didactic concept called for exclusively female trainers conducting the course.

The workshop was announced in the local newspaper. The mother-daughter teams and groups who signed up had widely varying background, particularly in media matters. There were persons who had never held a computer mouse before and others who used a PC every day at work. The expectations of the participants also differed greatly. One mother stated at the outset that she needed to overcome her fear of computers; up to now only her husband had used the family computer, and she hadn't seen any necessity to deal with it. The situation was similar for her two daughters, who had only come into marginal contact with computers at school. Another mother and her two daughters had had no previous contact with computers whatsoever. A family that came from

Kosovo wished to "catapult itself out of its 'Stone Age situation' into the present" (Schumacher, Kunz, & Freund, 2003, p. 8). One mother, experienced in the use of the computer, saw the workshop as an opportunity to do something constructive together with her daughter in their free time, while expanding her own knowledge.

Recreational Learning as a Field for Experience

Voluntary participation is the prominent feature of recreational learning activity. When acquiring knowledge is not dictated by work or school requirements, its motivation is of special significance and commands particular respect. While promoting media literacy, the mother-daughter workshop sequence attempted to create an enjoyable atmosphere for learning, including creative (or even playful) as well as socially satisfying elements that would encourage confidence and self-determination in accessing the media and using the internet.

Recreational media education, dissociated from any school context or curriculum, best takes the daily life realities of young people as a starting point. "It emphasizes experiential and learning processes that revolve around learning as the joy of self-discovery" (Niesyto, 2000, p. 11). Media skills that have already been more or less consciously developed elsewhere can be built upon, expanded, and differentiated. It is essential to create authentic learning situations in which learners can experiment creatively. Here, the emphasis does not lie on handling technical equipment, but rather on communication, self-expression, and articulating personal interests. Promoting subjective formation of styles and symbols is a major goal of media pedagogy. This includes, among other aspects:

- free choice of topics, forms of expression, and working techniques;
- a balance between emphasis on means (process) and ends (product), allowing time for social and emotional learning, for reflection and gathering experience;
- reinforcement of symbolic-presentational forms of expression (images, music, body language), particularly in the context of intercultural learning processes (Niesyto, 2000).

Media educators face the continuing challenge of developing project activities geared to the interests and daily realities of participants. Group interaction processes must be considered as important as media production processes, learning to learn seen as the basic prerequisite for acquiring any knowledge. The active and investigative dimensions of learning demand great attention, whereby everyday problems of the participants can be taken as a starting point; developing solutions requires that different perspectives be taken into account and techniques from various fields of activity be employed (see Röll, 2003, p. 369 for discussion, and Mandl et al., 2002, on situated learning). Because this is a recreational activity pursued during their free time, participants understandably wish to enjoy themselves—not just learn new things or be exposed to pedagogical concepts.

Curiosity and a sense of adventure play a major role, especially when young people choose their own media topics. In terms of motivation, some relevance to their own person is essential; there has to be a certain fascination at play. In the workshop sequence described here, the situation was different than in most media activities for young people, because mothers and daughters were participating together. However, they managed to find a topic that could be agreed upon by all, settling on the theme of "witches." Their goal was to produce a home page dealing with the subject that included stories, pictures, audio reports, and music composed by group members. The group outlined the following assignments for itself:

- informal opinion surveys on the questions:
  If you had magical powers, what would you do?
  Do you believe in supernatural energies?
- research of internet links about witches;
- research on the persecution of witches in their city;
- graphic surface of the home page with pictures of participants as witches in flight;
- suggestion of magical atmosphere through witch-like music;
- structure and layout of the homepage.

Learning Tailored to Participants

The idea of having the participants decide on the topics and forms of their work corresponds to what Röll (2003, p. 369) calls "tailored" learning. It is their interests and needs that are at the center of attention, not a pre-given curriculum formulated in general terms.

In order to maintain an overview and a certain transparency in such a course, it is very important that participants keep their overall goal, as well as their specific assignments, in view. At the end of each course unit, one or more elements—such as audio clips, texts, photo collages— were completed and presented to the group. Intermediate results were made note of on a flip chart, visible to all and discussed openly by the entire group. These techniques improve orientation, helping the group to keep to a rough timetable and avoid duplicating work. The preparation of the home page demanded a great deal of concentration on the part of the participants. It included the following technical aspects:

- introduction to the graphics program Paint Shop Pro7;
- use of digital cameras, recorders, and microphones;
- researching topics in the Internet;
- introduction to the World Wide Web and its services;
- introduction to the audio editing software Cool Edit;
- production of a radio clip (survey);
- construction of a homepage with Macromedia Dreamweaver as a tool.

The techniques were not presented to all participants at once; instead modular units were approached with individuals, according to their previous background knowledge and the tasks they had assumed within the group. During the workshop, questions about the protection of children and young people using the internet were discussed.

In the course of the workshop sequence, it became more and more apparent how greatly the participants enjoyed discovering media for themselves. On the opener of the homepage they launched (the outcome can be viewed in Action 7b at http://www.digital-dialogues.de), they wrote, "We worked magic with a digital camera, a recording device, various software, and our own creative ideas."

In carrying out this course, just as much importance was placed on the design of the learning environment and the creation of a pleasant learning atmosphere as on the teaching of subject matter and the successful completion of concrete tasks. Sufficient time was reserved for the exchange of ideas and experience among participants.

The mothers and daughters supported and supplemented one another in their abilities. They were proud of one another and of their newly acquired abilities and skills. Because the children in the group had more interest in experimentation, they were soon able to show their mothers what effects they were able to achieve with the photo editing program. The girls enjoyed painting with the computer most of all, printing the results and taking them home. The daughters profited from the concentrated and goal-oriented work with their mothers. The mothers took on tasks that the children thought boring and reminiscent of school, for example, writing information texts for the home page.

One significant factor contributing to the positive atmosphere in the group and among family members was the preparation of communal lunches during weekend workshops. In course breaks, the mothers developed good personal contact and decided to meet again after completing the workshop.

Rewards of Independent Work

This media education project was geared to the experience, interests, and abilities of the families—with regard to content, technical demands, and also social aims—while focusing on a gender perspective. The girls and women acquired new skills and confidence in media matters, experimenting freely with technical aspects while also exploring possibilities for personal growth. Participants not only articulated their own needs and interests, they also developed them in new ways through their media activity. Everyday experiences with media, in particular their own use of media, were discussed. Almost all of the participants emphasized that they had been interested in attending these workshops (among other reasons) because there would be no males involved. They hoped to gain better access to working with computers and other media and at the same time overcome gender-based role stereotypes that they found troublesome.

An Interactive Web Platform for Sound

The internet platform www.soundnezz.de is aimed at improving sensibilities in the area of sound and listening. *Soundnezz* has been in online since the end of 2001 and has created new contexts for communication and participation via internet. The platform makes networking possible among isolated radio projects or sound experiments initiated by teenagers and young adults across the state of Baden-Württemberg, giving them opportunities to present their projects to a larger audience and develop contacts and exchange. It encourages publication and webcasting opportunities for children, young people, and students. A database provides training materials for teachers. The platform has provided a stimulating focus for children's radio and audio projects, and a motivation to develop new ways of presenting and broadcasting audio products.

Four organizations collaborated on founding the audio platform: the Scientific Advisory Institute of the Youth Welfare Organization of Freiburg, and more specifically its Media Center; the Media Institute of the University of Education in Freiburg; the State Association for the Cultural Education of Youth in Stuttgart; and the Student Services Organization of Freiburg. All of the project partners had previous experience in digital media production, focusing on radio, music, and multimedia work. The project was partly funded by the State Media Authority in Stuttgart.

Character and Goals of soundnezz

Soundnezz is different in many respects from so-called "internet radios" and web sites. First and foremost, it is noncommercial: there is no advertising or commercial sponsoring. The platform is oriented toward specific target groups: young people and (media) educators whose professional work involves children and young people. This brings together internet users with similar interests and also it forms a basis for continued contact among these widely separated groups, making it possible for them to communicate, exchange ideas, and even to join in cooperative ventures—sometimes coming into actual personal contact with one another. These are aspects that are frequently undervalued.

Flat user hierarchies enable broad access to the platform, which is structured in such a way that individual groups have responsibility for their own homepages and can design and update them. In keeping with the goals of action-oriented media pedagogy (see Chapter 3), young people are encouraged not only to acquire skills relating to internet use and design, but also to develop networks and to cultivate a critical eye and ear for their own work and the work of others.

The specific aims of *soundnezz* thus included the construction of a regional internet junction as a platform for audio productions and a forum for their publication, but also other overriding goals: promoting acquisition of skills in communication and web technology; publicizing programs and materials valuable to trainers and teachers; formation of editorial teams to produce audio material; and combination with other broadcasting options (such as community radio stations).

Contents of the Internet Platform

Soundnezz was intended as a platform for the exchange of audio productions and training materials. It was initially an "empty platform," taking on contour through the materials uploaded by those participating. To provide orientation and a modicum of structure, these main areas were set up for contributions:

- web and radio projects: a space for audio material produced by young people
- music projects and publicity for young bands from the area: including original takes recorded at the sound studios of the Youth Welfare Organization in Freiburg
- archive and data bank: with search function to locate radio material according to topic, genre, or producer;

- event calendar: announcing courses, workshops, concerts, meetings
- source materials: exchange forum for media education information, references to publications (books and CD-ROMS) and to semi-official literature such as seminar plans, production and teaching aids.

To date, audio productions and web projects uploaded by young people constitute the major portion of the platform's content. The site can be accessed from any computer with an internet connection, and all contents can be downloaded free of cost.

During the design phase, it became clear that the heterogeneous target group of the platform would make compromises necessary with respect to structure and appearance. A rather serious, academic style might appeal to students, whereas a more colorful and varied approach seemed better for other young groups. Reaching an compromise was difficult, but in the end all the project partners were satisfied with the solution.

Building up Traffic and Contacts

Decisive for the success and quality of *soundnezz* is the extent to which it can attract potential users. In the first months it became apparent—as is true for the introduction of other internet sites—that the mere launching of a platform does not automatically generate traffic. The latter depends on a "snowball" effect—the users and their ability to attract others users. First contacts were established by offering information and workshops in youth centers or at universities (for detailed description, see Günnel & Klug, 2003). Whether through personal contact or coursework, once young people have become interested in and capable of media activity, they usually wish to present their productions. The internet platform permitted them to do this easily. This corresponds to "situated learning" as outlined by Mandl et al. (2002) in a particularly interesting form, combining physical and virtual presence in a way beneficial to motivation and progress in learning.

An illustration of this can be found at the Youth Welfare Organization in Freiburg. After attending workshops on radio journalism (conducting interviews, writing radio scripts and radio plays), a group of interested young people have continued these activities. Tutors accompany their work, and the results are uploaded onto the web platform.

Two 12- and 13-year old girls, for example, started off with a survey asking pedestrians who was the most handsome player on the local upper-division soccer team. They subsequently felt confident enough to actually interview their favorite prominent athlete, and then proudly saw to it that their audio clip was uploaded onto *soundnezz*. As the two later reported, their courage was boosted considerably, and with lasting effect ("and we played it off the website to all our friends"). What had begun with girlish giggling resulted in their presence on the internet platform with an original production that only they could have developed.

For those who are inexperienced, such projects can be a key to active media access. In fact, young people from socially disadvantaged backgrounds can profit even more greatly from such processes than those growing up with steady support, because the former relish the novelty of computer availability and personal tutoring, taking advantage of this new experience to learn quickly about the possibilities that digital communication presents.

Another typical instance was that of the young bands recording their music at the studio of the Youth Welfare Organization (set into in biographical perspective in Chapter 8 of this book). "Life is one big experiment," as a lead singer put it. He and three other band members from one of the more remote valleys of the Black Forest were trying out their own rock number with very personal lyrics, singing in several parts and using exotic instruments, such as the didgeridoo. After producing their own first complete track, they met other bands at a weekly forum in the studio. Together, they organized a "newcomer festival" and competition for young bands, publishing the entries on *soundnezz*. Those that were shortlisted played live at the festival event. The band "X-periment" took second place, establishing all kinds of contacts to other musicians and fans, and now the four are eager to upload new songs. "This really works," was the lead singer's comment.

Direct Access to the Internet Platform

One of the main considerations with regard to access was achieving a flat hierarchy easily entered. It was decided that a tree-like structure would be erected, involving tutors for communication along the branches. This would enable direct contact, alongside the virtual contact, and give a personal component to the digital learning environment. It would also simplify problem solving, distribution of passwords, and the like.

A system was developed whereby employees of the partner institutions are authorized to make changes in the opening page of *soundnezz*, to update information, upload training materials, and initiate new projects. Thus, they can introduce new participants to the web platform, assigning passwords and allotting space, so that password holders can upload data on their projects with all the accompanying multimedia files. In this way, the users are given as much freedom as possible. But they have an established contact to a tutor who can answer their questions and, if necessary, intervene in case of misuse.

To create a stable and active user structure, a concept can be recommended that was successfully applied in another project called *Media for Citizens*. The core group of project initiators recruits potentially interested persons for each area of planned activity. These "multipliers" can include, for example, social workers in youth organizations, open-minded teachers, or those active in music. The multipliers carry the basic idea of the project to a wider circle of interested people and, at the same time, reduce the work load for the initiators, who could hardly establish all these contacts themselves.

This approach has proven advantageous for running *soundnezz*, from the outset. The participating institutions responsible for the web platform are able to withdraw from day-to-day operations; cooperation between tutors and users functions well. Structuring web content with the aid of the editing system can be done by a person who is not involved in tutoring. In larger projects, user guidance can be delegated to several persons. Tutors can, within their particular area, grant certain rights to users and teach them how to work with the platform. These matters are set down in a user contract regulating internal responsibilities and clearly defining, in legal terms, what is possible or not possible on the platform. It also proved helpful to hire a person to answer both short inquiries (mostly by e-mail) and requests for more extensive support.

The Virtual Meets the Actual

The initial assumption that virtual contact via *soundnezz* might trigger actual encounter among certain culturally or socially defined communities proved accurate. Also, promoting media competence through workshops and continued personal guidance was absolutely necessary and desirable. Although young people sometimes possess astounding abilities to acquire, on their own, the knowledge necessary for creating web sites or producing audio material, that can be tedious—and isolating, as well. Workshops and other group activities help young people to attain a certain level of quality and to perceive the societal component inherent in media. Interaction within a peer group can also enhance motivation and improve individual learning success, as feedback from *soundnezz* participants confirmed. Within the framework of the participants' life contexts, self-directed learning combined with unobtrusive guidance (as outlined by Tergan, 2002, and Röll, 2003) proved highly successful.

Soundnezz can be regarded as part of what is defined as community media (see Chapter 2). The platform itself is noncommercial. It is "interactive and participative" (McQuail, 1987, p. 123) and offers open access to a range of groups, thus defining community both virtually (focusing on issues or common interests) and locally, or as a mixture of both. Due to its linkage of actual sociogeographic community structures with virtual networking, the *soundnezz* platform provides some practical data on the feasibility of such mixtures, which are novel and, as Hollander has suggested, "a matter for investigation" (2002, p. 41).

Out of their virtual contacts through *soundnezz*, young bands and musicians developed the idea of a newcomer festival, an event that was then realized. Thus the "community" integrated virtual and local face-to-face contacts and collaboration and developed media competence in a much wider sense than that of merely engaging in internet communication (see Baacke, 1997; Schorb, 1995; Schulz-Zander, 1998). Networking requires computer and internet competence, but also organizational, social, and communicative competence.

Very important seems—though up to now not often a subject of research—the merging of virtual and actual interaction for creating long-term and lively networking in nonvocational contexts largely based on interactive web sites. This assumption is corroborated by research projects on electronic and multimedia learning and teaching environments that emphasize the importance of blended learning, a combination of e-learning with various approaches of face-to-face learning (see introduction and Röll, 2003).

CONCLUSION

As the exposition of this chapter explained, building bridges across the "digital divide" was one major intention of the European projects *Creating Community Voices* and *Digital Dialogues*. Reflecting on the effects and outcomes of the activities that have now been depicted, the question arises as to whether and how they may contribute to that aim, at least as models. To what extent did the undertakings promote digital skills and media competence, as defined holistically by Baacke (1997), Schorb (1995), and Schulz-Zander (1998)? And in a more general sense, what could be transferred and adapted from these experiences to benefit future projects concentrating on similar objectives?

Each of the three examples that have been described contributes to the effort of overcoming the digital gap in a different way and in a different sector of digitalized media, attempting to avert the dangers sure to ensue if the existing cleft is allowed to widen between the "haves" and "have-nots" in handling information technology.

The instructional software for digital audio editing, our first example, was primarily (but not exclusively) intended for target groups at community radio stations. These groups often include persons who, due to their social and educational background, are unfamiliar with computers. The software that was developed established a learning environment that allowed participants to practice producing their own radio programs, supporting their efforts to take an active part in public communication. At the same time, they developed digital skills that are applicable beyond the radio context in other vocational and nonvocational areas.

The course sequence for mothers and daughters creating and publishing a web site, our second example, offered participants the opportunity to develop digital skills and to use the internet in an independent and self-directed way. They were able, at least in part, to rise above the gender stereotypes that still deter many women from handling computers and using the internet. Simultaneously, the course promoted communication and collaboration across generations. Mothers and their daughters worked toward mutual recognition of their differing interests and perception of media by making collective decisions on the content and the design of their web site. This helped them discover that by concentrating on complementary aspects, they could support one other in a constructive way, laying the groundwork for sustained cooperation and gaining confidence in using computers and the internet without the help of male relatives, friends, or experts.

Our third example was an interactive and noncommercial internet platform for sound called www.soundnezz.de. Directed toward two specific target groups—young people interested in presenting their own audio material to a wider audience and media educators working with these young people—it encouraged them to use the internet in a creative and self-determined fashion and to cultivate direct communication with one another in addition to their virtual contacts. This was intended to strengthen their communicative abilities and stimulate reflection on media production, with a special focus on the treatment and presentation of sound. *Soundnezz* developed into a site with considerable traffic, the younger target group members using the platform to publish their own productions, and the older addressees—teachers and media educators—exchanging teaching materials and information on training and workshops. Some of the contacts led to face-to-face meetings and personal cooperation. One example was the "newcomer festival" in October 2003 in Freiburg, Germany, organized by young musicians who had come into contact via *soundnezz*.

Perspectives for the Future

Addressing the question of what insights can be gleaned from these experiences for future projects, it seems likely that a few essential aspects could be valuable in a more general context. Firstly and most significantly, the orientation toward target groups implies a learner-centered approach, meaning that activities arranged by media educators must be congruent with the interests, needs, and life experience of the target group in question (situated learning).

All three of the cases depicted were based on this approach—even the first example, relating to the design of instructional software on digital audio editing. The development of this software was closely linked to the evaluation of workshops held for members of the target group before and during the conception of the software. A draft version was tested in workshops, the feedback of participants influencing the ongoing design of the software. Subsequent successful application of the software in workshops and individual learning situations seems to be related to this developmental strategy, which resulted in individual learning schemes adjusted to users.

Contrary to what one might expect in the shifting sphere of software applications, the success of the instructional software, published in 2000, has been enduring. An e-mail written in January 2004 by a representative of the city media center in Emden, East Frisia, states:

> Your Cutmaster CD-ROM is the best I've ever seen for interactive instruction. Congratulations, and I've recommended it to any number of interested people. Do you have any more intelligent software? Is there an audio program for kindergarten and elementary school children? Wishing you continued success in the future.

Another important aspect transferable to related projects would be the orientation toward action and production. In all three examples, it was essential that participants determine the planning and realization of their media product—whether it was a radio clip, a web page or a music recording presented on the internet. The theoretical approach of action-oriented media education (see Chapter 3; Baacke, 1997; Schorb, 1995) and the arrangement of "goal-based scenarios" in the context of electronic learning (Röll, 2003) seem to be highly productive.

Focusing on the arrangement for teaching and learning, all three examples can be characterized as "blended learning", alternating face-to-face interaction with periods of individual study enhanced by simultaneous communication or messaging. In their evaluation of the workshops, participants emphasized that direct interaction with trainers but also within the group itself was very important for their motivation and for successful learning. This corresponds to the discussion within the academic community on setting up successful learning environments, as summarized in the introduction to this chapter. The exchange among participants led, among other things, to critical discussion on media production—contributing to development of media competence in the broadest sense.

In the context of a comprehensive view on digital skills—including not only technical aspects but also media literacy and critical acumen—these three examples show how different target groups, and even marginalized groups, can be guided toward using electronic media in a creative, self-directed, communicative, and constructive way. These are viable alternatives to a pure consumer role for the media audience, supporting self-expression and counteracting the threat of a widening "digital divide" within society.

NOTE

1. Klimsa (2002, p. 5) defines multimedia not only by the integration of various media such as graphics, pixel pictures, text, video, sound, and so on, but also by interactivity, multitasking, and parallelism of media presentations.

REFERENCES

Baacke, D. (1997). *Medienpädagogik*. Tübingen: Max Niemeyer.

Baacke, E., Frech, S., & Ruprecht, G. (Eds.). (2002). *Virtuelle (Lern)Welten: Herausforderungen für die politische Bildung.* Schwalbach/Taunus: Wochenschau.

Castells, M. (1999). Flows, networks and identities. In M. Castells, R. Flecha, P. Freire, H.A. Giroux, D. Macedo, & P. Willis (Eds.), *Critical education in the new information age* (pp. 37-64). Lanham, MD: Rowman & Littlefield.

CCV (1999). *Creating community voices: Community radio and new technologies for socially disadvantaged groups.* Socrates Programme for Adult Education, Year 1 Report. Sheffield: AMARC Europe (brochure). http://www.digital-dialogues.de.

Conklin, J. (1987). Hypertext: An introduction and survey. *Computer, 20*(9), 17-44.

Eble, K., & Schumacher, I. (Eds.). (2003). *medi@girls: Medienarbeit mit Mädchen*. München: Kopaed.

Feierabend, S., & Klingler, W. (2003). Medienverhalten Jugendlicher in Deutschland. *Media Perspektiven, 10*, 450-462.

Günnel, T. (2002). Counteracting the gap: Strategies for teaching media competence. In N. Jankowski & O. Prehn (Eds.), *Community media in the information age: Perspectives and prospects* (pp. 333-358). Cresskill, NJ: Hampton Press.

Günnel, T. (2003). *Experiment Arbeitsweltredaktion: Bürgerradio im Kontext von Medienpolitik, Kommunikationswissenschaften und Pädagogik*. München: Kopaed.

Günnel, T., & Klug, A. (2003). *Soundnezz.de: Handbook on creating an interactive sound website and on training its users*. Freiburg: University of Education (brochure). http://www.digital-dialogues.de.

Hall, P. (1999). Changing geographies: Technologies and income. In D. A. Schön, B. Sanyal, & W.J. Mitchell (Eds.), *High technology and low-income communities* (pp. 43-68). Cambridge, MA: MIT Press.

Harrison, T., Zappen, J. P., & Prell, C. (2002). Transforming new communication technologies into community media. In N. Jankowski & O. Prehn (Eds.), *Community media in the information age: Perspectives and prospects* (pp. 249-270). Cresskill, NJ: Hampton Press.

Hollander, E. (2002). Community media and online communities: Towards a theoretical and methodological framework. In N. Jankowski & O. Prehn (Eds.), *Community media in the information age: Perspectives and prospects* (pp. 31-47). Cresskill, NJ: Hampton Press.

Issing, L.J. (2002). Instruktionsdesign für Multimedia. In L. J. Issing & P. Klimsa (Eds.), *Information und Lernen mit Multimedia* (pp. 151-176). Weinheim: Beltz.

Kerres, M. (2001). *Multimediale und telemediale Lernumgebungen: Konzeption und Entwicklung*. (2nd rev. ed.). München, Wien: Oldenbourg.

Klimsa, P. (2002). Multimedia aus psychologischer und didaktischer Sicht. In L.J. Issing & P. Klimsa (Eds.), *Information und Lernen mit Multimedia* (pp. 5-27). Weinheim: Beltz.

Klug, A. (2000). *Der Weg zum digitalen Schnitt. Lernprogramm für digitale Tonbearbeitung am Cutmaster*. CD-ROM. München: Kopaed.

Kubicek, H. (2002). Vor einer "digitalen Spaltung"? Chancengleicher Zugang zu den Neuen Medien als gesellschafts- und wirtschaftspolitische Herausforderung. In E. Baacke, S. Frech, & G. Ruprecht (Eds.), *Virtuelle (Lern)Welten: Herausforderungen für die politische Bildung* (pp. 53-65). Schwalbach/Taunus: Wochenschau.

Kuhlen, R. (1995). *Informationsmarkt: Chancen und Risiken der Kommerzialisierung*. Konstanz: Universitätsverlag.

Lenning, O.T., & Ebbers, L.H. (1999). *The powerful potential of learning communities: Improving education for the future*. Washington, DC: George Washington Graduate School of Education and Human Development.

Malina, A., & Jankowski, N. (2002). Community-building in cyberspace. In N. Jankowski & O. Prehn (Eds.), *Community media in the information age: Perspectives and prospects* (pp. 271-293). Cresskill, NJ: Hampton Press.

Mandl, H., Gruber, H., & Renkl, A. (2002). Situiertes Lernen in multimedialen Lernumgebungen. In L. J. Issing & P. Klimsa (Eds.), *Information und Lernen mit Multimedia* (pp. 139-148). Weinheim: Beltz.

McQuail, D. (1987). *Mass communication theory: An introduction* (2nd ed.). London, Thousand Oaks, New Delhi: Sage.

Moser, H. (2000). *Einführung in die Medienpädagogik: Aufwachsen im Medienzeitalter.* Opladen: Leske & Budrich.

Nadarajah, M. (Ed.). (2003). *Pathways to critical media education and beyond: Deliberations on media reforms and the Manila Initiative.* Bangkok: Asian Communication Network.

Niesyto, H. (2000). *Medienpädagogik und soziokulturelle Unterschiede.* Baden-Baden/Ludwigsburg: MPFS, SWR Medienforschung.

Röll, F.J. (2003). *Pädagogik der Navigation.* München: Kopaed.

Rötzer, F. (2003). Anmerkungen zur digitalen Spaltung. In G. Roters (Ed.), *Digitale Spaltung: Informationsgesellschaft im neuen Jahrtausend. Trends und Entwicklungen* (pp. 11-17). Berlin: Vistas.

Schorb, B. (1995). *Medienalltag und Handeln.* Opladen: Leske & Budrich.

Schulz-Zander, R. (1998). Multimedia und Netze in Schulen: Eine Chance für eine neue Lernkultur. In H. Kubicek, D. Klumpp, G. Müller, W. Neu, E. Raubold, & A. Rossnagel (Eds.), *Lernort Multimedia. Jahrbuch Telekommunikation und Gesellschaft, 3,* 139-147.

Schumacher, I., Kunz, C., & Freund, M. (2003). *Mothers and daughters learn about the internet.* Freiburg: Wissenschaftliches Institut des Jugendhilfswerks (brochure). http://www.digital-dialogues.de.

Tergan, O.S. (2002). Hypertext und Hypermedia: Konzeptionen, Lernmöglichkeiten, Lernprobleme. In L. J. Issing & P. Klimsa (Eds.), *Information und Lernen mit Multimedia* (pp. 99-112). Weinheim: Beltz.

Tichenor, P., Donohue, G., & Olien, C. (1970). Mass media flow and differential growth in knowledge. *Public Opinion Quarterly, 2,* 159-170.

Winterhoff-Spurk, P. (1999). Von der Wissenskluft zur medialen Klassengesellschaft? Möglichkeiten und Grenzen individueller Rezeptionsautonomie. In U. Bischoff (Ed.), *Mediengesellschaft: Neue Klassengesellschaft?* (pp. 28-43). Bielefeld: Gesellschaft für Medienpädagogik und Kommunikationskultur.

6

Networking Community Media: Web Radio as a Participatory Medium

Caroline Mitchell

Susan Jones

Brecht's vision of a "wonderful public communication system . . . capable not only of transmitting but of receiving, of making listeners hear but also speak, not of isolating them but connecting them" (cited in Lewis & Booth, 1989, p. 186) is often quoted in radio research. The potential of web radio and a wide variety of audio applications on the internet to deliver the two-way communication that he was espousing is particularly relevant when discussing the relationship between digital technologies and community-based media (Priestman, 2002, p. 11).

This chapter will consider a wide spectrum of web radio applications in the context of their current use as a communicative tool among and within grassroots communities. Positioning audio material on the internet can allow for either simultaneous or delayed reception, and thus for direction toward specific target groups or new audiences, whether through rebroadcasting or "listening on demand." Increasingly, such applications serve as an innovative tool for linking different parts of the community radio movement (see Chapter 2 for further discussion). This has the potential to connect people, issues, and causes locally and globally and to play an important role in helping dispersed communities to maintain sociocultural communication.

In order to contextualize developments in community web radio and audio on the internet, we will be exploring a range of different definitions, forms, technologies, and techniques of web radio and documenting some of the varied ways that the internet/web radio is being used by community radio broadcasters.

Martin Spinelli warns of the dangers of overpromoting the democratic nature of radio and the internet:

> Neither the Internet nor radio is a deus ex machina of democracy, community or education. The Internet is only an emergent medium, existing in a specific context with and within a real set of material conditions, and certainly with some real potential. (Spinelli, 2000, pp. 276-277)

In Chapter 5 we have already seen how the work of www.sound-nezz.de, the young people's interactive and noncommercial internet platform, has involved different uses of sound and the internet; and this chapter explored the training context that helps young people feel motivated and skilled enough to contribute to and benefit from such a project. Our research focuses on the experiences of a number of partners in the *Creating Community Voices* and *Digital Dialogues* projects particularly using web radio; including *Radio Orange* based in Austria, *Connemara Community Radio* in southwest Ireland, and *Radio Robin Hood* in Turku, Finland. We shall also refer to examples from the international community radio movement including activist web stations and archives as well as participatory women's web radio initiatives. Finally, we explore methods and practices in which web radio production was introduced to a group of refugees and asylum seekers in Sunderland, UK.

There has been very little documentation about grassroots-oriented use of web radio and the processes involved under the umbrella of adult education, training and development initiatives—including working in partnership, using web radio to support social groups, and similar initiatives. As Atton and Couldry remarked in their editorial for *Media Culture and Society*: "Perhaps the greatest challenge to alternative media research lies in how the World Wide Web is being used" (2003, p. 584). Wolfgang Kemptner from the community radio station *Orange 94.0* in Vienna (a partner in the *Digital Dialogues* consortium) sums up the community broadcasters' dilemma about how to approach the issue of new technology:

> The new technology . . . not only presents possibilities: it also creates a new processes of exclusion. Some radio makers might be internet "freaks" and use all the facilities the radio station has to offer,

while others would need training in order to take advantage of these facilities at all. The approach of the community radio movement has always included a democratic perspective on media production. Therefore, a community radio should be prepared to offer training to its radio makers. (Kemptner, 2003, p. 5)

Action-oriented training (see Chapter 3) that involves working in partnerships and with ongoing evaluation feeding back into the training process has been an important part of the work of *Creating Community Voices* and *Digital Dialogues* projects. In this chapter we explore the methods being used to introduce and train people in web radio use in different settings—in established and emergent radio stations and within the context of adult education and community workshops or initiatives. Our work on using web radio and all the skills that this involves has probably raised more questions than answers about how grassroots organizations interact with radio and the web: How do particular groups relate to ICT, radio, and the web? Can community web radio help to break down hierarchies of media use for individuals and specialist interest groups? Can accessible media training in this area change how people see the media as representing one group's interests over another?

The very "worldwide" nature of web radio has a particular significance and resonance for groups of people who have been displaced from their country of birth and who have crossed geographical borders and social, cultural, and religious boundaries:

> . . . whereas ethnic community media...continue to operate to meet the information and entertainment needs of their communities, they are increasingly expanding their communication activities to a transnational scale, altering in the process the experiential horizon of the ethnic communities they serve' (Tsagarousianou, 2002, p. 210).

DEFINING WEB RADIO

Web radio is developing at a time when radio is undergoing huge technological changes for both consumers and producers and, as Hendy notes, "Digitalisation—in all its aspects—is leading the radio industry into new and often unfamiliar territory" (Hendy, 2000, p. 59). Atton says that web radio resembles "conventional radio only in the notion of broadcasting sound" (Atton, 2002, p. 144). Arguably, there are as many positive functions of web radio as there are for the internet. It has the potential to transform the way that people find out and learn, create, communicate, and trade. Although web radio can be seen as "radi-ogenic" (Tacchi, 2000, p. 292) it is limiting to consider it as a radio add-on: "the potential of web radio is diminished if we treat it only as an imi-tation of what radio broadcasting has become" (Priestman, 2002, p. 232).

Web radio is the digital transmission of sound recordings via the internet. The most commonly used method for distributing web radio is streaming, where digitilized sound bits are compressed and encoded so that they can be uploaded onto an internet server and downloaded by any recipient with web access.

Most terrestrial commercial and public service radio stations use the web as a service in addition to analogue or digital transmissions in order to increase the reach of a station nationally and internationally. There are now hundreds of radio "stations" on the web: it is difficult to quantify how many stations there are, because many are personalized jukeboxes.

In his comprehensive overview and analysis of different ways that sound and radio interact with the web, Priestman outlines the main char-acteristics of the relationship between radio and the internet. He states that web radio has "an inherently interactive, horizontal infrastructure" (Priestman, 2002, p. 27). Of course this interactivity chimes with the aims and ethos of community stations that are specifically set up for commu-nity benefit and social gain: "Listeners can become increasingly more involved as contributors or makers of programmes if a web station cre-ates that opportunity" (Priestman, 2002, p. 234).

In this age of convergence, web radio co-exists with sites and plat-forms that enable multimedia access; web radio is one media form inte-grated with other communicative practices being utilized as a tool for activism and grassroots community communications. What seems to be clear is that web radio is a hybrid:

> These initiatives, in their intertwining and redefining of media forms, in their blurring of creator, producer and distributor, or broadcaster and listener, suggest hybridised forms of media production particu-larly well suited to the multimedia possibilities of the Internet and worldwide web. Hybridity in media form may also lead to a hybridity of intention, a hybridity of consistency and even, that Holy Grail of so many alternative media—a hybrid audience beyond the grass roots ghetto. (Atton, 2002, p. 144)

Web radio may well work best as a narrowcast or niche medium, and this space can be harnessed by community radio stations that may be not be able to find frequency space in the terrestrial or digital radio marketplace (Priestman, 2002, p. 233). Recent work by Kahn and Kellner recognizes the importance of the Internet and wireless technology as a "vital new space of politics and culture" (Kahn & Kellner, 2003, p. 27), supporting the emergence of international subcultures and activism that resist corporate globalization. This is played out particularly at a local level:

> The emergent mediated post-subcultures are also involved in the attempt to allow people the freedom to re-define and construct themselves around the kind of alternative cultural forms, experiences, and practices which radical deployments of the Internet afford. (Kahn & Kellner, 2003, pp. 2-3)

Carey, cited by Atton and Couldry, sets up the two opposing forces of the centripetal (structuring) force of "national media control space" and the centrifugal (fractured) force of the "diaspora of the internet" relating to minority media (Carey, 1998, p. 34, cited by Atton & Couldry, 203, p. 584). It is this latter space that we now turn to in exploring examples of web community radio practice.

FACETS OF INTERNET USE IN COMMUNITY MEDIA PRACTICE

Community radio stations that broadcast specialist music, language, political or cultural programming have used the web particularly effectively, attracting new audiences with similar interests in different parts of the world. Resonance FM is an example of this; it is a small experimental arts station that has a community license in London UK and extends its audience globally by webcasting and archiving past programs on its website.[1] It has attracted contributors from all over the world and could be said to have a global concern and purpose to provide a two-way communication between broadcasters and audiences interested in experimental music, arts, and sound.

The ability to "listen again" to archived programs allows people to access programs via their computer at a convenient time (or "time shifting" as described by Tacchi, 2000, p. 230). Listening on demand "transfers control to the listener" (Priestman, 2002, p. 234). In Britain the *BBC* has developed its web sites so that they provide extensive background information about programs, including opportunities to interact with and comment on program content and receive additional information that complements broadcasts. Many national public service broadcasters have extensive on-line audio libraries. The *BBC Listen Again* service[2] makes most programs available for a week after they are first broadcast.[3]

Most terrestrial radio stations can be listened to via live streaming on the web. Some stations are set up solely as web stations: *Street Radio* in Sydney, Australia,[4] for example, enables young homeless people to have a voice:

> "The biggest issue with these young people is the feeling they have of being on the outside of society looking in," said Captain Paul Moulds, director of Oasis.[5] "They're cut off from opportunities the rest of society enjoys. And the biggest illustration of this is access to technology." (Horin, 2004, p. 1)

In the past this has allowed people to circumvent traditional licensing regulations: Kemptner describes this as a "compensatory" mode of broadcasting for groups that haven't been able to secure an FM license (Kemptner, 2003, p. 5), and Tacchi describes setting up what she calls net.radio: "This is proving to be easier (no regulation, no conventions) and is more likely to succeed. Every restriction or limitation you come across with the Internet is temporary" (Tacchi, 2000, p. 293).[6]

These stations have the advantage of being able to set themselves up with lower capital costs (Tacchi, 2000; Priestman, 2002), often with no more resources than a room with a computer and a lone operator.[7] Wall argues that, from an idealistic viewpoint: "this should allow for a greater range of broadcasters, and for innovative approaches to be risked as the costs of failure are not so great" (Wall, 2004, p. 38). Until recently it has also meant that copyright payments for music have been avoided. However, since 2002, copyright organizations in each country have set up regulations concerning payment for music, which have led to many small operators closing down.[8]

Some stations use the internet in a very pragmatic way: at *Radio Robin Hood* in Turku, Finland, there is remote control of night programming via internet from a volunteer's home into the studio. This keeps the station running 24 hours, even when the studio is closed down, because they haven't got the personnel to staff the station constantly. At *Kothmale Community Radio* in Sri Lanka, the radio station helps bring web resources to wider communities by broadcasting a daily *Radio Browsing on the Internet* program where the listeners (who don't have internet access) request information and the broadcasters and their assistants browse the web and broadcast the results. The web is therefore a research tool (Pringle & David, 2002, p. 2). One of the more recent developments of web radio is the ability to use it for networking among community program makers and for program sharing, setting up web radio events linking broadcasters from around the world. Traditionally, community stations have made use of telephone, CD duplication, or satellite links to network news and specialist programs so that work by one journalist or production team can be received by more than one station's audience. This can happen on a "one-off" basis, such as the radio webcasts for *Voices Without Frontiers*, an international project linking campaign groups and broadcasters that aims to "mobilize the community media sector at a national and international level in broadcast campaigns against discrimination, for respect of migrants, refugees and minorities, and in celebration of cultural diversity."[9] At *Radio Orange* in Vienna, webcasting is part of grassroots media activism on the internet for bringing together feminist groups around March 8, 2003, which will be discussed later in this chapter.

The advantage of having a permanent web presence that complements webcasts is that there is a longer-term and continuing presence of audio archives, and text and visual images can be presented or discussion forums opened on station web pages. Listeners and station volunteers who want to know more about particular programs or events connected to the station have a high speed link to this. The web site can aid active volunteers to participate democratically in the station itself, for instance by publicizing and providing contextual information about station meetings and elections, or background on groups that create their own programs. A web site offers opportunities for a station to maintain its own publicity, independent of mainstream publicity sources such as local newspapers who may not want to publicize a community station's events and program announcements.

Live Streaming of Individual Events as a Form of Media Activism

Many community media initiatives lack the resources to transmit their programs on a steady livestream via internet, but nonetheless make use of this possibility on particular occasions—often in concert with other stations or media groups. Cooperation has evolved around various themes, including global, social, and political issues as well as questions of media policy and access. Instead of employing the internet as a means of direct dissemination, such cooperation can involve using the internet to transfer material from one station to another so that it can be rebroadcast from various points along the usual terrestrial channels. To illustrate the workings of such one-off events as simply as possible, let us begin with an action limited to one language and one region, organized within an existing contact group.

Political Positioning

In the spring of 2003, the association of free radio stations (AFF for "Assoziation Freier Gesellschaftsfunk") in Germany's southwestern federal state, Baden-Württemberg, organized a mutual public relations campaign in which all nine member stations were invited to participate. The overall goal was to gain state-wide recognition for the community stations and to draw attention to the licensing struggles then in progress. In comparison to licensing practices in other regions and countries, the conditions for noncommercial community radio in this German state may seem rather comfortable: Broadcasting licenses are granted for a period of eight years and can extend to 24-hour/7-day set-ups. The transmitting power and range, however, leave a great deal to be desired, because the community stations have sometimes been restricted to "leftover" frequencies, unattractive to commercial or public radio enterprises due, for example, to lack of wattage or interference from neighboring transmitters in Switzerland or France. Like many other small stations, *Free Radio Freudenstadt*, one of the German partners in *Digital Dialogues* and a member of AFF, has experienced such problems—all the more reason to participate in this initiative.

As the first eight-year licensing period in this state drew to a close and applications were being processed for the following period, AFF wished to call public attention to the framework in which community radio in the state was increasingly constricted: some stations were forced to share major air time with university or private media training programs or with religious groups, and their partial funding (a tiny fraction of the general subscription fees paid by all radio listeners) was a matter for continuing negotiation. But the German constitution, Article 5, Paragraph 1, states that "each individual has the right to state and disseminate his or her opinion orally, in print, or in images."[10] Where in the current media landscape, the AFF was asking, did the general public have the opportunity to exercise this right, other than in the few community stations serving only certain areas of the state?

Using their routine meetings and a one-day workshop for planning and preparation, the AFF members decided on a "Radio Tour" of the state in May and June 2003. A van with mobile transmission equipment was borrowed from a station in another German state and scheduled for a layover of several days at each of the community radios participating. Each member station planned a special program during the period when it would have access to the broadcasting van, so that a live take-up of a local event or from a street or pedestrian zone was possible. Transferred into the local studio via telephone or internet, this programming or a section of it was relayed via internet server to the other member stations for simultaneous broadcasting—meaning that the same program could be received on all participating stations within the state. The tour rounded up with a public debate on media politics in the state capital, organized and broadcast mutually by the AFF member stations. On this occasion, representatives of the media authority were invited as guests and were presented with a formal statement of AFF on questions of media policy, particularly licensing and funding.

To realize this plan, the AFF member stations were able to use a communication structure that was already well established. At meetings and in their e-mail groups, they agreed on a division of labor: organizing the server, designing a poster, setting the exact schedule. Because this organization holds a "radio camp" at the Lake of Constance every year in the spring for training and exchange among radio activists from German, Austria, and Switzerland, it was possible to hold a workshop there on studio handling in the broadcasting van and on technique for uploading a program onto a common server. Even under these positive conditions, conducive to cooperation and arrangements on details, a great deal of last-minute direction was necessary—in emergency messages or personal visits—and ultimately, not all nine members were able to participate. Still, the campaign was considered an overall success.

Contact Across the Globe

One detail that frequently causes confusion in discussing and planning such schemes should be addressed before we approach more extended forms of cooperation. First on the list of FAQs about this topic: If an internet server is being used to transfer signals from one station to another, why can't any willing listener just tune in to that server? This is technically possible, for example, when a station live streams its full radio program. It may, however, miss the point, namely that broadcasting "in chorus" along a number of terrestrial frequencies in different parts of the world is a form of informational presence usually not available to smaller or local groups.

They are not only linking content, but also cultivating a mutual public image, throwing in their own local prestige and authority to support for voices and topics that come from far away and perhaps presenting them differently than mainstream media do (if at all). This can be a valuable tool for grassroots movements, NGOs, minority communities, alternative media, and many others. It is a highly directed use of the internet, as opposed to the saturating effect of countless livestreams, and it is accessible to listeners without computers.

There are also a number of practical reasons why direct livestreaming is not always the method of choice. Firstly, cost-free servers set up by independent media groups or activists for this purpose are not designed for unlimited traffic. The hardware required for a server to support, for example, 20 simultaneous downloads is considerably less expensive than that necessary for 200 "listeners" to tune in—not to mention 2,000 or 20,000. Theoretically, a signal being transferred through such a server and headed for rebroadcasting could be tapped into by anyone who has information on the running time and the URL. But in practice, this remains a very limited possibility when using independent servers, due to the capacity involved.

Secondly, it may not be in the interest of a station to have the signal—being transferred via server to a group of recipients who have agreed on its use—made generally available 'as is'. If a station in Vienna is picking up a program from its colleagues at the Salzburg *Radio Factory*, a local presenter in Vienna will probably want to make an announcement to that effect. Some context would also be suitable on a program coming in from South America, for instance. And translation may be necessary, perhaps in the form of partial overdubbing, or as full translation involving delayed broadcast.

As emerges from this second point, it can be of advantage to store broadcasting material on a server, or in an archive, so that it can be downloaded on demand for renewed broadcasting. This enables combined programming that can mix locally produced material with items received from radio colleagues across the globe. Obviously, this technique for exchanging up-to-date reports on current events can just as easily be used for regular program exchange, an application we will return to later on. In all cases, as we will see, it entails communicating along several channels

Women World Wide

Both of the options just mentioned—livestreaming in the context of an international event, and program exchange among stations via archives—were given particular attention by the *Digital Dialogues* partner in Vienna, *Radio Orange 94.0*. The experience there with motivating and training radio volunteers to use these techniques is well described in Wolfgang Kemptner's handbook (2003). One of Vienna's activities can serve as an illustration of the broad reach this type of exchange can unfold and at the same time, an indication of the preparatory and supplementary communication it involves.

Some weeks in advance of the International Women's Day on March 8, 2003, *Orange* hosted the annual meeting of InterKonneXiones or IKX, a network of feminist media activists—worldwide in principle, but mainly including women from Europe, Latin America, and the Caribbean. The conference in Vienna included workshops on livestreaming and on the use of internet for program exchange via archives. One of the motivations was to initiate personal contacts among women at *Orange* and others in Europe and Latin America, centering on the feminist content of the programs they create. There emerged a variety of international exchange activities among radio makers who creatively adapted "audio in the internet" applications to their ideas and aims.

At the IKX conference, it was decided to attempt a live program connection on 8th March between *Radio Número Crítico* in Santiago de Chile and *Orange* in Vienna. After technical training and an enthusiastic exchange of ideas on content during the conference, the women remained in e-mail contact in the weeks leading up to the event. They arranged to meet one hour before the scheduled broadcast in an internet chat room, where they would be able to make last-minute updates on arrangements and decisions. While broadcasting locally as usual, Vienna streamed the program with reports and features on the events of the day in the Austrian capital. These were translated into Spanish in the studio in Vienna. Then, Santiago took over with the latest news from that end. This was translated into German in Vienna, using an overdub during the broadcast. Because each of the stations was broadcasting live and simultaneously streaming, the other station was able to take the stream directly off the internet without using an intermediate server. One participant reported:

> It was a great feeling the first time we took over the live-stream from Chile; to hear that voice again two or three months after the conference. Before that, we met in the chat-room and asked her questions, and on air she was answering these questions. It was just like an interview via livestream—a great form of communication. (quoted in Kemptner, 2003, p. 26)

The two-way stream was so successful that the women coordinated a second event two weeks later on the International Day Against Racism, this time including *Radio Lora* in Zurich. There were no previous personal encounters with the women in Zurich, as noted in an evaluation interview:

> So it can still work without knowing one another personally. I would suggest, though, clarifying the programmes in the chat-room or via e-mail, so that you know what's going on and what will be happening. For example, in the Swiss programme there was local news and I knew the people in Vienna wouldn't be so interested in listening to

local news, so I knew that when it started I could do other programming. (Kemptner, 2003, p. 25)

Later, two women from Vienna visited their Brazilian colleagues at
Radio Fala Mulher in Rio de Janeiro. They produced and broadcast a
one-hour bilingual program in Portuguese and German, which was
uploaded onto a server and broadcast a day later in Vienna.

Since 1998 FIRE (Feminist International Radio Endeavour) has a
strong presence on the internet—just one part of its raft of activities,
which include a radio station, training, and consciousness-raising
events. FIRE makes regular web broadcasts (including marathon webcasts lasting several days) in English and Spanish as well as archiving
previous events and interviews. Like many feminist alternative media
organizations, FIRE sees training of women and girls in radio production
and web site construction as a priority. FIRE has formulated a process of
teaching about technology that is part of an interactive methodology and
exchange designed to enhance the learning process and create new
tools for political activism and learning of technical knowledge and skills.

At a recent workshop in Costa Rica one participant said that
"although she has been doing community radio for many years, she had
never thought the internet could become an international radio station,
which is why she is so interested in working at FIRE" (internet newsletter on FIRE web site).[11]

Communication via Various Channels

As these examples show, cooperation along such lines requires
communication over and above the actual exchange of audio files: personal encounter, extensive e-mail correspondence, phone calls, and
chats among partners. Successful rebroadcasting also depends on good
rapport with and support from other groups within a local community initiative. Ideally, one-time broadcasts ought to receive local publicity in
advance, ensuring that there will be more listeners. But organizing that
publicity can be too much of an additional burden for those preparing the
event—producing a trailer to announce the broadcast, struggling with
the content management system on the radio station web site, or setting
out a press release for the local papers. This points toward the significance of frequent contact and steady backing within a station, where
colleagues will help shoulder that burden if they perceive it as serving a
mutual goal. As Wolfgang Kemptner, in Vienna, pointed out in an interview with a member of the DD evaluation team, the station provides a
macrostructure, but "the participants create their own infrastructure. It is
highly interactive, there's a lot involved."[12]

Maintaining Accessibility to Selected Programs

Once located at a specific address on a server, sound files can be fetched on demand and downloaded to another computer. Not only do large broadcasters such as *"BBC Listen Again"* make use of this to accommodate their listeners, the smallest do it as well. *Connemara Community Radio*, the *Digital Dialogues* partner on Ireland's Atlantic Coast, regularly posts several programs a week on its web site http://www.connemarafm.com, including local news and other popular shows that audience members may have missed. The material is posted in Real Audio format and is picked up, as feedback shows, in many different places. This is reflected on the station's web site, which offers information for a new community of listeners: Connemaran and Irish *diaspora* all over the world (particularly in the United States).

Some larger community stations upload most or all of their programming into an archive on their own server, where listeners can call up individual shows on demand. *Orange* in Vienna has practiced this successfully, even considering automation of the uploading process, despite all the exact timing this demands of the radio volunteers running their own shows.

The option of delayed reception is not restricted to listeners: colleagues at the same station can use archive material for reference or quotation, and other stations might download audio productions and use them for researching related topics or for rebroadcasting (on agreement). Such arrangements call for coordination, and although smaller stations would stand to benefit the most from interesting additional program elements, they often lack the resources to organize rebroadcasting. *Freies Radio Freudenstadt* in the Black Forest, for example, only manages to pick up two outside shows regularly: *Europe from down below*, produced in southern Austria twice a month and reporting on Eastern Europe and the Balkans, and *Free Wheel*, a weekly music show in English, made in Hamburg. Here, the internet as a ubiquitous "pick-up area" is a simplification compared to the older method of sending tapes or CDs through the regular mail.

Labels Make Audio Files More Manageable

The mathematics and logistics of exchange don't come into play until a certain volume and variety of material have been reached. Suddenly, systematic use of labels and key words become highly significant, because searching becomes necessary. Not only are file names and locations important: there may be worthwhile information or short clips inside a larger file, to be found only if the key concepts or names of interviewees have been tagged onto it. Independent or community radio servers normally use compressed formats for archives, such as mp3, rather than the (larger) formats common to consumer interfaces (e.g., Real Audio). Yet even when audio files are compressed they still take up a lot of space and are slow to download. Seen in relation, low-volume labeling enhances availability without notably increasing file size. To make for easier access, some system of content organization or additional communication on content is indispensable.

On a local level, this requires additional effort on the part of community radio employees and volunteers and is a further argument against automating the upload process. "If a radio station chooses a more horizontal approach aimed at spreading the use of internet widely among radio makers, it needs to motivate and teach its volunteers the skill of uploading and audio file onto archives 'by hand'" (Kemptner, 2003, p. 8). When volunteer radio presenters tag their own uploaded programs with subject markers, which may include names, index and search functions can be applied more effectively by listeners or colleagues wishing to tune in or download.

On a supraregional and international level, servers with thematic emphases or specific editorial approaches have been created (for a list of examples, see Kemptner, 2003, p. 13). In the following, we will discuss a system set up in the German-speaking part of Europe by community radio activists in Germany, Austria, and Switzerland.

E-mail Daily on Current Reports

Saving research and production time is an important reason to cultivate program exchange, as most volunteers at community radio stations have limited time. An even more significant reason, however, is the qualitative leap it enables, helping smaller or geographically remote stations to keep abreast of current events. Sharing editorial material also implies a direct exchange of information and opinions among the general population in different locations without a detour through any mainstream filter.

Community stations in central Europe have established a "free radio" web site—http://www.freie-radios.net—which is used for posting clips and programs. They can be downloaded and rebroadcast freely by other participants. These are usually speech items: reports, features, interviews, and editorials, typically including only short passages of music, for copyright reasons. Uploading privileges are limited to those who have clearance by the entire group, so that the web site can't be misused. Whenever new material is posted, basic data on it is distributed in an automatically generated e-mail that gives a link to the exact internet location of the clip. Typical earmarks (labels) are: title or topic, genre, length, and contributor(s); sometimes there is also a précis or a suggested introductory text for the presenter at another station. These "cue sheet" e-mails reach subscribers daily; the subscription list and uploading rights are administered by a webmaster collective.

Again, additional informational substructures are included in and supported by this self-organized system. A German-speaking radio volunteer interested in covering Latin American topics in his or her radio show can rely on the fact that, once a week, the *Onda* editorial group ("The Wave") will produce and distribute new programming with news and features, about half an hour with six or eight different topical reports that can be used individually or as an ensemble. This weekly offering is not located on the free radio server itself (instead on www.npla.de, run by the News Pool Latin America in Berlin-Kreuzberg); still, the weekly posting notices go to all subscribers on the free radio program mailing list.

International events, such as the *World Social Forum* in Recife, Brazil, in March 2003, are handled in the same fashion. Networking before the fact informs mail subscribers that colleagues attending the event expect to post reports on certain days or at given times (often using cell phones to upload the material). The advance planning allows for short-term pickup and better integration of the reports into programs.

zipFM

A major regret of many community radio participants has always been the sheer impossibility of dealing with up-and-running news. It demands good sources, editorial skill and speed, and, above all, more time than volunteers or employees usually have. This can become a source of frustration for socially and politically committed people who would like to articulate their ideas on topics of more than purely local interest. A cooperative effort developed among the German-speaking free radio groups helps to alleviate this problem.

On a Monday to Friday basis, volunteers at different locations produce up to half an hour of daily political coverage. This may consist of elements they produced themselves or include packages submitted from colleagues elsewhere. On a given day, one location is responsible for compiling the material and uploading by 5 P.M. If a delay is to be expected, notification comes in the course of the afternoon. Colleagues preparing an evening review-of-the-day show can proceed with their planning. Each station chooses the clips it would like to broadcast.

Even *Orange 94.0* in Vienna, the largest community radio in the German-speaking area with over 400 active volunteers, was formerly unable to sustain daily news coverage. Cooperation through zipFM has resulted in a Tuesday-to Friday evening show with political topics and news, produced by an editorial group founded specifically toward this aim. In his evaluative comments on this, Kemptner clarifies that technical fascination or prowess are not the driving force behind this, but that initial access to internet program exchange seems to get the ball rolling for further activities among volunteers: "It's quite clear that the main motivation of the radio makers for participating is based on the content of their production rather than on enthusiasm about IT. In general, a concrete project makes the exchange via internet more meaningful" (2003, p.12).

The German-speaking radio community of volunteers, activists, and trainers assembles yearly on lakefront (trade union camp) property not far from the three-way border between Austria, Germany, and Switzerland. Here, workshops are informal and productive—morning voice work, for example, may begin with casting pebbles into the calm lake and watching how the interference pattern of tiny waves develops, just like acoustic waves—and, the idyllic setting notwithstanding, the free radio server enthusiasts regularly set up temporary internet hook-ups there to teach new colleagues how to use the program exchange servers effectively.[13]

Training for the Web: Voices of Asylum Seekers and Refugees

> Refugees are particularly vulnerable to the denial of their right to freedom of expression—not only in terms of their general ability to express themselves on any matter of personal concern, but also regarding issues specific to their status as refugees. (Carver, 2001, p. 1)

Web training and production initiatives have provided ways for new and emergent communities in the United Kingdom to get essential information and to communicate with each other in their own languages: Refugees Online[14] has provided web space and training for around 80 refugee groups. The groups representing refugees are mainly from London, and there are also nationwide support and training groups. Community radio has been used by migrant communities to help build language-based and cultural communication. In Vienna, where there are well established migrant ethnic communities, *Radio Orange* has many different programs made by and for each of these communities. This is in the tradition of community radio stations in multiethnic communities: *3ZZZ* in Melbourne, Australia, has broadcast multiethnic and multilingual programming from over 60 different language groups since 1989.[15] The National Ethnic and Multicultural Broadcasting Council (NEMBC) in Australia advises members to be particularly sensitive to the needs of refugees:

> These communities are relatively small and may experience one of the following: high levels of unemployment, English language barriers, low-income status and other social factors that could be defined as special needs. More recently-arrived communities lack resources and they have not established regular media in their own language.[16]

Using an example of one of the *Digital Dialogues* projects involving refugees and asylum seekers in Sunderland in northeast England, we can now look at how community web radio initiatives might enable people to express their identities and maintain communications with their family, homelands, and culture(s) without succumbing to *a priori* dominant cultural representations. Since 2000, the British Government has adopted a policy whereby refugees and asylum seekers are dispersed from the capital to other parts of the country. The trend is that people are sent off to areas where housing shortages are less acute than in London and the South East.

Sunderland is one such place that has seen a large increase in the number of refugees and asylum seekers. In this predominantly white city, there has been a rise in incidents of racist abuse and physical attacks against asylum seekers and refugees. During the time of the *Digital Dialogues* project about a thousand asylum seekers were "dispersed" to Sunderland. The violence against asylum seekers over the years 2000– 2002 culminated in the murder of Peyman Bahmani, an Iranian asylum seeker, which the police described as racially motivated. Since 2003 the U.K. Home office has stopped sending people to the city. There have been several reports about unbalanced and inaccurate reporting on asylum seekers in the press (Speers, 2001; The Information Centre about Asylum and Refugees in the UK [ICAR], 2004). The ICAR report indicates the consequences of negative reporting—this statement came from "a representative of a leading refugee agency": "We have been told that a negative article one day equates to a fist in the face the day after" (ICAR, 2004, p. 2).

Many of the refugees and asylum seekers in Sunderland have poor language skills and often feel isolated within the overall civic community. Discussions with local agencies working with refugees and asylum seekers indicate that the need to develop oral communication skills is one of the main priorities for refugees whose language skills are poor. The increasing accessibility of the internet and development of new digital technologies opens up fresh opportunities to engage people in broadcasting and education. People can look for news, information, or music from their own cultures or interest groups.

One of the aims of the Sunderland project was to provide access to these new media and also to provide learning opportunities to enable people to become active contributors to digital media rather than passive consumers. For many refugees and asylum seekers food, shelter, and safety are the main priorities. Many have been dispersed to the area and have few friends. Some speak very little English, some have mental health problems as a result of trauma relating to separation from their families, bereavement, and social isolation. Most refugees and asylum seekers experience insecurity about their citizenship status, and their insecurity is increased by the lengthy and difficult process of assessment by authorities. While waiting to find out if they are to be given permission to stay in the United Kingdom, they have to attend numerous appointments with solicitors and be present at court hearings.

Assimilation or Distinction?

The British government's proposed adult education curriculum for refugees and asylum seekers rests on the foundations of increasing their language, ICT, and citizenship skills. In their research about asylum seekers, cultural difference, and citizenship in Brighton, Bellis and Morrice acknowledge the huge effect that displacement has on their lives and the "insecurity, trauma and culture shock" that increases their sense of displacement (Bellis & Morrice, 2003, p. 83). They recommend that a holistic approach to citizenship be taken that acknowledges asylum seekers as active learners and that involves adult educators, local community networks, and organizations that "play a vital role in facilitating the process of settlement and encouraging a sense of belonging" (2003, p. 88). They conclude:

> [W]e believe that the government approach reinforces an assimilationist and deficit model of citizenship education. According to this model, linguistic and cultural difference, rather than being valued, is perceived as a handicap, and the role of adult education is reduced to facilitating the process of assimilation into the values, norms and culture of the host society. (Bellis & Morrice, 2003, p. 86)

The suggestion from this is that citizenship and media literacy skills, combined with ICT skills in accessing the web, can enable people to produce positive, inclusive representations: ". . . inclusion should not mean assimilation or enforced homogeneity but a recognition of existing skills, talents and knowledge and a celebration of distinctive cultural identities" (Bellis & Morrice, 2003, p. 89).

Unsurprisingly, apart from learning English, formal learning is not one of the top priorities for refugees and asylum seekers. This raises the issue of "having a voice." It means that unless your basic needs are met, you are unlikely to be in a position to have your voice heard. The *Digital Dialogues* project found that it was difficult to address these through community radio while people were experiencing "human rights shortages." In these situations, "excluded" citizens/learners had primary needs and circumstances that had to be addressed before they were ready to engage on any sustained citizenship learning project (see Johnston & Coare, 2003, p. 193).

As outlined in Chapter 4, the University of Sunderland has well-developed community links that have been built up over a number of years. It is one of the most successful U.K. universities in terms of attracting underrepresented groups to study in its degree programs. The student radio station has in the past broadcast programs made by and for underrepresented groups in the student community, including using the web as a dimension to enhance local broadcasts. A program had been produced by and for Greek students and streamed simultaneously on the web. The program makers were primarily media students who already had radio skills. This was the only student program in the Greek language that was accessible to students and that dealt directly with their interests and music. The program was successful in that Greek students told us that groups of Greek students all over the campus were listening. It also enabled friends and relatives in Greece and the United States to listen in, and the web was used to relay requests and messages that were then used as part of the programs. We use this as an example of how a small station can effectively unite and link up members of a specialist audience. It was this philosophy that led the course partners to look at how the student station and web initiatives might be used to benefit refugees and asylum seekers.

The course partners were Sunderland Refugees and Asylum Seekers Support Network (SRASSN), a network of statutory and community organizations concerned with the needs of refugees and asylum seekers,[17] and two university departments at the University of Sunderland; the tutors were members of University Radio lecturing staff and a development worker from the School of Education and Lifelong Learning.

Careful Approaches to Building Trust

The development worker attended informal drop-in sessions for refugees/asylum seekers over a number of months. Half-day workshop sessions took place over a 6-week period at SRASSN premises and

Sunderland University Media Department; in addition many informal sessions took place at a church hall where the refugees and asylum seekers would meet once a week. The participants were refugees, asylum seekers, workers, and volunteers from SRASSN. A tandem approach to training was taken (see Chapter 4). A great deal of time was spent working in partnership with SRASSN to look at the best way of working with refugees and asylum seekers.

The participants had little experience of either web radio or community radio. This posed problems in planning workshops; how could people say what would interest refugees and asylum seekers if they did not know about the potential of the media? As one participant said "You need to know the basics of radio production before you can start getting on the web!" It also emerged that the refugees and asylum seekers faced issues and had needs that were very different from other groups with which the University team had cooperated in the past. The community workers' and volunteers' knowledge and understanding of refugees and asylum seekers' needs were critical factors in the planning of workshops.

Early on in the discussions with the refugee support organization, it emerged that workers and volunteers within the network had very little knowledge or experience of internet radio. Many did not have access to the internet in their workplace (interestingly, even if they were allowed access to e-mail, they were explicitly barred from using sound on the internet).

People in the project, including the asylum seekers themselves, felt that "telling the stories" of different asylum seekers' experiences in their home countries, during their flight from there and their stay in Sunderland, was an important part of representing themselves on the radio and countering the myths that had been built up in the media or views that were held by many people who lived in Sunderland. This was, in some cases, a very uncomfortable experience for the asylum seekers concerned. For example, when the trainers used the technique of role play in radio courses, getting trainees to interview each other, it replicated the unpleasant interview/interrogation sessions with authorities at various points during their journey. It could also be very difficult to talk about traumatic events that they had experienced. (During our project two members were deported, which in itself was unsettling for group members—these were people who had related to us horrific stories of violence and abuse against them and their families.) This comes on top of what has been for many a long journey fleeing danger, violence, and abuse.

Acknowledging these problems was a first step for the person towards feeling more comfortable about telling his/her story. Building up trust with trainers and group members about what would be done with the interviews was important. Learning digital editing skills so that people could feel in control over their own stories was also valued. Sharing the process of choosing music, being presenters and preparing the program in the studio—an important part of the process—was often the most pleasurable part of the course for the participants.

New Media Spaces for New Communities

> Adult educators should contribute to an anti–racist model of adult education by challenging racist assumptions in media coverage of asylum seekers or individual attitudes. (Bellis & Morrice, 2003, p. 89)

The planned end-products of the workshops for community workers, volunteers, refugees, and asylum seekers were an antiracism campaign about refugees in Sunderland and a world music program intermixed with refugee stories broadcast on *Utopia FM*, a student-run radio station based at the University of Sunderland.

The ICAR report cites several "myth busting" campaigns by The Refugee Council, Oxfam, the Commission for Racial Equality and others (ICAR, 2004, p. 86). It was this myth busting—counteracting inaccurate information that has been used as a slur on asylum seekers—that the Sunderland campaign chose to focus on. They used clips of interviews that asylum seekers had made with volunteer workers and with one another (thus changing the usual dynamic of the asylum seeker being the passive interviewee). A Sunderland resident was recorded repeating the myth that asylum seekers had been given free mobile phones. This was countered by the voices of the people themselves saying that they had saved up for the phone and how vitally important a mobile phone was for getting information, keeping in touch with each other, finding out what had happened to relatives, and generally for their own personal safety reasons as they walked around Sunderland. The mobile phone was a piece of technology that was being used in a positive way and gradually, over time, group members were learning to use radio technology and the web to name and define their experiences, to seek advice and information that would make their lives a little easier, and using community radio to articulate their needs, interests, and desires in a more positive way.

Through their experience of negotiating the allocation of airtime for their on-air campaign and program at the university station, they became conscious of some of the difficulties inherent in being involved with media organizations that have to serve competing audience interests. In the case of the University station, this raised questions about participation in decision making for the "mainstream" full-time student compared with the "part-time" temporary student from a community education workshop like the one the SRASSN students attended.

The ITC, web radio, and program-making workshops enabled the SRASSN group to gain access to educational and community media resources and acquire the confidence to discuss their position in the media landscape. Through being producers and editors of a variety of forms of radio programming on air and on the web, they began to imagine for themselves, and actually play, an active role in local media, rather than being solely consumers or "victims" of media messages.

OVERCOMING GEOGRAPHICAL
AND SOCIAL DISTANCE

Community radio is already being used by different subcultures in a number of original ways, from activists to grassroots movements or dispossessed groups. What is evident from our research is that the various ways that audio can be accessed and produced for the web often entails convergent and complementary forms of communication among those participating. This sets into motion new relationships and communication dynamics among groups seeking access to community media, radio stations and radio trainers, and community development workers.

As with any new media form, the uses and function of different types of web radio and audio applications on the internet are changing at a fast pace and are continuing to redefine radio, particularly with regard to its interactive potential. However sophisticated the technology, any training and development in this area still needs to start from a human angle and shouldn't ignore basics of radio production: applying conversational skills, telling stories, weaving creative narratives, and understanding the unique characteristics of radio's potential. Those involved in the various projects described above used the process of learning about radio and the web to articulate their interests and needs, and there is no doubt that the use of new media in all forms relating to web radio has enabled and encouraged communication along various other channels and on neighboring topics, including the resolution of conflicts encountered. Among other things, a new community/convergent media literacy can help trigger the realization that information is not simply there to be consumed, but that it is selected, formed, and disseminated—decided upon by individuals and groups. However, we concluded that people need to understand the context of community radio (and international networks) before they can understand the idea of web radio.

What seems clear is that the internet dimension of community radio activity at a local level can be seen as a response to the negative influence of the corporate globalization of media. Linking dispossessed groups via community radio can enable useful and often crucial communications between groups (e.g., refugees, activists) who have shared interests in the local or global dimension (see Kahn & Kellner, 2003). There is a balancing act involved in the role community web stations play in helping groups, for example, refugees and asylum seekers, to cultivate their own culture of origin while engaging in a new culture in their own way. The options offered them by community media can bring them into closer contact with both of these cultures, as they use interactive resources to edit, produce, display, and update audio material or text, as they follow up cultural links, document life stories, and much more—all this within the context of a civil organization structured by the new culture. This has a sociopolitical significance, implying as it does integration by means other than assimilation. It also has a global cultural meaning: these volunteers may even employ state-of-the-art technology to maintain contact with and build bridges of comprehension to very old cultures and ethnic traditions, some of which are endangered today. (A highly interesting variation of this type of oral history, intertwining communal with personal histories in the autobiographical telling of southern Italian émigrés, is described in Chapter 8.)

Much talk about web radio and audio centers on technology, and when it comes up at community stations, it may initially be seen as the province of those knowledgeable and enthusiastic about using technical equipment. The activities described in this chapter and other sections of this book have worked toward systematically subverting that effect—an approach quite in keeping with cybernetic thinking, where foreseeing reliable sources of error is standard procedure in handling all types of processes. From the outset they have approached technical handling as only one of the many flanks or tracks in a wide and variegated constellation of information exchange that newcomers are invited to enter. The escort over the (equally predictable) initial hurdles is provided by forms of training that open up the technical sphere of communication as a tool for those who, under other circumstances, might never have assumed an active role within it. Their motivation, which is to be kindled, is not dependent on a fascination with technology, and their trainers therefore look at motivation as being fed by human and social sources, life experience, and communicative abilities.

NOTES

1. See http://www.resonancefm.com/
2. http://www.bbc.co.uk/radio/

3. and there has been a spin-off in the realm of radio studies for radio teachers and students, who can access programs in different genres for study of texts and techniques.
4. http://www.streetradio.net/
5. A charity organization for the homeless, run by the Salvation Army.
6. See also Tacchi (2004) for description of Youth Internet Radio in Australia.
7. See http://www.irational.org/radio/radio_guide/ for do-it-yourself guide to setting up a web station
8. To see an example of copyright regulations in the UK, see http://www.ppluk.com
9. http://www.commedia.org.uk/voices/index.htm
10. "Jeder hat das Recht, seine Meinung in Wort, Schrift und Bild frei zu äußern und zu verbreiten . . . "
11. http://www.radiofeminista.net/agosto04/notas/tallerames-ing.htm
12. Recorded interview by Traudel Günnel, April, 2003, unpublished.
13. Some documentation on the same type of workshop, conducted in Vienna, is available in Kemptner (2003) and on the project web site http://www.digital-dialogues.de.
14. http://www.refugeesonline.org.uk
15. http://www.3zzz.com.au
16. http://www.nembc.org.au/
17. SRASSN's network consisted of around 60 local partners, from education, health-related, and voluntary sector organizations.

REFERENCES

Atton, C. (2002). *Alternative media.* London: Sage.
Atton, C., & Couldry, N. (2003). Introduction to Special Issue Alternative Media. *Media, Culture and Society, 25*(5), 579-586.
Bellis, A., & Morrice, L. (2003). A sense of belonging: Asylum seekers, cultural difference and citizenship. In P. Coare & R. Johnston (Eds.), *Adult learning, citizenship and community voices* (pp. 73-91). Leicester: National Institute for Adult and Continuing Education.
Carey, J. W. (1998). The internet and the end of the national communication system: Uncertain predictions of an uncertain future. *Journalism and Mass Communication Quarterly, 75*(1), 28-34.
Carver, R. (2001). *Voices in exile: African refugees and freedom of expression.* Report for ARTICLE 19 and the Global Campaign for Free Expression. Oxford: Centre for Refugee Studies.
Hendy, D. (2000). *Radio in the global age.* Cambridge: Polity.

Horin, A. (2004). DJs who really know the beat on the street. Retrieved November 2, 2004 from http://www.smh.com.au/artiles/2004/02/29/ 10779894 34839.html?from=storyrhs&oneclick=true (posted March 1, 2004).

ICAR (The Information Centre about Asylum and Refugees in the UK). (2004). *Media image, community impact*. London: King's College/ International Policy Institute.

Johnston, R., & Coare, P. (2003). Reflecting on voices. In P. Coare & R. Johnston (Eds.), *Adult learning, citizenship and community voices* (pp. 192-204). Leicester: National Institute for Adult and Continuing Education.

Kahn, D., & Kellner, R. (2003). Internet subcultures and political activism. Retrieved June 30, 2004 from http://www.gseis.ucla.edu/courses/ ed253a/oppositionalinternet.htm (posted March 23, 2003).

Kemptner, W. (2003). *Webcasting*. Freiburg: University of Education (brochure). http://www.digital-dialogues.de.

Lewis, P.M., & Booth, J. (1989). *The invisible medium: Public, commercial and community radio*. London: Macmillan.

Priestman, C. (2002). *Web radio—Radio production for internet streaming*. Oxford: Focal.

Pringle, I., & David, M.J.R. (2002). Rural community ICT applications: The Kothmale model. *The Electronic Journal on Information Systems in Developing Countries* [EJISDC], *8*(4), 1-14. http://www.ejisdc.org.

Speers, T. (2001). *Wales Media Forum, welcome or over-reaction? Refugees and asylum seekers in the Welsh*. Oxfam/Cardiff Report on Asylum and Media in Wales.

Spinelli, M. (2000). Democratic rhetoric and emergent media: The marketing of participatory community on radio and the Internet. *International Journal of Cultural studies, 3*(2), 268–278.

Tacchi, J. (2000) The need for radio theory in the digital age. *International Journal of Cultural Studies, 3*(2), 289-298.

Tacchi, J. (2004). Researching creative applications of new information and communication technologies. *International Journal of Cultural Studies, 7*(1), 91-103. .

Tsagarousianou, R. (2002). Ethnic community media, community identity and citizenship in contemporary Britain. In N.W. Jankowski & O. Prehn (Eds.), *Community media in the information age: Perspectives and prospects* (pp. 209-230). Cresskill, NJ: Hampton Press.

Wall, T. (2004). The political economy of internet music radio. *The Radio Journal, 2*(1), 27-44.

7

Live Broadcasting of Public Events

Susan Jones

The youth center in Freudenstadt, a town in the Black Forest in southeast Germany, has been temporarily closed for over a year due to changes in city personnel and the development of a new concept for youth social work. To encourage the revitalization of the center, the local radio station, Freies Radio Freudenstadt (Free Radio, or FRF) has planned an evening of live music for the Saturday of the Easter weekend. The youth office and a volunteer organization that supports the center have joined with FRF to organize a program for the target group, 14- to-25-year-olds. Five local "beginner" bands have been invited to present one set each between 7 p.m. and midnight.

FRF is a community radio station with its work space in the youth center—a main reason why the partnership for the event makes sense. It will be possible to transfer the sound signal from the concert into the studio via cable within the building, thus eliminating the problems of transferring the program via telephone lines. This in turn means that the radio team managing the event will be able to concentrate on presenting an attractive program for an age group often neglected in this rural and tourist area of Germany. The majority of the team—about two dozen will be actively involved in the evening—are themselves under 25.

They have long been busy with preparations—the design and printing of posters and flyers, press releases and internet publicity, negotiations with authorities, attention to neighborhood concerns about noise and an influx of people, security measures at the door, as well as arrangements for the use of sound and lighting systems, delivery and sale of refreshments, payment of royalties, and much more. But they have found time to record interviews with the young local bands performing in the show, and can use these as an opener for their broadcast an hour before the live music begins.

The evening turns out to be an overwhelming success; the venue in the youth center is sold out with an attendance of more than three hundred. Admission is inexpensive at ∈2 a ticket and there is an enthusiastic teen audience. A number of adults are around, and there are no problems with security. The sound system is working efficiently, as is the signal transfer into the studio and onto the broadcasting line. No deficit will be incurred: The city authorities have made the hall available at no cost, and the support organization for the youth center is covering the insurance.

Satisfaction all around, and—a few days later—the young production team gets together and looks back. Most knew beforehand what their role was to be, but some tasks had been overlooked or underestimated. "Cleaning up!" "Looking after the musicians was more work than I'd expected." "Nobody showed me how to use the DAT (digital recorder)." "I had no time for a break—everybody else got one." Everyone was glad to have taken part and learned a lot, agreeing that next time more detailed planning was needed, a clearer division of tasks within the team, and a greater degree of mutual toleration. As to the on-air presentation, it needed to more clearly explain the event to listeners. The bands themselves had obviously gotten valuable experience and publicity.

WHO WILL BENEFIT?

The event described above took place at the end of March 2002 and was the first in a series of live broadcasts produced by FRF together with local organizations as part of Action 3 of *Digital Dialogues*. The experience contains a number of strands that will be explained and discussed in this chapter. They include the training and the educational assumptions that underpinned it, the social and cultural role of the radio station within its locality and the editorial, logistic, and technical issues that have to be taken into account in the live broadcasting of a public event. These are standard considerations in planning live coverage, but were selected to be part of *Digital Dialogues* in the form of training needed to put on a type of broadcasting that is a vital part of the operation of any community radio station.

To briefly describe the actual setting in which FRF operates, Freudenstadt is a town with a population of some 25,000 surrounded by woods and hills in the northern Black Forest in Baden-Württemberg. The nearest cities are the state capital, Stuttgart, the second administrative center, Karlsruhe, and Strasbourg across the border in France, all some 80 km distant. The local economy still includes the sale of raw lumber, but prices have fallen radically due to international competition, making light industry and tourism increasingly important. For over a century, the fresh mountain air has attracted wealthy guests from all over Europe for health cures, and even after WWII, health insurance organizations kept the sanatoriums well filled. This guaranteed employment until about 20 years ago, when health reform set in. Now the economy must cater to more conventional modern forms of tourism and hope to attract international meetings, sporting events, and conferences.

The geographical isolation of Freudenstadt dictates that social life revolves mainly around local clubs, church communities, or village events. In these traditionally oriented structures, members of minority or socially disadvantaged groups may not feel readily included. And from the point of view of young people growing up in the area, the emphasis on tourism and the need to keep up a hospitable front does make it feel as if the place is someone else's playground.

The radio station is therefore a focus of interest for young people and for new arrivals to the area; both groups are strongly represented within the radio project. For them, radio work is an attractive hobby that links with musical interests and brings rewards in terms of the acquisition of technical, communication, and self-presentation skills similar to those described in Chapter 4 (Sunderland and Turku) and in Chapter 8 (Freiburg). Broadcasting of public events yields, in this case, the extra benefit of bringing radio volunteers in contact with local organizations they would not otherwise have approached, presenting opportunities for integration.

A community radio station like FRF attracts a variety of volunteers. Some are good talkers and good at getting others to talk; others are experts in a particular field or hobby and can communicate their enthusiasm—a particular sort of music might be their interest. Such people can end up running a regular program, and their contribution is the stronger and more reliable if they have the backing of an organization or a team behind them. Still others just like helping to make things happen, are good at organizing rosters or keeping resources checked, whether it be coffee or equipment. Yet others—and these are often young men— are fascinated by the technical aspects of radio.

All these types of people participate in an operation like community radio and sometimes, profiting from the lack of hierarchy or demarcation of labor, they will move from one area of work within a station to another as they gain sufficient skills or confidence to see what else they are capable of. There is an element of chance about who becomes involved, but again the chances are that some groups will not become active of their own accord: older people, people with disabilities, people from minority groups, and women and girls—these last for reasons that we have seen, in the Chapter 4 account of women in Sunderland, can be overcome: lack of confidence and a social conditioning that makes regular escape from household tasks and childcare unimaginable.

The balancing of access to a community media project between those who seek it and those who do not (but would benefit from the experience) and whose participation can only be solicited through affirmative action, is an important decision. A radio station like FRF has a relationship with a number of communities, or "community segments" in the words of Hochheimer, who poses some key questions in his discussion of the problems of organizing what he calls "democratic radio":

> Who serves whom? Is the function of the station to serve its constituent community segments? Or do the communities act as resources for the station to present to society as a whole? . . . Who speaks for which community interest? Who decides what are the legitimate voices to be heard? . . . What happens when power, or people, become entrenched? (Hochheimer, 1993, p. 477)

The possibility of a random encounter with a radio project is one reason why, for the station itself, the station's presence at a public event is important. It is an opportunity to be seen in action for the first time by many people, both those who know of the station only through listening, and those who have never heard of it and perhaps have no idea that their lives and occupations, their leisure interests and their opinions are the stuff of local community radio. Chance conversations around the mobile unit can turn into research projects that end in programs. There is an opportunity here, too, for feedback, the collection of names of people who might want to become radio volunteers, and the distribution of leaflets and program schedules.

For organizations running social, cultural, or political events, simultaneous broadcasting considerably enhances the occasion. It obviously widens their audience and heightens their significance by giving organizations a media platform within the public sphere. This kind of broadcasting brings local initiatives and organizations into direct contact with their community media and can lead to cooperation over longer periods of time. In this respect, the relationship somewhat resembles the Tandem partnerships described in Chapter 4. In Freudenstadt, "cooperation partner" became the shorthand term for the organization with which FRF established a working relationship for the purpose of a live broadcast. Such partners are usually busy with their own organizational work and cannot invest the additional time required to master the technical and editorial aspects of radio broadcasting. The arrangement with the community radio station puts at their disposal equipment and the skills of radio volunteers and paid personnel. Successful cooperation of active groups inside and outside the station can result in mutual recognition, pooling of energies, and a collective contribution to local public life and civic exchange.

THE TRAINING CONTEXT

The technical equipment necessary for low-cost transmission of the broadcasting signal into the radio studio (using computers and telephone lines) was purchased and tested in advance of the *Digital Dialogues* project. A small group of volunteers was trained in October 2001 and ran broadcasts of three events in October and November of the same year. This experience formed a basis for the project activities beginning officially in January 2002 and leading to the first event within the training program, described at the start of this chapter. It was the intention to extend the pool of volunteers so that, to use a football metaphor, a wider "squad" might be formed, any of whom could be selected to be in the relatively small production team for a particular event.

In the first phase of the action (year one), the broadcasts were generally arranged with groups that had cooperated with the radio station in the past. This phase served to train teams for the live broadcasting situation, to observe the most frequent difficulties that arose, and to find solutions that could be attained through improved training and better advance preparation. Work stages leading to individual broadcasts were documented, to be developed subsequently as a handbook for use by other community stations and groups wishing to prepare a live broadcast of a local event.[1]

The events covered during this period included:

- an environmental fair including panel discussion with politicians/experts;

- a benefit concert for the handicapped with live music and program inserts;
- a disco program presented by young local DJs;
- the traditional local trade union meeting on May 1;
- an apprenticeship fair at which young people are offered vocational opportunities;
- an African culture festival;
- an international sports event held locally, the world championship in sail-gliding;
- two mixed cultural programs at the city youth center, with music performed by local groups.

One of these last events has already been described, and for both of these FRF, having its studio in the same building as the event, was the main organizer. The live broadcasts ranged in length from four to sixteen hours and included a period of two weeks with a daily broadcast of one to three hours duration during the sport event.

The training concentrated on the practical application of technical matters and on the coordination necessary in advance of an event. Major attention was given to these areas, which the next section will consider in turn:

- **public relations**: establishing viable contacts with other organizations, planning and publicizing the event itself;
- **logistics**: selection of proper equipment, coordination at the site of the event, testing and trouble-shooting;
- **editorial concerns**: preparation of interviews, writing and presenting links, and choice of suitable music;
- **teamwork**: successful cooperation before and during a broadcast.

Public Relations

An event broadcast produced under live conditions is a mutual public relations effort linking a community station to local activists in other fields. Once a partnership has been initiated, it often leads to a continuation. But in the initial phase, it has a tentative character. Do the representatives first establishing contact with the radio station have the full backing of their organization? Can publicity be managed together, the division of labor arranged sensibly? Will cooperation partners be able to participate in presentation during the broadcast or be too busy managing their event? Are they willing to acknowledge the commitment of radio personnel and volunteers as opposed to simply using the radio team in a functional manner for the duration of their event? Questions such as these need to be addressed early, because they affect the public perception of the broadcast. Indeed, a community media initiative has to consider Hochheimer's questions: what organizations it wishes to be associated with and which facets of public life it chooses to support actively. Selecting cooperation partners has a political dimension, too. As Wolfgang Kemptner pointed out in relation to *Radio Orange 94.0* in Vienna, "the content of the live event will have to be compatible with the political values of the radio station" (in his article appendixed to Jones, 2003, p.27).[2]

Resources being limited, not any and every event can be handled. Weighing the options and making decisions can be difficult, because positive results are hardly quantifiable and negative effects difficult to make good. Alongside the publicity benefits for the organizers, including the radio station, relevant internal factors include scheduling and the availability of individuals from the production "squad". External aspects to be taken into account might relate to the status of a cooperation partner. Investing time and energy in support for a group that does not normally receive much publicity, rather than a well-established organization, may not benefit the radio project significantly. However, its endorsement of a marginal group can help create public interest in the group's activities. Ultimately, a gesture of inclusion or solidarity sheds a positive light on the radio project, at least within a certain sector of the public.

Proximity with certain local initiatives will seem more or less desirable to different individuals involved in community radio work. On the other hand, a general debate within the media project over selection criteria could be counterproductive or even paralyzing. Relating the planning of individual events back to the initial rationale for acquiring equipment and skills is one method of creating a context for decision making. Another helpful technique is overall scheduling for a year's time. A list of events coming into question over a period of at least several months makes it simpler to achieve balance and variety in the programming and ensures that personal contacts or favoritisms won't lead to one-sidedness.

The importance of detailed exchange on the plans and intentions of an event's organizers was so apparent that FRF tried to arrange meetings with cooperation partners as much as six to eight weeks before a broadcasting date. This permitted, under favorable circumstances, research on a theme and advance production of interviews or clips that were used to advertize the event and the broadcast, and that could in part be integrated into the live broadcast itself. Interviews with those participating in an ecological trade fair; "talk" sessions with members of a young local band produced a few hours earlier and then blended into a live broadcast during their break between sets of a punk concert: there is no end to the possibilities for using radio coverage to enhance and complement the published information about a local occurrence. The teams prepared a written broadcasting sequence that integrated the program of the event with approximate starting times, the editorial items designed for in between, music sources and other "fillers," as well as full names and functions of the speakers and interview guests. This plan, clearly showing planned shifts between stage program and radio presentation, was available to team members working at the venue and those in the studio. The latter also had written information on the event to use in short announcements, and filler materials in case of an interruption in the signal transfer.

Logistics and Handling of Technical Equipment

Until recent years, technical and bureaucratic hurdles made on-site broadcasting from outside a studio essentially unmanageable for community media initiatives. Before digital phone lines were available, signal transmission from a live event into the studio had to be handled on a separate radio frequency individually approved by media authorities—a process that made broadcasting from external venues practically accessible only to large stations and networks. Probably for reasons of quality, even these broadcasters used cable connections as extensively as possible, involving telephones and acoustic couplers only for short interviews or live reporting. Their typical scratchy quality became one of the aesthetic "signatures" of radio. Even in the age of high fidelity, reduced sound quality was tolerated because it signified a live event.

Digital sound and telephone technology changed all that, making it possible to feed not only spoken language, but also music in acceptable quality through cable connections that are almost universally available in the public telephone network.[3] Community media have begun to take advantage of this inexpensive option, setting up mobile studio components at an external venue and feeding their signal through a high-speed modem or computer into a digital telephone line or broadband cable. In the studio, the signal can be decoded and broadcast conventionally or streamed directly onto the internet. Aesthetic criteria, incidentally, have changed along with technology: the general public, now accustomed to listening to music listening in digital quality, expects high fidelity even from community media. Providing state-of-the-art broadcasting opportunities to local organizations grants them a new form of access to media coverage.

At *Radio Orange 94.0* in Vienna, it was possible to initiate live event broadcasts as part of an overall "quantum leap" in terms of technical infrastructure and programming interests. In the course of digitalizing studio production, the nonprofit radio station (the only one of its kind in the Austrian capital) had installed its own server. This was to be used for various purposes: documenting the daily programming and making specific sections available on demand as archive material; uploading preproduced elements for broadcasting; improving program exchange; and encouraging webcasting schemes together with other noncommercial stations on a national and international level, including alternative news servers (see Kemptner, 2003). Ethernet cables being almost universally accessible across the urban area, the Viennese colleagues realized that to broadcast from an external venue, they need only set up mobile studio equipment at the location and connect it through a computer to a broadband socket. The signal would then be transferred via internet to the station's own server or, alternatively, relayed through another server called *shoutcast* providing free service for this application, both alternatives known to deliver stable connections without "stuttering."

They reasoned that, using equipment already at their disposal, they would be able to provide a new service that would be paid for by event managers. The income, even if modest, would cover training and personnel costs for the event broadcasts, support the overall infrastructure required for the other activities being pursued, and at the same time strengthen the station's presence within the local scene. Also, the skills to be learned for local event broadcasts are nearly identical to those necessary for other forms of program exchange via internet. Thus, opportunities for participation in international webcasting events would improve as well. These hopes have, in fact, been realized on frequent occasions, such as International Women's Day, with live material from Latin America, and globally organized independent media broadcasts with alternative programming on summit meetings or political rallies (as treated in Chapter 6). On a local level, it was possible to promote cultural festivals, urban development projects, and more.

Freies Radio Freudenstadt chose the other technical alternative for signal transfer into the studio: the digital telephone line. This method was better suited to the rural environment in the Black Forest in southern Germany, where broadband cables are the exception rather than the rule. Relying on an ethernet/DSL connection would have limited the number of locales from which broadcasts could be undertaken, whereas employing ISDN lines meant availability for a wide variety of different cooperation partners in all parts of the area. In situations where no digital telephone line was available, a temporary one could be installed by the phone company at short notice and at relatively low expense (not possible for broadband connections in that region). Using digital phone lines for several hours isn't costly, and they usually provide a stable connection, although one financial drawback of this method was the initial investment for high-performance modems.

This was outweighed, however, by the perspective of being able to broadcast from practically any spot within several hundred meters of a telephone simply by having a temporary extension added to the existing line. This would enable cooperation at outdoor events or remote locations, which appeared significant in the rural context. Many organizations, it was considered, would not perceive a live broadcast of their local event as undesired competition (drawing away paying guests), but rather as an enhancement, making it accessible to those unable to attend—public transportation often presenting a problem on evenings or weekends, particularly for the younger generation and the aged.

Editorial Concerns

The most challenging aspect of live broadcasting from local events derives from the fact that every event is different: the program is unique, the cooperation partners all have their own special interests, and the venue may or may not be familiar from a previous broadcast. An event with a set agenda can be handled well, because the greater part of the program sequence can be planned in advance. If the proceedings at an event cannot be reliably predicted, program elements can be prepared in advance, later to be used flexibly. Some event managers will accommodate radio colleagues by agreeing on definite times and arrangements. Other broadcasts may depend entirely on planning done by the radio station. This is the case at informal events or when the station itself is managing the event. This transfers the emphasis of preparation work from dealing with a (more or less realistic) plan presented by an external partner to detailed organization done exclusively by the radio team.

In all cases, one basic tenet has to be observed, the starting point for preparing team members for any and all live broadcasts: the *broadcasting* sequence is not identical with the *program* sequence at the venue. Obvious as this may seem, it addresses the most frequent misunderstanding about live-event broadcasts. Even experienced radio programmers make the initial mistake of equating the event program with the on-air program and assuming that technical preparation is all that will be necessary. A minimum of reflection will reveal that this can hardly apply: Spectators at an event can see, and perhaps also participate in what is happening, but the radio audience needs a narrative in order to follow the event—description of sights, smells, and atmosphere. Also, at intervals, it is important to identify the radio station and inform listeners about the event, where it is taking place, and what will be happening next.

Inevitably, there will be gaps in an event program that need to be filled on the radio—perhaps while the stage is being rearranged, a sound check completed, a guitar string replaced, or while everyone is busy eating lunch. A major speaker can be delayed in a traffic jam, or (particularly at an outdoor event) a thunderstorm may come up. In fact, even a broadcast from an indoor event can be interrupted by a thunderstorm (blackouts are not that rare in the Black Forest).

For such unforeseeable situations, including breakdown of the telephone or cable connection during signal transfer, there must always be a person back in the station studio to react to unexpected situations and to pick up calls from listeners. Ideally, however, a broadcasting team will not be taken off guard, but rather will have discussed various options on program elements of their own, keeping in mind that they represent more than just a technical medium for transmitting a sequence of events determined by others.

Teamwork

Feedback among the team members in the Freudenstadt training period generally took place during a meeting after the event and was briefly documented in writing. Overall, the reactions show that the success of a broadcast and the satisfaction of the active participants are greater when a clear division of roles is accepted by the team, that is, when delegation of tasks is successfully undertaken. In cases where one or two persons attempt to handle all aspects of broadcast preparation, this tends to result in insufficient preparation, lack of communication, and general frustration. On the other hand, teams working on a basis of mutual respect and open communication can manage broadcasts successfully with a minimum of written preparation.

The broadcasts themselves illustrate these observations: solidarity within the team is actually audible on the radio. Short pauses are then filled with music or informative messages, and the atmosphere remains relaxed even when delays or mishaps occur. The responses of cooperating partners also corroborate this. The broadcasts carried out by a well-disposed radio team are those that have prompted positive feedback from the event managers and audiences. This is expressed in the wish to continue cooperation on the occasion of another event.

The live broadcast is a much more complex communicative situation than exists generally during studio work. This suggests that close attention should be given to acquiring the necessary skills and applying them in an exposed public context, because an unsuccessful broadcast will have negative consequences for both the radio project and the cooperating organizations. As experienced trainers confirm (Werner & Günnel, 2003, p. 33), a systematic approach to conducting interviews is the core of preparation for practically all radio work, and in this particular context as well. It not only enables radio amateurs to deal better with all types of conversational situations at a live event, at the same time it improves the quality of their research and programming decisions in advance of an event. The art of conversation—in this case of structuring verbal encounters so that they can incite the interest of others—emerges as the most versatile tool.

Training offered for live broadcasting teams necessarily entails treatment of technical topics, such as handling the hardware and software required for signal transfer into the studio, assessing acoustic conditions at a venue, or treating various sound sources simultaneously—stage sound, background atmosphere, radio presentation. If action-oriented training methods (see Chapter 3) are being applied, this may involve simulating a live situation in advance. This is only possible to a certain degree, as a "dry run" can hardly approximate an actual event. Therefore, written documentation on technical experience gathered in individual locales is very valuable for future reference and training.

Some Lessons Learned

In the period of training planned within the Freudenstadt action, two events were marked by insufficient preparation and communication by the coordinating persons. In both cases, other colleagues managed to rescue the day. In two other cases, technical difficulties occurred that could not have been foreseen by the teams preparing the broadcasts. Here, the difficulties were handled with ease and good humor (and additional equipment that had been transported in reserve or could be fetched quickly from the radio station).

With regard to documentation, it is noticeable that when communication is not functioning within a team, notes are no longer taken, summaries are never written, feedback and evaluation are avoided. On the whole, however, the documentation was more than sufficient for its stated purpose within the action, which was to provide subsequent teams preparing broadcasts with a broader base of experience from which they could profit.

Another difficulty to be faced is that of conducting training in such a way that it is applicable to the wide variety of broadcasting situations later to be managed. There are enormous differences in the events and the venues, and thus the editorial and technical challenges can vary greatly. Experience showed that workshops centering on the live broadcasting equipment may be unsuited for beginners: In fact, the most successful participants of these workshops were those who already had extensive experience with studio equipment and with editorial tasks of various kinds. They are also more pragmatic than beginners, that is, more able to size up a broadcasting situation realistically and make plans that can actually be carried out. Newcomers need to be encouraged to participate, but also informed frankly about the limitations they will almost surely encounter.

THEORETICAL REFLECTIONS

In 2002, Freies Radio Freudenstadt was awarded the Baden-Württemberg Media Prize for its overall programming and open access for diverse social groups. The preceding account has shown how that access works for two sets of groups and in two directions: a station recruits and/or attracts as volunteers individuals who seek to be included in activities; the resulting trained team points an important part of the station's programming towards a range of organizations, in effect offering each an amplification system to reach a wider public. In the other direction, the organizations, "contracted" as "cooperation partners," may or may not themselves learn media strategies, may or may not become longer-term partners, but are inescapably caught at least for a day in a broadcasting schedule of a certain character that gives their event a meaning through association beyond any original intent.

"Programmes," Scannell and Cardiff observed, "remain the final register and bearers of institutional intentions and assumptions about the scope and purposes of broadcasting and about the audiences to whom they speak . . . they are the point of exchange between the producing institution and society" (Scannell & Cardiff, 1982, p.170). Their point is as true of a community radio station as of the subject of their comment, the National Programme of the prewar BBC, and the program schedules of both have something in common in their variety, even if the relation with the audience is entirely different. In Freudenstadt, the cooperation partner's event is heard on air as part of FRF, while, as already mentioned, the station has to weigh strategically what are the advantages and disadvantages of being seen—and heard—to choose an organization as a cooperation partner.

The comparison with the prewar BBC can be continued. In their *Social History of British Broadcasting*, Scannell and Cardiff speak of the BBC's becoming "a central agent of the national culture [through] its calendrical role; the cyclical reproduction . . . of an orderly and regular procession of festivities, rituals and celebrations—major and minor, civil and sacred—that marked the unfolding of the broadcast year" (Scannell & Cardiff, 1991, p. 278).

FRF's live broadcasting endeavors may not have the cultural centrality and regularity of the BBC but there is no question that their coverage is a contribution to the local public sphere. Speaking of Radio

Dreyeckland, a community radio station in the same *Land* of Baden-Württemberg whose purpose is similar in aiming to foster communication between diverse groups of the population, Lewis speculates that the "program schedule could be read as a schematic representation of the common meeting ground—a part of the local public sphere—afforded to the producers and listeners," and asks "to what extent this schema acts as a 'roadmap for listening' and for putting the different groups in touch with each other" (Lewis, 2002, p. 57). The FRF experience confirms that this "putting in touch" goes on for the individual volunteer as well as for the organizations that, whether on a one-off basis or as part of the annual calendar, are enrolled in the FRF schedule.

Public sphere theory puts into context the social and cultural role of the station, an example of the "non-profit and legally guaranteed media institutions of civil society . . . run voluntarily and held directly accountable to their audiences through democratic procedures" whose existence Keane urges as a necessary accompaniment to a reformed public service (Keane, 1991, p. 158). But as was observed at the start of the chapter, the Freudenstadt experience contains a complexity of strands. Training for live broadcasting of events was the main contribution FRF made to the *Digital Dialogues* project. It is clear that the experience offered the trainees reproduced many of the key features of action-oriented media pedagogy (AOMP) as outlined in Chapter 3.

The training arose out of an expressed need for more a more effective live broadcasting system, and thus was related to the learners' real-life situation. Product orientation was emphatically illustrated by the fact that their production was not only published over the airwaves but occurred under the eyes of the public and was the result of a planned collaboration with a particular organization. The process was equally action-oriented: trainees "in creating their own media products . . . develop[ed] their skills and knowledge on a technical, creative, and content level and at the same time strengthen[ed] their self-confidence and their autonomy" (Günnel, Chapter 3). Günnel, following Schorb (1995), includes "acquisition of self-confidence in different social situations" as an aspect of AOMP: "participants learn how to act in different roles, such as conducting interviews with prominent personalities, and to reflect on such experiences with other members of the team" (Chapter 3). For a young person to find her/himself, microphone in hand, controlling the words of a local dignitary is indeed an empowering experience.

Up to a point, the training adopted a learner-centered approach in that it traded on the young volunteer's desire to be involved in broadcasting. More accurately the training might be described as group-centered insofar as the need for teamwork and mutual toleration was a hard lesson to learn, yet one patently needed to achieve a successful outcome. Johnston underlines the need for exactly this kind of experience in discussing studies of community contexts (as opposed to individualized activity) providing access to adult education:

> The particular relevance of social learning to social inclusion . . . is its focus on the collective, its commitment to innovative learning and its emphasis on problem-solving at a group, network, institutional or community level. In terms of learning processes, it identifies the four axes of social learning, as being the processes of action, reflection, communication and cooperation. (Johnston, 2003, p. 56)

Finally, a key element of Freirean pedagogy can be recognized in the mode in which the training was conducted, that of dialogue. It is possible to see, in the young team's evaluation of their handling of the musical event described at the start of this chapter, that reflection among peers and in a group, facilitated by the trainer, was the driving force for improvement and further learning.

CONCLUSION

Cooperation with other organizations in the context of live events brings with it a number of solutions to problems that are common in community radio:

- It draws attention away from individual presenters who can all too easily reduce programming to varying forms of self-portrayal, directing it instead towards the particularities and special interests of groups outside the media project. This also creates an opportunity for media activists to appear publicly—in person and through broadcasting—as a unit with a collective (non-corporate) image.
- It broadens the perspective of community media volunteers, requiring them to research local event calendars long in advance and take careful note of activities pursued by others. Because selection and decision making is needed, it promotes exchange on the overall goals of the media project and its role within a regional constellation.
- In compressed form, it makes maximal demands on the equipment and skills accrued within a radio project, spurring participants to take on tasks they otherwise would not have attempted, often with surprising and satisfying results.
- It provides the excitement and fascination of a live broadcasting situation, without treating that as an end in itself. Instead,

this tension serves toward endorsing and supporting other local initiatives, including both mainstream and marginalized sectors.

- It helps cultivate liaisons on a local level, granting new groups insight into local media activity and inroads to accessing it. Simultaneously, radio volunteers receive first-hand information about local initiatives and their target groups.

- It ultimately helps overcome the negative effects of standardized approaches to community media activity and of stereotypes in general. This applies not only to technical and editorial aspects, which differ greatly from one event to another. It applies to the social dynamics, as well, leading away from hierarchical structures based on status. Club functionaries or radio staff accustomed to "running the show" function poorly in this type of team effort, which relies heavily on work behind the scenes. Members of partner organizations usually have no experience that would enable them to size up the broadcasting situation. To estimate realistically what needs to be done, they are often entirely dependent on the radio crew, in which some of the most competent and reassuring members may actually be teenagers from minority groups. For many, this is a refreshing reversal.

Unexpected alliances among "strange bedfellows" sometimes result from these cooperative schemes, but other effects can be predicted more reliably. Defining a new facet of the public sphere on a local level will position the partner organizations anew in the perception of audiences, who also become participants. This will not escape the attention of communal authorities and functionaries, who receive an opportunity to overcome wariness toward free media (which they sometimes mistrust and hesitate to acknowledge as a partner on the sociocultural scene). Radio volunteers will see new reason to learn more about the craft, some of them concentrating on technical installations, software, and acoustics, others becoming interested in mastering challenging forms of journalistic presentation. Particularly younger team members often begin to expand their mental images of professions potentially available to them.

Seen individually, each of these effects represents a small victory for the unfettered imagination. In their entirety, they show how authentic experience can arise within a public context valuing both process and product, suggesting to all involved that personal integrity and creativity are not private matters to be developed as fetishes and pitted against others, but rather constructive elements within a social and political structure being reformed constantly and collectively through imaginative contributions made by its constituents.

NOTES

1. A detailed description of these activities can be accessed on the project web site, *http://www.digital-dialogues.de*, by following the links to Action 3 and its handbook.
2. *Radio Orange*, as a partner in *Digital Dialogues*, also conducted training in live broadcasting and contributed to the handbook referred to in footnote 1.
3. Major broadcasters have advanced to wireless transmission via satellite—a technology that is, however, not practicable for local applications.

REFERENCES

Hochheimer, J.L. (1993). Organizing democratic radio: Issues in praxis. *Media, Culture & Society, 15*(3).

Johnston, R. (2003). Adult learning and citizenship: A framework for understanding and practice. In P. Coare & R. Johnston (Eds.), *Adult learning, citizenship and community voices* (pp. 53-67). Leicester: National Institute for Adult and Continuing Education.

Jones, S. (2003). *Local events on a "live wire"*. Freiburg: University of Education (brochure). http://www.digital-dialogues.de.

Keane, J. (1991). *The media and democracy*. Cambridge: Polity.

Kemptner, W. (2003). *Webcasting*. Freiburg: University of Education (brochure). http://www.digital-dialogues.de.

Lewis, P.M. (2002). Radio theory and community radio. In N. Jankowski & O. Prehn (Eds.), *Community media in the information age: Perspectives and prospects* (pp. 47-61). Cresskill, NJ: Hampton Press.

Scannell, P., & Cardiff, D. (1982). Serving the nation: Public service broadcasting before the war. In B. Waites, T. Bennett, & G. Martin (Eds.), *Popular culture: Past and present* (pp. 161-188). London: Croom Helm with the Open University Press.

Scannell, P., & Cardiff, D. (1991). *A social history of British broadcasting: Serving the nation. Volume One: 1922-1939*. Oxford: Blackwell.

Schorb, B. (1995). *Medienalltag und Handeln*. Opladen: Leske und Budrich.

Werner, U., & Günnel, T. (2003). *Der Radioschein: Radiojournalistische Basis-Ausbildung für Laien. Praxishandbuch für Lehrende*. München: Kopaed.

8

*Telling It Like It Is: Autobiography as Self-Definition and Social Identification**

Beatrice Barbalato

Karin Eble

Collecting, archiving, and broadcasting autobiographical heritage is a way of safeguarding community voices, of bringing the constituent parts of a group, a community, or an association into dialogue with themselves, of giving them cohesion. In this essay, after a theoretical excursus to make clear the social character of autobiographies, we describe two different examples of autobiographical accounts that come from two situations poles apart. One relates to the long-standing village-based culture of the Daunia-Irpinia (Southern Italy) and the wish of the area's many *émigrés* to identify with this tradition; the other involves adolescents from Freiburg, Germany, musicians who frequent a Media Center belonging to a Youth Aid Organization.

The *Digital Dialogues* project had the aim of observing, in the Italian group, how individual accounts reveal a substratum of metanarratives, and to what extent the groups of young people in Germany were able to situate themselves in a wider context, putting together a collection of material within the available time and suggesting a method for archiving and circulating the material.

---

*Translated from the French by Peter M. Lewis

In the final section of this chapter we reproduce some extracts from the autobiographical accounts of these two communities—quite different in their economic profiles, their contexts and their cultural models, and yet each, in its own terms, showing evidence of a more-or-less voluntary use of interpretive frameworks common to the membership group. Drawing on such sources to mold one's own identity, as we will show, is a central aspect of autobiographical narratives. For people to tell their story does not mean they are telling the truth about themselves, but shows how they feel about their own past and who or what they would like to be. Community radio, which clearly has a mission to put itself at the service of a community, can find in these accounts interesting program material to broadcast.

There is no doubt that emigration from the one place (the village and environs of Panni) and the social *anomie* in the other (Freiburg) have profoundly changed the way people identify themselves in their community. Nevertheless, telling one's story remains one of the most classic forms of remembering, of passing on a picture of oneself. In these narrative structures it is possible to recognize the codes by which people communicate their own identity.

The stories reproduced in the final pages of the chapter are very different in the two cases, but all point in the direction of the collective, toward the "glue" that unifies the group. There is also a symbolic reason for recording, side by side, the testimony of these two communities: it is a metaphor for an imaginary union between old and young, between the south and the north. It's a question of two extreme situations that we want put on record as marking the social significance of the biographical and autobiographical experience—two expressions that end by being the same thing.

Within these two cultures, we can see two different forms of regarding one's own individuality as something belonging to a community: one is closed and coherent, the result of sedimentation over centuries, the other fragmented but with a multitude of connections open for exchange; each gives evidence of cultural practices, of work *in* and *of* its time. As we've said, the wish to develop a collection of autobiographical accounts for *Digital Dialogues* and *Creating Community Voices* contributes to the project of setting up archives of oral and autobiographical memory.

Those reading and listening to these stories, both now and in the future, are called upon to undertake a work of interpretation, because the individual accounts are singular, of necessity limited in scope, and do not immediately reveal similarities. It is only when they are examined as a whole that it is possible to understand the connections that underlie the different forms of telling one's own story.

THE SOCIAL VALUE OF AUTOBIOGRAPHY

Writing About the Self and its Value for the Collective

> To the Nietzschean question, "Who is speaking?" Mallarmé replies—
> and constantly reverts to that reply—by saying that what is speaking
> is, in its solitude, its fragile vibration, in its nothingness, the word
> itself—not the meaning of the word, but its enigmatic and precarious
> being. (Foucault, 1966, p. 333)

The trend towards producing autobiographical writing that was strictly individualist and self-sufficient reached its peak due, above all, to the influence of two fields: psychoanalysis and 20th-century literature. The two disciplines pushed to an extreme the idea of an exclusive and unique individuality. Clearly this corresponded to a *ratio,* a particular relationship between the two: on the one hand, psychoanalysis with its focus on the patient insists that personal actions (even if they take place in the context of varied interaction) are recognized as having strict boundaries. On the other hand, literature, especially from the 20th century onwards, constructed a genre that is still with us today, in many variations. From Goethe's *Sufferings of Young Werther*, through Proust and Joyce to Musil, the "I" becomes an absolute protagonist. It was at the beginning of the 20th century that the framing that used to accompany a story disappeared: formerly, the narrator would give the reader an explanation about having found a manuscript or a collection of letters, and one read the work in the context of this framing. From the Romantic movement onward, there is a complete correspondence between the author of a novel and the *persona* of the narrator.

The character of "auto-fiction" present in many of the novels of the 18th and 19th centuries, leads the naïve reader (a) to believe that a story told in the first person is a form of testimony and that there is a correspondence between author and narrator, and (b) to shrink the space between autobiography and autofiction to the point where they become the same thing. And yet, as Philippe Lejeune (1975) explains, every author sets out an "autobiographical contract" that provides a key for the reader to understand the particular form of autobiography, which is in fact for the most part self-interpretation. What it comes down to is that autobiographical writing subscribes to a code of pretence based on a selective presentation.

Jean-Jacques Rousseau, in his famous *Confessions*, promises to tell the truth, and he asserts that no one is capable of writing a man's life except himself.

I undertake a work that has no other examples, and will have no imi-
tators. I wish to show my fellow men a man in all his naked truth; that
man will be me myself alone. I know my heart, and I know mankind.
I am unlike anyone I know, and I dare believe that I am not made in
the same way as anybody else that exists. If I am not worth more, I
am at least different. Whether nature operated well or badly in opening the shape into which it thrust me can only be judged after having
read me. (Rousseau, 1959, p. 5)

In the great majority of such cases in literature we are dealing with stylistic conventions. In his essay "The Right to Biography" Jurij Lotman
(1985) explains the characteristics of a true biography. He cites as an
example how, at the beginning of the 19th century in Russia, the lives of
famous people were constructed on the model of military records. In
other words, models of a specific historical period with their particular
metanarrative structures provided the mold for biographies and autobiographies.

Each Period Has its Autobiographies and Biographies

Someone once said that biographies are lies told as truth. The same
could be said about autobiography. From the 16th to the end of the 18th
century biography was a reconstruction of the life of a person recognized
as someone who deserved to be the object of a biography. In
Transparency and Obstruction, Jean Starobinski remarked that J-J.
Rousseau "instead of confining himself to reconstructing his own biography, told his story in the process of reliving that history at the same
time as he wrote" (1982, p. 308)—an act of truth that Rousseau intended should stand the test of time, even calling on God as his witness.

Also, autobiographies express a different intentionality according to
the social class that produces them. The better-off and better-educated
have a tendency to hand down a memoir that is tidy and constructed. As
Blasco-Martinez and Rubalcaba Pérez emphasize:

The ruling classes . . . not only create their own image and their own
personal identity, using to this end intimate diaries, memoirs and
travel journals, in which the authors put forward their own subjectivity and opinions; they also elaborate the particular tradition of the
social group of their origin which justifies their power. Memoirs of this
kind can be constructed partly from old elements that rely on the
sub-strata of tradition, but they seek a new identity, one that is considered, loved, desired. (Blasco-Martínez & Rubalcaba Pérez, 2001,
p. 113)

Federico Fellini said one day, "I invented a life and a childhood for myself so that I could tell people about them," and Gabriel García Márquez (2002) gave his autobiography the title *Living to Tell the Tale*. The idea that one can live in order to construct one's own image belongs to the domain of cultured individuals, whereas ordinary people have a world view which is the absolute opposite; and it is often in writing that they have the feeling of taking shape. One can see this in The *Notebooks of Luisa*. Luisa (2002) writes an intimate journal to give substance and content to her life. For her, the intimate journal becomes a means of survival and a way of constructing of an identity.

The value that literature of every kind, in the 19th and 20th centuries and today, assigns to individuality as a sort of unique testimony was unknown in antiquity. Lessing, in *Laocoon*, points out how Helen is never directly described in Homer's Iliad, but only through the feelings for her awakened among older men:

> Homer himself, who so carefully avoids any detailed description of physical beauty and can hardly bring himself to say, in passing, that Helen had white arms and beautiful hair, still knows how to give us an idea of her beauty far more effective than anything art could achieve in a matter of this kind. (Lessing, 1964, p. 117)[1]

This is a concept well explored by Mikhail Bakhtin when he analyzes autobiography and biography in the ancient world and draws attention to the fact that, in antiquity, there was no cultural custom of thinking about the "I" outside of a context (1979, pp. 277-293). In Graeco-Roman literature, individualization resulted from another's gaze. Paul Ricœur's *Soi-même comme un autre* (*Oneself as Another*) helps us to understand this dynamic. Ricœur speaks of narrative identity, of how one can construct oneself through telling one's own story, a story that is always an act of interpretation (1990, p. 198).[2]

In her novel *Orlando*, Virginia Woolf annihilated, reduced to zero the idea that chronology has meaning in a life story. Does time serve to portray an identity or a biography? Is there a progressive development in an individual's life capable of being conveyed in a story that follows a temporal sequence? It is with irony that Virginia Woolf writes:

> It was now November. After November, comes December. Then January, February, March, and April. Next is September. Then October, and so, behold, here we are back at November again, with a whole year accomplished. This method of writing biography, though it has its merits, is a little bare, perhaps, and the reader, if we go on with it, may complain that he could recite the calendar for him-

self and so save his pocket whatever sum the Hogarth Press may think proper to charge for this book. . . . life, the same authorities have decided, has nothing whatever to do with sitting in a chair and thinking. Thought and life are as the poles asunder. (Woolf, 1970, p. 240)

Reflexive thought and life experience are, in fact, polar opposites. Biography and autobiography are constructed on the basis of categories of time and space, in which an author locates him/herself in relation to other people. The thousands of boring 19th-century biographies of a sociological or historical nature are the result of a belief that history moves forward, and they are the fruit of the conviction that a coherence exists between life and writing. It is an idea much debated and rejected by the Russian Formalists who, as far as literature is concerned, put the emphasis solely on stylistic values.

Nowadays, as Abraham and Török neatly say (1996, pp. 208-209), there is on the one hand a tendency to regard the "I" as a crypt or stronghold, and on the other hand a mass culture presenting images that only appear to be individual. For example, a person telling his own story on television as if it were something distinctive often (this is Maurizio Grande's interpretation, 1987, p. 155) transforms his appearance, adapting it for the audience as he waits "in the wings," and has a tendency to "present himself in a borrowed identity, making his personality totally fit the topic at hand, conforming to the social type and setting implied by the program."

That is to say that, increasingly, media presentations offer the illusion of something new and remarkable, while at the same time deferring — exactly like the picture painted by Guy Deborre (1988)—to a society that makes a spectacle of false originality, failing to recognize and systematically undervaluing the aspects of a culture that are common to all. This is a feature of society described also by Mario Perniola (2000, pp. 82-83). Put simply, it is a way of consistently reducing these cultural aspects to folklore; people talk more and more about ethnic cuisine and ethnic music—words whose meaning is lost because every culture, whether native or hybrid, evinces a character. People like the word ethnic: it protects them from the temptation to go beyond an exotic façade.

On the other hand, in the empirical reality of text and context, this capacity to make connections is at the root of cultural evolution, a molten mix of the old with the new in ever differing proportions. From this capacity to connect, identities are derived, a theme the writer has recently discussed (Barbalato, 2003b).

Codification has its part in telling one's story, as several recent socio-anthropological studies show. In *The Polish Farmer in Europe and America*, William Isaac Thomas and Florian Znaniecki analyze how peasants who emigrated to the United States in the 1920s, describing their life in letters home, used phrases taken from oral greetings and rituals remembered from the culture of their origin (1968, pp. 32-42).

Danilo Montaldi, in the 1960s in his book *Autobiografie della Leggera* (Autobiographies of the Down and Out), stressed the social value of life histories: "even the reactions of an individual, responding to what begins as an act of analytical understanding in a matter in which he is directly involved as a subject, depends on the general consciousness of the society in which he lives" (1961, p. 39). Montaldi's book includes the transcripts of five autobiographical accounts. It is an important work, both because of the collected testimonies, and for the preface in which Montaldi emphasizes the transition from individual to collective consciousness. He has outlined two opposite ways of telling one's story that can be taken as poles of reference: the *submergé* (overwhelmed) and the political militant.

The *submergé* "in writing his own autobiography has already, in revenge, accepted even his own failings as virtues, in accordance with a reversed consciousness which allows one to accept a personal situation which is negative and integrate the repression of political passivity" (1961, p. 40).

In contrast, the political militant (Montaldi, 1971) has a tendency to depersonalize the facts and to refer to others in stereotypes, such as "young people," "opponents," "people who don't know." In this case the boundaries between the Self (described on the basis of the chosen political values) and the Other follow very evidently. Again, we must note that it is a question of a narrative strategy aimed at taking shape and forming one's own image.

We find a similar perspective in Pierre Bourdieu, who offers his own autobiography as if it were a matter of no importance: "In adopting the analyst's point of view, I required (and authorized) myself to retain all the features which are relevant to the sociological point of view, that is, necessary to a sociological explanation and understanding—and those alone" (2004, p. 12).

The Experience of Creating Community Voices

As the philosopher Mario Perniola remarks, writing about Nietzsche: ". . . to read, think and write is not to express subjectivity, or to create oneself, but on the contrary to lose oneself, to feel oneself to be a tool, a gateway for something different and foreign" (1990, p. 48).

To talk of recording and giving weight to ordinary people through autobiography brings us naturally to the *Digital Dialogues* project. Community radio stations, which are set up to help protect a community's cohesion, can find in such a framework more scope for interpretation, less room for solipsistic concern, for nostalgic regret or indulgent fantasizing. And the autobiographical theme is given special attention in the *Digital Dialogues* project, developed as it is in the contrasting realities of life in rural and highly industrialized areas, cultures that are ancient and those of young people. The project throws light on the ritual elements that can be discerned in these life stories, like furrows in which several different lines of thought are inscribed.

Our north-south twinning, Panni-Freiburg, shows us, on the one hand, how old people from a small village in the south of Italy give a consistent and coherent account of their life stories, unconsciously using stylistic patterns that are recognizable only at second or third reading, and on the other hand, how young musicians in Freiburg seek out for themselves forms of communication that are in circulation on the internet, either manipulating them in remakes or creating quite new forms of expression. In this expressive bricolage the work, even if it is fragmented, does not reflect the world's discontinuity: it creates it, as Mario Perniola observes (1998, p. 107). The young people search for an identity through music, rejecting the idea that life is ordered by a plan, a final intention. They are not interested in telling a story centered around a theme; rather they prefer to comprehend and reconstruct a fragmented world, modeled on that of music stars. These are not finished models referring to a single person or idol, but wide open structures granting opportunities for contact and allowing the young people to function as a conduit—a bridge, but not an end, exactly as Friedrich Nietzsche said (". . . eine Brücke, aber kein Ziel") in the *Genealogy of Morals*.

The 'look' as a facet of youth culture is a sign of the transition from style to performance, from appearance to a manner of being.

> The look . . . sets up a space, better described as a landscape. The world in which we encounter video-music, trekking, the look, but also other manifestations of cultural activity like dance performance, break-dance, diverse artistic and literary forms—these are no longer spectacles, they are landscapes. What does that imply, a landscape? Rilke put it very well when he observed that, faced with a landscape, we feel ourselves at the mercy of something which is incomprehensible and distant: we are in fact conditioned to think that behind every gesture there lies an act of will, whereas a landscape makes no demands on us. (Perniola, 1990, pp. 59-60)

In a survey of various European cities conducted in the 1980s, most of the young drop-outs interviewed attached the greatest importance to space, to a choice of venue, rather than to the temporal dimension characterized by a structured life plan, and they attached more importance to the remake with its possibilities for playing with and commenting on a text, rather than on the aura of the original, which was out of reach (Barbalato, Liperi, & Scialotti, 1985).[3]

The "I" on the Computer Screen

A study carried out by Philippe Lejeune on intimate journals also recalls the human-bridge idea in certain significant aspects. These are diaries circulating on the internet, for whose authors the personal exchange serves an important function. The study gives insight into the psychological expectations of young people, particularly on the formation of their own individuality. The research shows how a self-description on the internet means short-cutting as much as possible the distance between the deeply intimate self and the outside world. For many, explaining oneself amounts to a self-description in parallel tracks, rather than providing a picture that is unified but hieroglyphic. The internet seems to facilitate the diarists' awareness in regard to autofiction and self-presentation. In the absence of personal handwriting, communicating in public without personal exposure modifies the canonical forms otherwise familiar in first-person accounts. The idea of an interpersonal exchange is certainly present, but it is a relationship that is more virtual than real and that leads to seeing oneself differently and sometimes to creating an alter-ego, a double:

> The Internet presents us with the paradox of writing without "difference" which is closely akin to the immediacy of speech, and to an intimacy which lacks an interior since apparently everything is instantly out in the open. The individual me which is created by internalizing social structures (the deep self) seems here to work in the opposite direction. (Lejeune, 2000, pp. 193-194)

A mirror-making system for writing about the Self is put into place. A sort of *multiple me* is deployed in different forms of journal written by the same person. Nathalie says "I like the distance you get from the screen, as if I was looking at myself from the inside and the outside at the same time." (Lejeune, 2000, p. 153)

One quarter of Philippe Lejeune's informants (17 out of 69) prefer their intimate journal to remain virtual: "Before their eyes, on the screen, this text which appears and disappears at will is as fluid and immaterial as their consciousness" (2000, p. 37). To choose the fluidity of the screen rather than the fixedness of the written page, the anonymity of typeface rather than the personal touch of handwriting, the dimension of one web page rather than of another, the wish to remain unknown or to insist on being read: these are all signs that need interpretation. "I went from an easy-to-hide notebook to the A4 format, legible at a distance of 100 meters in the fog. What that meant was 'It's my business, and to hell with you all'" (Lejeune, 2000, p. 156).

Anna's case is also interesting. She tells us how, through using email, her style changed from a formal and conceptual point of view. Dialogue, *the other*, alters the self-image. "I make myself into a person," writes Claire. Writing on the computer means for her tearing herself away to write about herself and for herself, a mode in which the other is just hinted at. "As a way of forging my identity, talking about my self was a method which no longer satisfied me. It caught me up in a bundle of old-fashioned attitudes." And "writing on the computer makes things more universal. She sees herself both as a spectator and an actor." comments Philippe Lejeune (2000, p. 127).

It's a question of a spiritual tattoo: "our life is a parchment on which living leaves its trace" (Lejeune, 2000, p. 407). "With my suicide attempts, I am as unstructured as my journal is structured"—the words of Maria P., who claims to have written a pyramid of words (sticking strictly to letterhead format and font size 13) on shifting sand. "Making her life a work of art conferred a unity upon it," a sort of repair job, was Lejeune's comment (2000, p. 99).

This style—negotiated, indirect, external—seems a common characteristic in much of youth culture. In mass culture, too, there is a trend to profit from the urge to speak in the first person. Reducing communication to confession is a successful formula for avoiding the impression that testimony is fictional. In the media, constant recourse to overused, first-person speaking is noticeable as a means to make various forms of communication more credible (see Barbalato, 1997).

From *Stories in the Mirror*, broadcast in Italy by RAI from 1978 to 1981 (see Sellari, 1985),[4] to the first-hand accounts reported by Philippe Lejeune in *Cher Ecran* (*Dear Screen*) (2000) or the interviews with dropouts in a number of European cities in the 1980s, and indeed in many other pieces of research: the idea of gathering life stories in particular contexts and building up a significant collection seems a positive way of rescuing history. It is not a question of preserving or petrifying cultures, but of pointing toward ways and means of mutual recognition.

The idea, on the one hand, of collecting autobiographies and building an oral archive in a small village in the Daunia region of Southern Italy, and, on the other, of understanding how young people using a cultural center in Freiburg interpret, identify, and construct an image of themselves has a double value for the *Digital Dialogues* project: it is a matter of facilitating the creation of oral archives and autobiographical accounts and of encouraging the use of radio and internet for these efforts.

SELF-DEFINITION THROUGH MUSIC

The *Soundcheck* project was conceived and carried out at the Media Center of the Wissenschaftliches Institut des Jugendhilfswerks Freiburg, a nonprofit youth service organization whose mission is to try and combat social discrimination by giving adequate and individual assistance to young people who participate in various activities there. Project activities were offered outside of school hours and were linked to the youth service program. They aimed to attract as potential participants particularly those with (usually for reason of social class) limited access to and motivation toward formal education and vocational training.

Soundcheck arose from the idea of accessing the internet and taking advantage of its interactive features to exchange sound and music files produced by and for young musicians. This would include the possibility of recording, uploading, and presenting their own music productions, unlikely to be accepted for conventional radio broadcasting or by the commercial music industry.

During the *Digital Dialogues* project, young music groups and performers—men and women—were interviewed about their hopes and individual ambitions in regard to the internet. The interview extracts allow a better understanding of the value placed on music. This individual perspective is the point of departure for the autobiographical project.

Throughout the project, music productions recorded in the studio of the Media Center with young bands and soloists were uploaded onto the audio platform *www.soundnezz.de*, which has been described at greater length in Chapter 5.

Concept and Goals of the Project

The Media Center has been carrying out projects in the area of music since 1999. These offerings are aimed at children and young people (up to the age of 21, in accordance with the German Youth Assistance Law), who, in whatever form, are or would like to be involved in making music, or are interested in sound technology or organizing music events. In this project a central role is played by the recording studio where young musicians can record and edit their own music without expense and with as much guidance or technical assistance as may be necessary.

On a organizational level this is part of the cooperative venture *soundnezz.de,* which was initiated by the Media Center together with the Landesvereinigung Kulturelle Jugendbildung Baden Württemberg e.V. (Association for Youth Education and Culture in the State of Baden-

Württemberg), the Medieninstitut der Pädagogischen Hochschule Freiburg (Media Institute of the University of Education), and the Studentenwerk Freiburg (Student Assistance Organization). *Soundnezz* evolved from an earlier cooperative effort of these four agencies called *"Haste Töne?"* (roughly translated: "got sumpn to say?"). The cooperating partners share server space for all kinds of project materials and outcomes, audio files, and current information. It was conceived as a platform where young people would have the opportunity to present, preserve, and document their own productions on the internet. The partners direct the project in cooperation with one another. A server has been configured to accommodate these goals, and the partners confer on content and design of the platform. The "internet music archive" is part of this larger audio platform and can be reached via *http://www. soundnezz.de*.

Why Music?

In a certain sense, music can be regarded as a harbinger of globalization. Since the 1950s, young people—particularly in countries with an orientation to the West—have contributed to the formation of overall cultural currents. Popular musical styles and the icons of pop culture have overcome geographical and political borders with relative ease and have become a focus for global communication, further promoted in recent years by the internet. The music industry was quick to recognize and exploit this development by advertising and marketing its products via the net. Alongside the multinational companies, however, smaller record labels and even independent producers have used the internet to enlarge potential audiences. The prospect of publishing their own music in this medium is associated, for many young people, with a sense of belonging to this multifarious and free-wheeling cultural carousel. (Baacke, 1998, presents several authors treating aspects of this development within the German context, including Vouillème, 1998, p. 433, on "Rock Goes Online" or Berg, 1998, p. 169 ff., with an interesting statistical contrast showing inverse trends in traditional musical activities among German youth, such as singing in a choir or glee club.)

At the same time, music offers young people opportunities to develop their personality and promotes their integration into peer groups. The experience of music is an active process. Especially in the area of popular music, the distinction between performers and audience is usually not clear cut. A rock concert, for example, can only be a success if the audience actively participates in it as an event. An audience that just sat there passively, taking in the music, would signify a total failure of the concert's intentions. As an interactive medium, the internet further reduces the distinction between producer and consumer, presenting diverse possibilities to develop activity: from aimlessly surfing the net to creating one's own homepage or participating in chats and mail-lists, each person can determine just how active he or she wants to be. Within this framework, music enjoys a status as a universal "language" of young people and is of interest to almost everyone. Fiske (1992, p. 30), referring to Bourdieu, shows how productivity and participation carry meaning for music fans and how selectively they choose among the commodities of popular culture; the cultural capital they produce is the most highly developed and visible of all (p. 48).

Many areas of popular music are closely tied to the latest trends. What's new? What titles are at the top of the charts or—even more exciting—will be there tomorrow? These are questions that young people want to talk about. Here, the internet is without rival as a medium that is modern and fast. Using the net is, of course, easier once a young person has mastered some of its technical options (which are not self-explanatory) and can enjoy them. In general, it is an accepted part of this culture to employ state-of-the-art technology wherever possible. This is true of the production, but also on the receiving end: interest in and enjoyment of new technologies is very pronounced, and it is often closely linked to or even generated by the wish to communicate through music.

Lifestyle Orientation and Forming Identity

Young people often see their music as a kind of "counterculture" in which provocation and self-expression play an essential role. Music that triggers enthusiasm within a certain age or peer group can become a significant social factor and can even take on educative functions, sometimes surpassing the influence of parents. Today, young people's questions about identity or about "the meaning of life" are often not asked (or answered) within the framework of the family or the school, but include other "authorities." Popular music is among them, creating as it does, an ethos of "telling it like it is."

In more than on respect, this music has a narrative quality. Firstly, the lyrics often tell stories or evoke images of lives and life situations. These may be socially and geographically very far removed from the audience, but are nonetheless experienced as "close to home"—similar to the more old-fashioned phenomenon of reading a novel and feeling as though one had lived through the story oneself. Secondly, mentioning music groups they feel an affinity toward has become a frequent, almost a standard way for young people to identify and describe themselves to one another. This can be observed in chat-room exchange, or when teenagers producing radio broadcasts on community media play their favorite bands as a way of letting the audience know "who they are."

In the context of self-definition and self-description as discussed in the introductory section of this chapter, music plays a particularly fascinating role, both for those who incorporate it into their mental picture of themselves and for those who witness this process. Music, it seems, is capable of creating new mythologies in an overrationalized world. These mythologies constitute multiple reference points for young people, in relation to which they can model their lifestyles. A collection of thirteen extensive interviews, "media-biographical narratives" of young Germans, reflects their perception of taste in music as a "central statement" about themselves, linking media involvement to personal success (Baacke, Sander, & Vollbrecht, 1990, p. 127).

Perhaps such effects are, in part, made possible by the nonverbal messages of music, which allow for shifting images and evade the assignment of labels and categories. At times, the dichotomy between the everyday reality of young people and the musical "roles" or identification figures they embrace can be extreme.

An illustration of this was provided in the 1990s by "gangsta rap," as countless European teenagers began identifying themselves with members of street gangs 10,000 kilometers away in Los Angeles, imitating their clothing, body language, and "underdog" attitudes (which included inverted racism, machismo, and proclivity to violence). This development was particularly bewildering because, in addition to the usual coupling of commercial music marketing with fashion trends, it entailed an aspect of social and mental manipulation that was objected to publicly by other rappers: the *Lifers' Group* at the maximal security prison in Rahway, NJ, not only began producing music with the basic message "no, it is not cool to be a criminal" (their first CD was nominated for a Grammy), they also initiated a hot line into their prison for telephone contacts and built up a role-play program in which teenage groups visited Rahway and interacted with inmates. The effect on a few young listeners who were associated with *CCV* activities in Germany was a split, some continuing to tow the "gangsta" line, others contacting Rahway and reporting on the *Lifers'* activities within their community radio show. At least the latter group had made a step away from an "object relationship" (simply using music to imagine another life for themselves) toward personal activity and interaction, and along the way had also gained some insight into the nature of manipulation.[5]

Although critical reflection on such processes is surely indicated, the *Soundcheck* project initiated within *DD* did not directly address the topics of mistaken or fictitious identity, manipulative intent or content in commercial music. Instead, in accord with Graebe (1998, p. 419), it placed emphasis on developmental options, encouraging young people to learn to produce music themselves and use the internet to circulate it (see Eble & Heinzel, 2003, on the training and production sessions). At the same time, the project provided opportunities for personal encounter among participants in meetings, studio sessions, or public events, which by their very nature suggested the value of integrity and accountability and also promoted critical discussion.

The development of personality is one of the main tasks young people have to face. In this phase of their lives, young people are increasingly able to determine their own cognitive and emotional development. They see themselves as individuals who have many traits, interests, or tasks in common with others, but who are also different from others in many essential respects. These similarities and differences that form the individual person are key aspects for them. At the same time as young people are becoming aware of this framework, they come under increasing pressure to confront their own future and the demands of society (i.e., parents, peer groups, school, profession). In addition, they have to deal with physical changes in their own bodies, making it necessary for them to confront their own sexuality. Thus young people face a difficult task: dealing with their own personal development and at the same time thinking about their relationship to the world and the world's relationship to them. *Soundcheck* hoped to promote this development by supporting activities that were both self-expressive and relational, combining their interest in music with their interest in the Internet.

Perspectives of Young Participants

Basti, 21, is a law student and guitarist in the group *Chinese Box*. His enthusiasm about publishing the band's music on the internet was typical:

> Ah, first of all it's everyone's dream to be sent around the world, I mean what you produce can be made accessible to everyone and that really makes me happy, when other people are able to hear my things and I can show my friends "Hey, there we are in the internet, that's us; we're right there!" That's really a feeling of confirmation that we as a band are accessible and not just playing alone for ourselves in some rehearsal room but for others; that others can judge our music and can write something—I dunno, maybe a critique or an opinion. We're also planning out the material that we recorded here—in the hope that our dream comes true and we'll get a guaranteed spot on Soundnezz.de, and maybe get some response to it, "Oh, they're on the internet; they've done something; they've got ambition" and "let's go on the net and see how their music sounds;

what do they look like?" I mean, we can mention this and use it as a reference for producers, record companies or concert organizers.

Two young people recording at the Media Center were asked what music meant to them:

> Music actually means everything to me because, if I couldn't make music, then I wouldn't be the person that I am today. At the moment there are only a very few things in my life that are more important. It's not an easy question to answer, but I would say that music will always be close to me, or in any case, not far away. (Conni, 17, school student, singer in *Backbeat*)

> Music means everything to me; that's why do it. I started a long time ago, exactly when I started, I can't quite remember. I must have been 13 or 14; I started with guitar lessons and since then, it has just come more and more into my life and become more and more important; and naturally I dream the dream that everyone does; it's not very realistic, but you dream it anyway (laughs) because it's so much fun to dream it; I mean, to stay a musician your whole life, which is really difficult. When you study law you have to set some priorities and when you're getting ready to take your final exams you have to say "OK, I can either make music (laughs) or get bad grades." But music means everything to me. (Basti)

Not only the music, but also the lyrics of rock and pop songs can be a powerful reflection of young people's thoughts and action. The lyrics, for the most part, have less to do with critical or argumentative ways of thinking and more with emotional confrontation or trying to understand individual problems. Music can help to create a consensus about communicating emotions and experience in the everyday world. Two participants described how music expresses their emotions:

> The lyrics in my songs are usually about girls or love. Or when I'm sad. Or what it was like to come to Germany alone and have to leave my family. Just now I have written a song about a child, for my brother, because his wife is pregnant. They're all sort of "I-stories." Everything that pops into my head. (Arben, 19, apprentice, solo singer performing in English and Albanian)

> Music is something that reduces my aggressions, that helps me to deal with my life. Maybe it's sort of a way of finding your way in the world. When something's bothering me, I withdraw into music and there I can let it out so that it doesn't eat away at me. (Conni)

On many internet pages one can find remarks about music embedded in a multitude of references to other areas of life. The language of this self-definition—stating one's musical preferences and distinguishing them from those of others—emerged when a musician was asked to describe the style of his band:

> Difficult question! Well, I think there's a lot of punk influence in it, but then there's a lot of pop influence too. The songs are written by two people: Marcus, the singer, and me; and he comes more from the pop direction and listens to people like George Michael, and I come more from hard core, the Punk corner with "Weazer." I used to listen to all the grunge groups like "Nirvana" or "Pearl Jam"; that's more my direction; and he listens to all the popular stuff, although we also have a lot in common like the Beatles, for example, which we all like. When we write a song—one of us usually has the idea, and then we work it out together in the band room. For this reason it is unavoidable that my influences sort of flow into his music and his influences into mine; that's pretty clear. I think the mixture is really interesting; it's kinda like, I would say, a mixture between punk and "Chili Peppers" or "Fu Fighters" and all the pop bands; and the hard groups like 'Nirvana' and popular stuff like "Bon Jovi" to some extent. We are really open. (Basti from *Chinese Box*)

For those actively involved in making their own music, situating themselves within the "landscape" of popular music is clearly a question of identity and development of individuality. But even for those who don't create music of their own, these aspects are of great importance. As members of a fan group on the internet or a newsgroup, in visits to a music chat room, they can affirm their identification with a particular group or star and be confirmed in it by their virtual correspondents. Also, they can attain recognition as "experts," which again has a positive effect on their self-esteem. The enormous number of music-related subject headings on the internet and the existence of special interest sites such as Musicnet would seem to indicate that self-confirmation plays as important a role as informative or entertaining aspects.

AUTOBIOGRAPHICAL NARRATIVES
FROM PANNI

In the community of Panni, autobiography is a running topic. This little village in the far South of Italy is classified as "at risk of extinction." The majority of the people are elderly, the young generation emigrates to find employment. Until the 1950s, residents numbered 4,500; today Panni has a population of 900.

Panni is a member of the Mountain Community of Daunia-Irpinia, an organization that links villages with similar human geography and mountainous characteristics. Despite the difficulties that the older people have had to face, they are very proud of their own values and culture. Knowing how to tell their own story is a marked feature of this pride and of the construction of their own personality. A genuine feeling of attachment and of belonging to their own land is present among all the inhabitants. The area around Panni has a scattering of agricultural activities, and the use of dialect is still very much alive.

The *Creating Community Voices* and *Digital Dialogues* projects have been closely tied in to the constitution of the Archive of Autobiographical Heritage and Historical Memory in Written and Audiovisual Form of the Daunia-Irpinia Area.[6] In a region that has suffered from the effects of emigration on a large scale, clearly everything to do with the memory of language and tradition is valued. The basic idea, then, was to create an oral archive that could be a reference point for transmitting histories, developing reactions, making contacts, and exchanging information (see Barbalato, 2002, 2003a). All autobiography and all personal history is linked to the wider characteristics of the collective culture, or, one should rather say, is a dialectical response to it. No one's story can be read without taking this wider context into account. Dialect, which is an essential element in the life stories, is of central importance.

There are a number of reasons for collecting life histories. Nowadays everything changes very rapidly and there is a tendency to forget, to leave things behind. This creates a risk that the relationship with the future may be badly damaged. Memory constitutes a basic part of our being. Without a starting point, without an anchorage or a past, no creative endeavor can have echoes or produce resonance.

Rescuing life testimony allows one to define, categorize and gain a historical understanding of the development of phenomena, and is a special way of constructing a community's memory. Protecting the traces of evidence means placing a value on the collective consciousness. Gilles Deleuze expressed it precisely: "Evolution is a matter of geography, of orientation, of signposts, of exits and entrances" (1977, p. 8).

From the interviews recorded in Panni, we will select a sample: a woman who emigrated, a peasant, and a farm laborer. The contextual framework is the village and the collective; all those interviewed, each in his or her own way, see themselves as inside the confines of Panni. Even Carmela who returned from Montreal, one of a family who had emigrated and who has lived now for many years back in Panni, talks of feeling different and of the wearisome business of integrating herself in

Montreal. But everything in her story is told from the viewpoint of Panni. Her narrative style is teleological.

> Yes, everybody was looking at me, waiting to see how I would say "good morning," and sometimes I didn't, but it wasn't because I didn't want to. Nowadays I'm a part of things: I know everyone and I say "good morning" to everyone. I fit into their world. Back then I didn't understand any of this. It was very difficult.

As we've said, the Panni life stories are embedded more in the village's geography than in its history. This is the way Donato speaks of his grave being very beautiful. At the top, his name is carved, DONATO DE STEFANO. And Pietro Cocciardi talks of his late wife in the present tense. She's alive, a fundamental part of his existence. To put it another way, what we see here is a mythical, circular type of thinking.

Here, we've chosen some significant pieces of testimony to represent this dimension of the bio-/autobiographies. These life stories confirm the force of the bygone culture, despite the emigration. The interviews don't have the somewhat rhapsodic character shown by the young people in Freiburg; rather they are couched in parables. One might note of these stories:

(a) Despite the singularity of every life experience, each story carries within itself techniques of self-presentation that are framed in the community and its values. (b) Language and dialect have a fundamental importance. This establishes whether or not someone is a member of the community circle. One interviewee (whose words are not among the texts reproduced below) said that his having lived in colleges and acquired different intonations there excluded him from the village's "community of dialect." His writings (dramatic scripts, poems, autobiography) are consequently viewed as suspect, in the same way as has been noted elsewhere (Radtke, 2002, p. 62).[7]

External parameters do not play a key role in the Panni story. Television and its models, the influence of economic wealth, where it exists, do not play a significant role in people's speech. What does have a very great significance is the past. Among elderly people one doesn't see radical change. Territorial membership has a greater influence than experience, which is often dramatized. The storytellers evoke habitat and context—a real amphitheatre in which to situate their own actions. The following are significant example.

Pietro Cocciardi, Agricultural Entrepreneur

Pietro's whole story tells in depth of the meeting with his wife, now long dead. It is one of the most interesting narratives both because of its use of dialect (which unfortunately one loses in the translation) and because of the story's structure. Pietro speaks of the time when he went to find his future wife in Milan where she emigrated with her parents when she was very young. He describes the people of Milan as if they were foreigners (the open country is a "desert," he meets a passer-by who speaks "like an African," etc.). In this way he reverses his own foreignness by putting his own cultural-anthropological context at the center of the narrative. Moreover, the structure of his story presents three tests that he has to pass, a feature of the fairy tales which were analyzed by Vladimir Propp in *Morphology of the Folktale*. Finding his wife after these three obstacles and being in an exotic land results in a miracle, to all appearances.

I met my wife when we went dancing at her grandfather's. "Excuse me, do you want to dance?" "Yes, yes . . . " As we danced, as we danced, I said to her, "what a beautiful girl!" I asked her, "Are you engaged? Are you not engaged? Do you want to get engaged? Do you not want to get engaged?"
. . .
It was August when I met her. September, October, November followed after.
In November I wrote to her.
"I ought to think about it, to turn it over in my mind" (she said) and that was that, she was sending me packing: but when she came to the end, she left her address.
"Now if you really mean it, etc."
I was working in a municipal restaurant in Foggia. It was at this time, at All Saints, seeing that she'd written to me, I said to myself, I must go to her.
"Do you want to tell your father, if you want me to come to Milan?"

The journey
So I packed a suitcase full of grapes. In November there's the Ermedia grape, a late one, hard, etc. The suitcase was a big one, 50 kg. It was going to be a fine present. When I arrived there, in Milan, (arriving in Milan, it's not like arriving in Panni) . . . It was like that because with a storm overnight everything was stuck in the mud. There are these narrow alleyways, like our sheep-tracks. I had worked out the way to get there, even the taxi driver had understood the way to go. He turns a corner, and 150 meters in from the corner there's a bar. We go in and ask, "Good morning, good morning all, excuse me Madam, where is the Via Messina?" She replies, "150 meters after the turn and you're there."
"We're there, do you understand? " (says Pietro to the taxi driver).
"Yeah, yeah, don't upset yourself" he replies.

Turn around. He takes the corner, we go nearly a hundred meters, and all these sorts of . . . When in the morning I got off the train, it was just before half past nine and there was this damn whatcha-ma-call it? (the fog). In the night there was rain and we were crossing these alleyways, you could see puddles, ditchfuls of water. One hundred, two hundred meters, I saw the lights but I didn't see the street-sign for the Via Messina. A leaf was covering it. The storm had filled the Via Messina with puddles.

"yes, yes, you've got there . . . " But what if we'd taken exactly the street she'd said?

"But no, it's there, it's there . . . " Oh well.

He'd sent us to the café and we went round a second time.

We entered another little street and we found everything shut and went back on our tracks. We found an old man who spoke brianzolo [dialect from the Milanese suburbs, Ed.].

"Excuse me. . . ?"

"O ba ba ba." Who could understand him? He spoke like an African.

"What? Via Messina? It's there, it's there . . . "

There were two or three cross-streets. We found a lane, a dog-leg. Who could say? There were leaves from the trees. It appeared there was a street-sign. The moment we entered the lane, two or three hundred meters in, there was a puddle of water as big as a river. The fog was intense, there was a bit of smog, it looked like a desert.

The street ended like that, but when we turned a corner, we saw Peppe, my father-in-law's brother. He had two or three goats, little ones and a couple of sheep. Quite soon he revealed who he was, but when I first saw him I said to the taxi-driver, "we've found a peasant."

"But how come you know him?" he said.

And afterwards, there was a great welcome.

In fact, she wouldn't let me go . . .

She said, "I don't like Milan. If you marry, you've got to go back to the South."

We got married. . . .

Maria Paglia Procaccini

Fifty years ago she emigrated to Canada and afterwards to the United States. Her memories stop at the moment of departure. Her story has the aim of reconstructing an image of the family, to create a contrast concerning certain things shared with family members who still live in the village.

They said it—with an air of sympathy, but at the same time, there are always those who . . .

My father poured himself a glass, he showed it. On the other hand, there was one of the others who felt it but didn't show it. And they put the blame on my brothers. Oh . . . when the two girls left who were always sitting on the stairs, they complained. "They're about to go, and they're drunk!" You know, that made me feel really bad, I heard it with my own ears.
And, anyway, lots of other things.
They said he'd stopped boozing, and it wasn't him. Doesn't matter what it was, they blamed everything on him, and because of him, people blamed his friends . . .

Donato de Stefano, Farm Worker

Donato is 65. He is still working and proud of it.

Work
Life in Panni . . . and there was the time when we were children. Life was hard when we were little. Compared to other families, we were better off because my grand-parents owned some land, that is a couple of fields, with two houses, so we had enough bread to eat.
During the war, when people didn't have bread, we did, and we lived well. OK, we still worked. Even nowadays, you can see, still working, but I wear myself out doing it.
. . .
After that I did military service at Udine. And when I finished military service, it was straightaway off to Frankfurt to work on the railway! We worked harder than slaves.
. . .
After that I was working on the chapel at the cemetery: have you been to the cemetery? You can ask the care-taker and he'll let you in, it's all behind there. Very beautiful!

Young and old
Nowadays they seem like leaves in the wind...and that means they don't have that drive any more. Young people twenty, thirty years old, they don't come . . .

CONCLUSION

In the two communities, statements and reflections assume a central significance because they are an intentional display of rationale, of will-power. Confession, self-portrayal—there is very little that is intimate or private about either.

At Freiburg, what comes out clearly is the considerable value given to musical choices as a deliberate expression of life-style and a means of cultural orientation. The stories have certain characteristics in common, evidence of the young people's will to live.

The situation in Panni is very different, where the testimonies are based on an ancient tradition of story telling. (The word "ancient" here indicates the persistence of a transmission model which goes back to the dawn of time). Are these deliberate choices? Yes, fundamentally, but there is also something subterranean about them. They are grounded in the place, they belong to its history, to the development of this community.

So it is that these radically subjective accounts, positioned at opposite poles of a sociogeographical axis, have been collected and archived in accordance with the value each community places on autobiographical story telling. However different the accounts may be, one factor that unites them is the urge of those doing the telling to rectify or structure their life experience in one way or another—omitting or emphasizing details, perhaps "ironing out the wrinkles" in their lives, or dwelling on individual moments whose reverberations last for years.

Another interesting parallel that emerges is the importance of idiom: in Southern Italy, correct intonation of the local dialect is a signal that a story should be taken seriously, and among the young people in German, it's the musical idiom that can generate sympathy and attention. This parallel shows how specific a framework or listening context may need to be if personal narratives are to be appreciated.

The differences between the two projects also led to several observations. There is no doubt that radio stations thrive on being up-to-date, on presenting current material: push a button; and there it is. However, downloading documents from an archive is not like turning on a tap, quite the contrary: selection, reorganization, and presentation are necessary. In musical productions such as those initiated in Freiburg, modern technical equipment and software plays a central role. By contrast, the Italian life narratives depend almost entirely on the human voice, its timbre and its melody—the direct and often intimate connection it can create between speaker and listener.

Indeed, the voice and its quality are fundamental to radio. This cultural aspect is often forgotten. The grain of the voice (to borrow the phrase of Roland Barthes) has a value of its own, quite apart from being a cultural sign.

Systematically collecting material of this kind and classifying it to make it available to others seems to be a key moment in the development of community radio. All these factors contributed to the emphasis, within the *Digital Dialogues* project, on the central function of memory, its workings and its work.

NOTES

1. Lessing cites the *Iliad*, Book, III 156-158, where Homer says that "when the (elders) saw Helen coming towards them they spoke amongst themselves, saying 'You couldn't possibly blame the Trojan and Greek armed forces for suffering for a woman who looks like the immortal goddesses.'"
2. "In a philosophy of the *ipse*-identity such as ours, one must be able to say: possession is not what matters. What is suggested by the limited cases produced by the narrative imagination is a dialectic of possession and dispossession, of care and carelessness, of affirmation of self and effacement of self. . . ." (in chapter on "Personal Identity and Narrative Identity," Ricœur, 1990, p. 198).
3. Barbalato et al.'s book is a synthesis of research carried out with 300 young people in five European cities (Rome, Naples, London, Paris, and Berlin) and underlines the emphasis on space rather than time: most of the young people said that it mattered to them *where* they were positioned and *not when*, because they didn't want to adopt a temporal way of looking at the world. Denying time also means rejecting history: for example in the field of art, the majority of interviewees said that a copy was preferable to the original. Questioned about the *Mona Lisa,* they said preferred an electronic copy because they could interact with it.
4. A television series presenting typical life stories, which the production framed in a sociohistorical context. The word "mirror" was not only a reference to the act of confessional interview, but also to the idea of the audience seeing itself reflected there. There was a strong emphasis on the theme of the representative nature of autobiography and biography.
5. The interchange between Calvin Bass as president of the *Lifers* and young people from Freudenstadt in the Black Forest was mediated/ translated by SJ, Ed.
6. Archivio del Patrimonio Autobiografico e di Memorie Storiche Scritte e Audiovisive dell'area Daunia-Irpina.
7. Linguistic membership plays a foreground role: "The territorial aspect, as an anthropological constant, has been neglected in linguistic circles. Human beings organise their social character in space, that is to say, in the structure of their territory. Visual perception, which is necessarily related to space, counts for more than touch, smell or feeling. Human beings conceive of the world spatially, which conditions their behavioural perspectives. In linguistics, the speaker's ability counts for more than the spatial value of communication, and the linguistic identity is judged as important as the spatial dimension. Thus, linguis-

tic provenance becomes identifiable through variations in speech" (Radtke, 2002, p. 62).

REFERENCES

Abraham, N., & Török, M. (1996). *L'écorce et le noyau*. Paris: Flammarion.

Baacke, D. (Ed.). (1998). *Handbuch Jugend und Musik*. Opladen: Leske & Budrich.

Baacke, D., Sander, U., & Vollbrecht, R. (1990). *Lebensgeschichten sind Mediengeschichten*. Medienwelten Jugendlicher, Vol. 2. Opladen: Leske & Budrich.

Bakhtin, M. (1979). *Estetica e romanzo*. Turin: Einaudi.

Barbalato, B. (1997). *Variations biographiques et médias: L'identité narrative du "je" dans les medias*. Brussels: Emile Van Balberghe Libraire.

Barbalato, B. (2002). *Autobiografie orali per un archivio delle voci*. Panni/Foggia (brochure).

Barbalato, B. (2003a). *Autobiography: Thought and action*. Rome: Mediapolis-Europa (brochure). http://www.digital-dialogues.de.

Barbalato, B. (2003b, July 15-19). *Identità e diversità nella trasposizione in video della scrittura autobiografica: Quale linguaggio per parlare la prima persona altrui?* 18th Symposium of the Associazione internazionale per gli studi di lingua e letteratura italiana (AISSLI) "Identità e diversità nella lingua e nella letteratura italiana," Louvain, Belgium.

Barbalato, B., Liperi, F., & Scialotti, S. (1985). *La fine del futuro*. Montepulciano: Editori Del Grifo.

Berg, H.W. (1998). Jugend und Laienmusik. In D. Baacke (Ed.), *Handbuch Jugend und Musik* (pp. 155-172). Opladen: Leske & Budrich.

Blasco-Martínez, R.M., & Rubalcaba Pérez, C. (2001). Sueño de una sombra. In A. Castillo Gómez (Ed.), *Cultura escrita y clases subalternas. Una mirada española* (pp. 109-131). Oiartzun: Sendoa.

Bourdieu, P. (2004). *Esquisse pour une auto-analyse*. Paris: Raison d'agir.

Deborre, G. (1988). *Commentaires sur la société du spectacle*. Paris: Lebovici.

Deleuze, G. (1977). *Dialogues*. Paris: Flammarion.

Eble, K., & Heinzel, M. (2003). *Soundcheck*. Freiburg: Wissenschaftliches Institut des Jugendhilfswerks Freiburg (brochure). http://www.digital-dialogues.de.

Fiske, J. (1992). The cultural economy of fandom. In L.A. Lewis (Ed.), *The adoring audience—fan culture and popular media* (pp. 30-49). London and New York: Routledge.

Foucault, M. (1966). *The order of things: The archaeology of human sciences*. London and New York: Routledge.

Graebe, H. (1998). Praxis der Musik–und Tonproduktion: Konzeption und Technik im Studio. In D. Baacke (Ed.), *Handbuch Jugend und Musik* (pp. 401-420). Opladen: Leske & Budrich.

Grande, M. (1987). Il trucco e la maschera. In G. Ferroni (Ed.), *I modi del raccontare* (pp. 154-166). Palermo: Sellerio.

Lejeune, P. (1975). *Le pacte autobiographique*. Paris: Editions du Seuil.

Lejeune, P. (2000). *Cher écran*. Paris: Editions Le Seuil.

Lessing, G.E. (1964). *Laocoon*. Paris: Hermann. Original edition (1766) *Laokoon*. Berlin.

Lotman, J. (1985). *La semiosfera*. Venice: Marsilio.

Luisa (2002). *I quaderni di Luisa—Diario di una resistenza casalinga*. Piacenza: Editrice Berti e Terre di mezzo.

Màrquez, G.G. (2002). *Living to tell the tale*. New York: Knopf.

Montaldi, D. (1961). *Autobiografie della leggera: Vagabondi, ex-carcerati, ladri, prostitute raccontano la loro vita*. Turin: Einaudi.

Montaldi, D. (1971). *Militanti politici di base*. Turin: Einaudi.

Perniola, M. (1990). *Enigmi*. Genoa: Costa & Nolan.

Perniola, M. (1998). *Disgusti: Le nuove tendenze estetiche*. Genoa: Costa & Nolan.

Perniola, M. (2000). *L'arte e la sua ombra*. Turin: Einaudi.

Radtke, E. (2002). Il napoletano: Varietà di prestigio? In T. Krefeld (Ed.), *Spazio vissuto e dinamica linguistica* (pp. 63-74). Frankfurt/M: Lang.

Ricoeur, P. (1990). *Soi-même comme un autre*. Paris: Editions du Seuil.

Rousseau, J.J. (1959). *Les confessions*. Paris: Gallimard.

Sellari, M. (1985). Storie allo specchio. In M.I. Macioti (Ed.), *Biografie, storia società* (pp. 224-241). Naples: Liguori.

Starobinski, J. (1982). *La trasparenza e l'ostacolo*. Bologna: Il Mulino.

Thomas, W.I., & Znaniecki, F. (1968). *Il contadino polacco in Europa e in America*, Vol. 2. Milano: Comunità. Originally published 1918-1929 in Chicago.

Voullième, H. (1998). . . . and Rock Goes Online and CD-ROM—Rockmusik und interaktive Medien. In D. Baacke (Ed.), *Handbuch Jugend und Musik* (pp. 421-443). Opladen: Leske & Budrich.

Woolf, V. (1970). *Orlando*. London: The Hogarth Press.

Section III

Discussion

9

Monitoring and Evaluation

Peter M. Lewis

"Did it work?" or, to put it another way, "how effectively did the projects fulfill their aim?" Earlier chapters have pointed towards answers to these questions as far as they concern CCV and DD. This one attempts rather to explain *how*, in general, one might set about answering them; it is concerned with the methodology of evaluation.

After some introductory remarks about the context of the two projects and the rationale for participatory monitoring and evaluation, this chapter looks at some of the techniques used in CCV and DD and the extent to which ethnographic methods accord with the action research approach. In conclusion, the discussion is related to the theoretical context of pedagogical theory.

The field to be considered is something of a no-man's-land between, on the one hand, areas where a vast amount of experience and literature exists on the subject (e.g., the evaluation of projects aimed at reducing poverty in the developing world), and others where little evaluation at all has been attempted (e.g., community radio). Then again, it must be recognized that the skills training undertaken in the projects, whose success was relatively easy to measure, was but a step towards something more intangible: the creative use of digital, web, and broadcasting technology in a setting, community media, dedicated to the empowerment of people whose voices are not usually heard in the mainstream media. Those who become empowered as a result of this experience are changed and are rarely content with exercising their new-found self-confidence and strength only in a media context. For many, there are consequences in their family and domestic lives, and enlarged perspectives and ambitions at a social and political level. Political and social change is, after all, the *raison d'être* of most community media. These kinds of consequences are familiar to those working in the field of continuing or lifelong education where the range of evaluation is long-term and often extends beyond the duration of the particular course or project that requires evaluation.

JUDGING EFFECTIVITY

The CCV and DD projects had their origins in community media where there have always been problems about assessing the effectiveness of projects. The restricted financial circumstances of most community radio stations, for example, have meant that their managements have rarely, if at all, conducted research on their own behalf, and the application of conventional audience research methods is inappropriate, considering the programming style and limited reach of most of the stations (Lewis, 2003). Yet surely participatory media deserve a participatory method of assessment, and the same applied, the CCV and DD partners felt, to the training to make use of participatory media. That is why the key feature they drew on from the field of development studies was participatory monitoring and evaluation. PM&E, as it is known for short, has a long history and there is considerable literature in this discipline (Estrella & Gaventa, 1998). There is, moreover, currently a lively interest on the part of international agencies and funding bodies in developing ways to assess the impact of a growing number of projects that aim to alleviate poverty by bridging the "digital divide," particularly in the developing world. In this context the challenge is to overcome infrastructural deficiencies and a historical lack of access to education as well as new technical skills associated with contemporary broadcasting and internet work.

A recent attempt to gather indicators of impact can be found in a report for OneWorld International on a series of case studies in South Asia, Southern Africa, and Central America in which the use of information and communication technologies (ICTs) was evaluated (Op de Coul, 2003). "Impact" was considered in relation to "promoting opportunity," "facilitating empowerment" and "enhancing security"—the first two being outcomes especially sought in the projects described in this book. Under the heading of "opportunity" the OneWorld assessment looked at skill-building that led to educational and employment opportunities as well as to access to markets. Empowerment was considered at the individual level where self-confidence and self-esteem, independence, emancipation, changed power relations (e.g., within a family) were factors, and at the organizational level where increased efficiency and better networking could be observed. Estrella and Gaventa cite Narayan-Parker's (1993) summary of the differences between conventional and participatory evaluation (see Figure 9.1).

From this neighboring field, then, the participatory element of evaluation seemed a useful and appropriate strategy. It followed that in CCV and DD each project partner should be involved in the design and execution of the evaluation, and that the trainees, participants, or target groups themselves should also have a say in the process. A considerable degree of *self*-evaluation was necessarily involved and in any case mitigated the effects of the constraints of time and budget and conse-

FIGURE 9.1.
Differences Between Conventional and Participatory Evaluation

	CONVENTIONAL	PARTICIPATORY
Who	External experts	Community members, project staff, facilitator
What	Predetermined indicators of success, principally cost and production outputs	People identify their own indicators of success, which may include production outputs
How	Focus on "scientific objectivity," distancing of evaluators from other participants; uniform, complex procedures; delayed, limited access to results	Self-evaluation, simple methods adapted to local culture; open, immediate sharing of results through local involvement in evaluation process
When	Usually upon completion of project, sometimes also mid-term	More frequent, small-scale evaluations
Why	Accountability, usually summative, to determine if funding continues	To empower local people to initiate, control, and take corrective action

(Narayan-Parker, 1993 cited in Estrella & Gaventa, 1998, p. 17)

quent limitations on opportunities for the evaluation team to observe work in progress.

The formally designated evaluation team for both CCV and DD consisted of Traudel Günnel, coordinator for both projects, Nicholas Jankowski, and the present writer. The last two both had experience in observing community media projects and applying action research methods (e.g., Jankowski, 1991; Lewis, 1993), and during the course of the two Socrates-funded projects, both separately and together discussed evaluation and research methods in publications and at conferences (Jankowski, 2002, 2003; Lewis, 2002; Lewis & Jankowski, 1999). These papers partly contributed to, partly drew on, the communications exchanged within the CCV and DD partnership as they related to evaluation.

The Organization of Evaluation Within CCV and DD

The data on which evaluation could be based was in the first place structured by the requirement for each "action" within the projects to produce a descriptive and normative handbook, an outcome promised to the European Commission. The proposed structure for the handbooks was outlined by the coordinator immediately after the overall project was set up and discussed by e-mail within the partnership to make sure that it suited the different actions and allowed for adjustments before final agreement. The outline structures had the aim of encouraging all partners to reflect on and record their proposed outcome as a continuing process while designing, carrying out, and evaluating their actions. The handbooks in their final form were to include a statement of objectives, the prerequisites for participants, a detailed outline of the activities or training, pedagogical and methodological instructions / comments, technical equipment and material required, and the proposed methods of self-evaluation. Early versions of the handbooks were exchanged among partners, monitored and evaluated by the evaluation team, and further developed. At the meetings within DD, separate sessions were held to assess and discuss the draft versions of the handbooks.

Thus each action was invited to define its own aims, objectives, and methods, which were then used as a benchmark to assist evaluation. In addition, the evaluation team called for[1] other data in six different, but overlapping, forms: (a) reports from trainers and action leaders about administrative aspects of their training courses; (b) self-evaluation by trainees; (c) reports by trainers on their own courses; (d) reports by trainers on colleagues' courses; (e) observers' reports; and (f) discussion of the above data in face-to-face project meetings. I discuss below what was expected under each heading.

Reports from Trainers and Action Leaders

We requested copies of publicity/recruitment documents describing the aims of courses, target trainees, and so forth, the recruitment procedures for trainees, details of equipment used during training courses, the course programs themselves (including intended learning outcomes and content synopses), any special arrangements made to facilitate access (e.g., childcare, transport), brief details of funding or contributions in kind and resources (if other than the main Socrates funding), and any reports that stakeholders (i.e., associated or co-funding organizations) may have produced.

Self-evaluation by Trainees

It was left to trainers to determine how they gathered this information and how many of the suggested questions they asked, because in most cases the time available would determine how much could be discovered. Questions adapted from a *Women on Air* report were used to illustrate the approach:[2]

- For you, what part of the course was different from what you expected?
- In what ways did this "difference" help your own learning and development?
- Identify two or three aspects of the course which you feel will enable you to participate in radio work in the future.
- Has the discussion about "women's radio" changed your views on your position as a woman in society? If so, in what way?
- What do you think are the barriers to women working in radio?
- What are the five main things you have learned from the course?
- What were the main aspects of the course that were least useful?
- Any other comments?
- What particular suggestions have you made for changes in the design of the course? What response has there been from the organizers?
- Other general comments about the design of the course.
- What, if anything, has really inspired you about the training?
- This time next year, where do you imagine you will be in terms of employment generally or radio work specifically?
- What help do you think you will need to achieve that?

A different but complementary set of questions was used by Caroline Mitchell[3] for a course, *Airing Our Differences,* organized in the EU-funded *Permanent Waves* project. She asked trainees to complete a short mid-term questionnaire, followed by a more detailed questionnaire and discussion at the end of the course. Overall, this included evaluation under several headings.

The course itself, which comprised units on radio production (pre-planned and live), background to radio industry, IT for radio, independent work:

- What was the best thing?
- What improvements could be made?
- Additional comments about teaching methods, resources, etc.

The experience of actual broadcast work:

- Describe the range of things you did for the station.
- How prepared did you feel for what you did?
- What new skills did you learn through making the program?
- Did you feel you had enough support in what you did for the program?
- What additional support would have benefited you?
- What was the best thing about your involvement in the program and the station?
- What was the main thing you learned from the whole experience?
- If you were to get involved with a/the radio station again, what changes would you make to (a) the program you worked on (b) other programs on the station?
- How do you think the experience prepared you for future work in radio?

Where next? Trainees were asked to say in which areas they needed more tutoring or skills, more practice, more experience, more work experience in specific roles, to name a preferred radio station in which they might seek work placement, and so forth, under the following headings:

- radio skills;
- confidence;
- knowledge of the industry;
- working independently;
- IT skills.

Planning for the future: Trainees were asked to state what they would like to be doing—in six months' time, in a year's time, and in five years' time.

Reports by Trainers on Their Own Courses

Trainers were expected to comment on administrative arrangements, the age, background, expectations, and radio experience of the trainees, the success of the methods used, the content and the pace of instruction, and on the outcomes—immediate, as in the acquisition of skills and the evident or reported self-confidence of the trainees, and longer-term outcomes, such as further courses taken, certificates gained, a job in radio, or other types of employment.

As evidence of this elusive data (long-term effects), trainers were encouraged to note the informal comments of trainees—an illustration of the growing articulation of an ethnographic approach.

> The last point—longer-term effects—is something that we expect may be illustrated by anecdotes, quoted remarks by trainees, and so forth. This is the area of "gossip" (in the original positive sense of the word)—the information that emerges from the equal exchanges of people talking informally and establishing relationships over meal breaks, traveling to the course, talking afterwards over a drink, and so forth. The kinds of things that would usefully throw light on the effect of the training are:
>
> - What was the trainee's prior experience of formal education?
> - What has been the attitude of partners, friends, work colleagues before, during, and after the training?
> - What, on reflection, do trainees feel has been the effect of the course on themselves? (Such reflections might be prompted by getting them to look again and comment on their original, end-of-course, self-evaluation form.)
>
> It may be possible to arrange group discussions, including one or two with former trainees on similar courses. All this would provide useful evidence. (e-mail circular April 28, 1999, see footnote 1, above)

Reports by Trainers on Colleagues' Courses

These were arranged through bilateral visits, one of which is discussed in more detail below. It was expected that they would cover similar ground to the trainers' own reports summarized above and, in addition, comment on the trainer's teaching and technical skills and relationship with trainees.

Observers' Reports

It was not expected that these reports be made exclusively by experienced training evaluators, although at a later stage, early in the second project (DD), there was a suggestion that attempts should be made to involve a local college or university in monitoring and evaluating the training. The hope was that an action might be adopted as a project for students. Students could be given the task of designing questionnaires under the guidance of their tutors and the project trainers, and of applying and analyzing them, as well as helping as interviewers or observers. Although the idea has worked well in other contexts, disappointingly it was not taken up in the CCV and DD projects.

Face-to-face Meetings

Finally, direct exchange at meetings provided the opportunity for methods and findings to be discussed in a group. For example, at the final meeting of the DD project in Turku, Finland, in October 2003, the partners spent some time in "mutual interrogation" of each other's work before each gave a brief presentation summarizing the highlights of their action and their disappointments, explaining what s/he would do differently if restarting the action and how the action might affect future work.

By this time self-evaluation, supported by communication via email, had become routine, as the example in Figure 9.2 illustrates. This was a "distance tutorial" sent out by the evaluation team during the early stages of DD.

FIGURE 9.2
A "Distance Tutorial" from the Early Stages of DD

We will be using a range of methods to evaluate *Digital Dialogues*, but with the very limited budget there will be little chance for us to visit you. So we see our task as assisting you to use appropriate methods to monitor and evaluate what you are doing—that is, to use *self-evaluation*.

We expect to use, with your help, four main methods for the monitoring and evaluation:

1. Examination of documents
2. Observation
3. Interviews
4. Questionnaires

FIGURE 9.2
A "Distance Tutorial" from the Early Stages of DD (continued)

1. **Examination of documents** Please take care to keep copies of all documents relating to your Action. These might include—
   - publicity for the Action—leaflets, posters, video or audio recordings of TV or radio programs in which your work is mentioned; press cuttings, etc.
   - planning documents, proposals for activities
   - training materials, scripts, agendas for meetings, program schedules
   - scripts, transcripts, "products" of various kinds, e.g., stories, poems, examples of archival material or of music, references to websites and printed pages which illustrate the website; logs (records) of PC or internet use, etc.
   - evaluation materials, e.g., completed questionnaires, reports for funding agencies, etc.

2. **Observation** This is a matter of making notes of what you, or some other observer, see is going on, and recording your reflections and ideas as you go along. You might, for example, note what works, and what doesn't, or whether the expected outcomes do in fact happen. Here, too, you can write down things people say which you think are significant.

3. **Interviews** These might be formal or informal, structured or semi-structured. For example, you might decide to cover the same ground with each interviewee, using a brief list of headings to prompt you. While questionnaires might be given to all participants, trainees, trainers, etc., you would want to interview only a selection. If you record interviews, you may decide to transcribe the most significant parts or summarise the content as a whole.

4. **Questionnaires** Those of you who were also involved in Creating Community Voices will have used brief questionnaires for completion by trainers and trainees. Some good examples can be found in the Appendices to Action 3 in the Year One report of CCV at www.digital-dialogues.de.

AN ETHNOGRAPHIC TURN

From the first, the planning for CCV and DD had described its approach to evaluation as action research, and this was in line with the qualitative research methodology favored by Jankowski and the present writer. Günnel, in her Chapter 3 summary of German research trends (e.g., Baacke, 1989; Fabris, 1989; Kübler, 1989; Maletzke, 1988) shows how media research moved from a quantitative empirical approach with its focus on more general representative communicator or audience surveys towards a holistic approach that focused on the process of media communication in detail; taking into account the subjects involved and their life situations; that is, social, psychological, and environmental factors. As ethnography, field and case studies acquired increasing importance, different empirical research tools, "qualitative" methods such as observation in the field, narrative interviewing, group discussions, diaries, and so on, became necessary.

What became increasingly clear as the projects progressed was the suitability of an ethnographic approach to the necessary data gathering, an approach that emphasizes the importance of what in some research contexts is dismissively referred to as "anecdotal evidence." Properly contextualized and interpreted, evidence of this kind—the stories people tell about themselves—is a valuable complement to other data.

Support for this approach in evaluation methodology came from Lewis's experience, during the final year of the DD project, in Sri Lanka. This was an evaluation of the *Kothmale Community Radio Internet Project* (KCRIP). Funded by the U.K. government (Department for International Development, DfID) in partnership with UNESCO, its purpose was not just to assess the effectiveness of a well-known project, but also, and mainly, to develop a methodology for evaluating small-scale community media projects in rural areas of the developing world. The work was undertaken by a team from the interdisciplinary media@lse group of the London School of Economics working with the Queensland University of Technology.[4] Excerpts from the final report to DfID about the Sri Lankan experience as well as the general methodological approach were used to explain to the DD team the meaning and value of ethnography, its relation to action research, and the need for what the authors called a "research culture" to be built into any project. For example:

Ethnography can be understood simply as a mode of reflection in which people use many of their normal ways of gaining knowledge with more awareness and more systematically. This means valorizing project workers' existing knowledge and experience; treating their own everyday practices and interactions as material that can be analyzed; and supplementing this with some training in the range of ethnographic research methods and analysis. . . . Ethnography involves a balance between closeness and distance: one aims at complete immersion for full understanding, but the entire approach recognizes the value of not being an actual member of the community, the advantages of being a "stranger" who has to learn the culture and therefore takes nothing for granted, asking questions about things which members take entirely for granted or which may be invisible to them. Staff participation moves a participant from closeness to distance and reflection. (Slater, Tacchi, & Lewis, 2002, p. 63)

"Staff participation" referred here to the involvement of project staff in the process of monitoring and evaluation. As the *Ethnographic Action Research* handbook put it:

The aim is to build up a *research culture* in your project, in which research and documentation is an integral part of its everyday operation. Everyone contributes to and learns from research; it is discussed at your meetings; staff and volunteers think about research when planning any activities. (Tacchi, Slater, & Hearn, 2003, p. 25)

The handbook goes on to explain how action research means a "tight connection" between the activities of a project and the research process in three ways: the active participation of the beneficiaries; action-based methods ("the activities and experiences of participants produce knowledge alongside, or in combination with, more formal methods"), and the way that research generates action as in planning or in problem solving (Tacchi et al., 2003, p. 25). As Günnel has pointed out, citing König and Bentler (1997), the application of these principles "corresponds to the tradition in media-pedagogical research which integrates the question of 'the underlying practical intent'" (Günnel, 2003, p. 138).

Ethnography in Evaluation: Two Examples from CCV and DD

Two examples illustrate how this approach was carried out in practice. The first comes from the "Powerful Voices," Action 3 within the CCV project. This has been referred to at several points in preceding chapters (e.g., Chapters 3 and 4) and was concerned with training women to use community radio in Ireland (Connemara and *Women on Air*—WOA) and the United Kingdom (Bradford and Sunderland). A strong interest and movement to increase the involvement of women in community radio had its focus at this time in AMARC Europe,[5] and because the individuals knew one another it was natural step for the CCV evaluation team to arrange reciprocal evaluation visits between the partners. The particular evaluation exchange examined here was that of the representative of *Women on Air* who reported on Sunderland.

The Value of Informal Sources

Women on Air was the title of a NOW[6] project whose partners included Connemara Community Radio (also a CCV partner), University College, Galway, and Ireland's Independent Radio and Television Commission (IRTC). "Independent" in the Irish context means distinct from the state broadcaster, RTE, and includes both the small number of community radio stations licensed by the IRTC and the commercial radio sector. WOA was intended to address the underrepresentation of women in this sector by means of research, policy development, and training, and its detailed and thorough evaluation procedures had been designed by an experienced training evaluator.[7] This experience, in the person of Margaret Tumelty, was brought to bear on the "external evaluation" of the two-day "taster course" held at the Bridge Women's Education Centre and the University of Sunderland. The course content is summarized in Chapter 4 where some of Tumelty's comments are reported. The focus here is different; it is to note how personal observation and informal conversations were a crucial complement to the scrutiny of documentation and of completed questionnaires.

It is necessary to amplify a point made above. Mutual evaluation by people and/or organizations familiar with each other could in some circumstances be a reason to doubt the validity of the exercise; mutual evaluation could easily turn into mutual admiration, or at least damage limitation. However, in this case, the degree of honesty coupled with an ability to relate sympathetically to another's situation was, in this observer's view, characteristic of a democratic and professional approach found among the majority of community media practitioners, a product of three decades of development of new ways of working, to which feminists have made a vital contribution.

Moreover, both the training activity and its evaluation were holistic, a term whose application by Caroline Mitchell, leader of Action 3 in CCV Action 3, was cited in Chapter 4:

> Parallels might be drawn between a holistic approach to training and feminist consciousness-raising. For instance, they shared the objectives of instilling confidence and re-skilling women, raising women's awareness of women's oppression, working collectively, developing women's creativity and networking. (Mitchell, 1998, p. 80, cited in CCV, 1999, p. 23)

Tumelty's evaluation report[8] was based on personal observation, scrutiny of planning materials, and informal conversations with Mitchell, the tutors, and a number of participants (trainees) during the day of her visit.

The personal exchanges made it possible to see the effectiveness of a day that gave women a "taste" of the work to come, as well as preparing them for a visit to the university on the second day of the course. Childcare was provided, the room was welcoming, with chairs in a circle and time allowed for chat over coffee. Very important, in Tumelty's opinion, was the presence of the "Year 1 women," that is, the women who had completed the whole course, taster days and radio production included, the year before. They had been centrally involved in the planning of this next year's course and, in sharing in its delivery, were able to reassure the new trainees and to demonstrate, with jokes and stories about their failures and successes the previous year, their confidence in handling the technical equipment and with interviewing. The day allowed time for practical exercises and for mistakes, for reflection, for checks by the trainers to see if the trainees were happy with how the day was going. Running through the structure of the course was the message that "your voice, your opinion, your story is worth hearing."

Tumelty noted the way the Sunderland staff let the Year 1 women take over the running of small group activity. In these sessions they paced their teaching sensitively: for example, the use of a microphone with no tape running in the recording unit allowed handling competence to be learned without the distraction and embarrassment that most people feel on hearing their recorded voice for the first time. Then, while interviewing skills occupied the groups, they themselves interviewed trainees about their impressions of the day, thus unobtrusively getting them to listen to their own voices. Feedback from this small group session showed how the trainees felt at ease in reporting their discussions and feelings, and a final group evaluation was further evidence that the course had made a connection with the trainees' own experience, and that the time allowed for action and reflection had resulted in the desired learning outcome.

In Mitchell's opinion, the use of participatory evaluation methodologies is important when building up trust, continuity, and accountability between partners, trainees, and trainers, as well as sharing practice between wider projects in the European network. The methods used—diaries, summarizing progress and problems in e-mails, conducting interviews, observing each others' workshops and courses, and sharing notes of meetings—bear out an observation made in the *Ethnographic Action Research* handbook:

> There is never a simple division between "us" (researchers) and "them" (research subjects). Rather, research involves many different roles and different kinds of conversations. Hence, you can involve participants as both informants and as fellow researchers. Action

research should be a way of listening carefully to what people know from their experience, helping to structure this more clearly, and bring it into the processes of planning and acting. (Tacchi et al., 2003, p. 5)

Learning About Hidden Obstacles

The second example of ethnographic method comes from Finland where the CCV project at Radio Robin Hood, based in Turku, has already been mentioned in Chapter 4. Three years after the course mentioned there, Riitta Haapakoski, the Radio Robin Hood trainer, reflected on her experience of training the metal workers union members in the handbook *About Participating in Digital Practice* (Haapakoski & Hurme, 2003), an outcome of *Digital Dialogues*. Strictly speaking, this is not an example of ethnographic method in the formal process of evaluation, but the whole piece, less of a handbook than an essay or *apologia*, is a remarkably honest reflection on the difficulties encountered over a decade of training union members to use the radio station. Haapakoski had recently read Paolo Freire's *Pedagogy of the Oppressed* and had come to realize that her training methods, like those of many community radio workers, had all along drawn on the Freirean *zeitgeist*. The learning processes she encouraged and which the handbook mirrors "appl[ied] the three-stage investigation method of Paolo Freire: naming, reflection, action" (Haapakoski & Hurme, 2003, p. 19). In Haapakoski's model—and it is no coincidence that it echoes the Sunderland pattern described above and in Chapter 4—the trainees first learn to define the characteristics of community and mainstream media. Next they learn to analyze and question the existing publicity work of their own organization—a trade union. Finally, they produce material for broadcast and are encouraged to find a form that suits them rather than imitating standard mainstream formats.

The problem the essay identifies—and which underlies the handbook's whole approach to training—is one of motivation. The station is formally supported by the Metalli 49 branch of the Finnish Metalworkers' Union (as well by other NGOs); goodwill abounds at every level, and the situation seems ideal: a union branch has a radio station at its disposal. Yet Haapakoski asks at the outset: "Why does a group remain silent although there is a medium available for their use?" (2003, p. 4). The answer, at a personal level, is "low self-esteem, the underestimation of abilities and skills, passivity and short-sightedness brought on by hard times, a lifetime of being taught to keep quiet." At an organizational level, among the reasons offered by workers themselves was that there was no incentive for them to produce their own publicity; there was uncertainty about who was allowed to speak on behalf of the organization; they were afraid of being held responsible for leaks; and their underestimation of the importance of their own views and creative ideas was reinforced by the belief that the presentation style and content of mainstream media was the model they should imitate.

The suggestions in the handbook for overcoming these obstacles are sensitive and ingenious. For example, to encourage trainees to "question the existing reality of the media industry," Haapakoski helps them to see that journalists, no less than metal workers, have to work within the conditions set by an employer, which may lead to the production of reports supporting the owner's interests. But beyond the training models offered, the handbook is valuable for two less obvious reasons. First, it is a record, not of failure, but of difficulties frankly acknowledged, something often more useful than records of successful projects. And it would be wrong to assume the problems should be laid at the door of Radio Robin Hood. The ship-building industry, which was the metalworkers' main employer, was—and is still—going through a difficult period of adjustment, not only in Finland but in the rest of the industrialized world. Competition for a diminishing number of orders, or for new types of ships, is intense and affected by global factors far beyond the control of a union branch. Feelings of powerlessness on the one hand, and on the other of unwillingness to make trouble for fear of the ultimate reprisal—being dismissed from one's job—are understandable in the circumstances and permeate a whole community dependent for its livelihood on the success of the company.

But more to the point of our present concern, the role of ethnography in evaluation, the handbook illustrates the importance of a skill or habit that is easy to neglect "in the field," that of keeping a notebook for reflective comment on the day-to-day experience. It is not enough to gather documentation and questionnaire results, carry out observation or interviews. The *Ethnographic Action Research* handbook is emphatic on this point:

> When we talk about documentation . . . we do not mean reports, summaries or things you might write after the data analysis. We mean the raw material of your research; detailed notes, transcripts and other material. Documentation means three things: (1) write it all down . . . (2) organise your notes . . . (3) read your notes regularly: ethnographic action research is a continuous process. Your further research is guided by what you are finding out now. You do not wait until all of your research is completed before thinking about and starting to make sense of it. (Tacchi et al., 2003, pp. 35-36)

The same applies to evaluation, and the powerful reflection in an essay such as Haapakoski's can only be achieved by reliance on a record of experience, which in turn depends on an allocation of time for the task.

THEORETICAL CONTEXT

By way of conclusion, it may help to set the evaluation attempted in the CCV and DD projects in a theoretical context.[9] First we should note that it was based on a heuristic understanding of science. As Kleining puts it, "academic heuristics is the development and application, guided by set rules, of processes of discovery" (1995, p. 225). This heuristic understanding of science is characterized by openness within the research process and towards the subjects of the research (in our case the trainers and participants of the workshops and seminars), so as to be able to explore new and unexpected aspects.

At the same time, this open attitude ought not to be interpreted as researchers being able to approach the research task without any pre-assumptions. Oswald is certainly right when he pleads for researchers to be concerned with a wide range of theory prior to their investigations:

> The recommendation that in order to discover new things one must approach a field without prejudice is often taken to mean that one shouldn't do any reading on the topic, that one should know as little as possible about it in advance. This misunderstanding is based on the premise that research can be done without previous assumptions. The contrary is true. We all enter the field with background knowledge and experience, with pre-assumptions and prejudices. (Oswald, 1997, p. 85)

König and Bentler support this view when they emphasize that "research results in educational studies cannot be dissociated from the observer's perspective, i.e., they are always a product of the underlying theoretical frame of reference and its research methods" (König & Bentler, 1997, p. 90). Evaluation, too, must have a position in advance of assessment, for example on criteria and indicators. There must also be a selection of which courses in which projects to subject to evaluation. The CCV and DD projects chosen for evaluation can be characterized as explorative case studies (see Oswald, 1997, p. 79) in the sense that Cresswell (1998) uses in his review of different approaches of qualitative studies.[10]

The evaluation of CCV and DD was designed to explore a social field in its complexity while being close to what was going on. This entailed an empirical approach using qualitative methods for data collection, analysis, and interpretation in which an ethnographic approach is often, though not necessarily, found. Cresswell in this context stresses that the complex and holistic view is essential for qualitative research. In his definition he also refers to methodological traditions:[11] "Qualitative research is a process based on distinct methodological traditions of inquiry that explore a social or human problem. The researcher builds a complex, holistic picture, analyzes words, reports detailed views of informants, and conducts the study in a natural setting" (Cresswell, 1998, p. 15).

A final point unites theory and practice: the significance that well-timed participatory monitoring and evaluation can have for the effectiveness of the activities on which it is directed. There are many examples of this in the CCV and DD projects, for example in relation to the CD-ROM on digital audio editing (Chapter 5), in the successive improvements built into the courses for women at Sunderland (Chapter 4), and in the experience passed on from one team to another in training teams for live broadcasting in Freudenstadt (Chapter 7). This type of evaluation treats the process and its participants neither as objects of post-hoc scientific study, nor as recipients of training or funds passively awaiting a verdict delivered at the end of a project, but, as Narayan-Parker's table introduced at the start of this chapter reminds us, as people whose continuous feedback and reflection allow them to take control and corrective action.

NOTES

1. The following section summarizes an e-mail circular to CCV partners "Action 3: Draft Guidelines for Monitoring and Evaluation" (PL, April 28, 1999).
2. *Women on Air* report of June 30, 1997, by the trainer Margaret Tumelty.
3. Mitchell was involved in *Permanent Waves* before becoming the leader of Action 3 in *Creating Community Voices*, and was also a partner in the following *Digital Dialogues*.
4. The original project team consisted on Nick Couldry, Peter Lewis, and Don Slater from the LSE, and Jo Tacchi from QUT. Two members of the team went on to develop, with a QUT colleague, a handbook on ethnographic action research for use in the evaluation of projects (Tacchi, Slater, & Hearn 2004).
5. The European division of the World Association of Community Radio Broadcasters, known by its French acronym, AMARC.
6. New Opportunities for Women, a program proposed and funded by the European Commission.
7. Adrienne Boyle who, as a consultant experienced in work for the United Nations and the European Commission, was brought in to comment on the evaluation of Action 3 as a whole (see CCV, 1999, p. 33).

8. The report is summarized in CCV, 1999, p. 29; the full report can be read at Appendix 3.5.
9. The following passage draws on Günnel, 2003, pp. 138-142.
10. Compare also Flick (1991) and Lamnek (1995).
11. Explicitly, Cresswell mentions the following traditions: "The historian's biography, the psychologist's phenomenology, the sociologist's grounded theory, the anthropologist's ethnography, and the social, urban studies, and political scientist's case study . . . " (Cresswell, 1998, p. 15).

REFERENCES

Baacke, D. (1989). Sozialökologie und Kommunikationsforschung. In D. Baacke & H.D. Kübler (Eds.), *Qualitative Medienforschung* (pp. 87-134). Tübingen: Niemeyer.

CCV (1999). *Creating Community Voices. Community radio and new technologies for socially disadvantaged groups.* Socrates Programme for Adult Education, Year 1 Report. Sheffield: AMARC Europe (brochure). http://www.digital-dialogues.de.

Cresswell, J.W. (1998). *Qualitative inquiry and research design. Choosing among five traditions.* London: Sage.

Estrella, M., & Gaventa, J. (1998). *Who counts reality? Participatory monitoring and evaluation: A literature review.* University of Sussex: Institute for Development Studies, Working Paper 70.

Fabris, H. (1989). Von der Medien- zur Kommunikationsforschung. In D. Baacke & H. Kübler (Eds.), *Qualitative Medienforschung* (pp. 72-86). Tübingen: Niemeyer.

Flick, U. (1991). Stationen des qualitativen Forschungsprozesses. In U. Flick et al. (Eds.), *Handbuch Qualitativer Sozialforschung. Grundlagen, Konzepte, Methoden und Anwendungen* (pp. 147-173). München: Psychologie-Verlags-Union.

Günnel, W. (2003). *Experiment Arbeitsweltredaktion: Bürgerradio im Kontext von Medienpolitik, Kommunikationswissenschaften und Pädagogik.* München: Kopaed.

Haapakoski, R., & Hurme, S. (2003). *About participating in digital practice.* Freiburg: University of Education (brochure). http://www.digital-dialogues.de.

Jankowski, N. (1991). Qualitative research and community media. In K. Jensen & N. Jankowski (Eds.), *A handbook of qualitative methodologies for mass communication research.* London: Routledge.

Jankowski, N. (2002). Epilogue: Theoretical perspectives and arenas for community media research. In N. Jankowski & O. Prehn (Eds.),

Community media in the information age; Perspectives and prospects (pp. 359-374). Cresskill, NJ: Hampton Press.

Jankowski, N. (2003). Community media research: A quest for theoretically grounded models. *Javnost/The Public, 10*(1), 5-14.

Kleining, G. (1995). Methodologie und Geschichte qualitativer Sozialforschung. In U. Flick et al. (Eds.), *Handbuch qualitative Sozialforschung* (2nd. ed., pp. 11-22). München: Psychologie-Verlags-Union.

König, E., & Bentler, A. (1997). Arbeitsschritte im qualitativen Forschungsprozess—ein Leitfaden. In B. Friebertshäuser (Ed.), *Handbuch Qualitative Forschungsmethoden in der Erziehungswissenschaft* (pp. 88-96). Weinheim, München: Juventa.

Kübler, H.D. (1989). Medienforschung zwischen Stagnation und Innovation. In D. Baacke & H.D. Kübler (Eds.), *Qualitative Medienforschung* (pp. 7-71). Tübingen: Niemeyer.

Lamnek, S. (1995). *Qualitative Sozialforschung* (3rd ed.). Weinheim: Beltz, Psychologie-Verlags-Union.

Lewis, P.M. (Ed.). (1993). *Alternative media: Linking global and local.* Paris: UNESCO Reports and Papers in Mass Communication No.107.

Lewis, P.M. (2002). Whose experience counts? Evaluating participatory media. Paper presented at conference of the International Association of Media and Communication Research, Barcelona.

Lewis, P.M., (2003). Est-ce que ça marche ? l'observation et l'évaluation des radios communautaires. In J-J. Cheval (Ed.), *Audience, publics & pratiques radiophoniques* (pp. 83-94). Bordeaux: Editions de la Maison des Sciences de l'Homme d'Aquitaine.

Lewis, P.M., & Jankowski, N. (1999). *Developing participatory research methodology in the context of local radio training programmes.* Paper presented at conference of the International Association of Media and Communication Research, Leipzig.

Maletzke, G. (1988). *Massenkommunikationstheorien.* Tübingen: Niemeyer.

Mason, J. (1996). *Qualitative researching.* London: Sage.

Narayan-Parker, D. (1993) *Participatory evaluation: Tools for managing change in water and sanitation.* World Bank Technical Paper Nr. 207. Washington, DC: World Bank.

Op de Coul, M. (2003). *ICT for development: Case studies.* London: OneWorld International and http://www.digitalopportunity.org/article/view/72469/1/

Oswald, H. (1997). Was heißt qualitativ forschen? Eine Einführung in die Zugänge und Verfahren. In B. Friebertshäuser (Ed.), *Handbuch Qualitative Forschungsmethoden in der Erziehungswissenschaft* (pp. 71-87). Weinheim, München: Juventa.

Slater, D., Tacchi, J., & Lewis, P. (2002). *Ethnographic monitoring and evaluation of multimedia centres.* Report of a research project funded by Department for International Development, UK (DfID), in collaboration with UNESCO (unpublished).

Tacchi, J., Slater, D., & Hearn, G. (2003). *Ethnographic action research: A user's handbook developed to innovate and research ICT applications for poverty eradication*. Paris: UNESCO and http://cirac.qut.edu.au/ictpr/downloads/handbook.pdf.

10

Local and Global Participation

In this final chapter we raise a number of questions about the experience described in the book. These cover the areas of pedagogical theory and method, adult education, and the implications for community radio policy and practice. The discussion of each in turn leads to a global postscript.

PEDAGOGICAL THEORY AND METHOD

It will be clear by now that the training offered in *Creating Community Voices* and *Digital Dialogues* taught far more than the acquisition of technical skills. Günnel's theoretical justification for action-oriented media pedagogy (AOMP) and related approaches in Chapter 3, based on her considerable prior experience in media training, was already central in the project proposals to the EC's Socrates Adult Education Programme, but it did not need her theoretical arguments to convince the other project partners to use methods already widespread in community media practice. Nevertheless, trainers themselves need, in a spirit of Freirean reflexion, to theorize practice. To do so means putting experience—

whether the experience of a trainer or of the individual trainee—into a historical and theoretical context. It is a kind of sharing that adds strength to individual perception and experience. A trainee might feel "others have been here before" or "I can make more sense of my situation now I see it's part of a wider pattern." Equally, trainers, adapting methods and techniques from a variety of different contexts—for example from professional broadcast training, from nonformal adult education, from women's consciousness raising—and proceeding like most teachers by a process of trial and error, find reassurance in standing back to see how the courses they have developed relate to a wider pattern. In the theoretical exposition of Chapter 3 Günnel makes the connection between a quarter of a century of training tradition in community media and the parallel trends in pedagogical theory, allowing contemporary exponents to recognize their debt to both strands of development.

The exploitation of situational factors and the use of "blended learning" (the combination of methods such as self-teaching, distance learning, and face-to-face interaction) discussed in relation to the teaching of digital editing by Eble and Günnel in Chapter 5 is a useful example of the way these teaching approaches actually depend to a high degree on the participatory monitoring and evaluation (PM&E) that, as pointed out in the previous chapter (9), supported the work of both projects. The continued inclusion and application of insights derived from feedback, mid-course review, and self-evaluation strengthens the effectiveness of the methods used. As Eble and Günnel remark, "one of the important evaluation findings was that what initially seemed plausible and logical at the planning stage did not always correspond to the learning experience of individuals."

The same chapter includes other examples of achieving the right blend—of explanation and practice in the case of audio editing, of virtual and actual encounter in the context of the *soundnezz* platform, of formal and informal elements in the internet adventures of mothers and daughters. In Sunderland (Chapter 6), the familiar technique of teaching radio interviewing ran into the difficulty that interviews recalled for asylum seekers the traumatic experience of being interrogated, and ways round this, in order to build trust, had to be found. In the training for live broadcasting in Freudenstadt (Chapter 7), it was found necessary to support the practice and preparation of routines with documentation—a record of decisions made, equipment needed, and so forth. In each case the trainers were learning at the same time as the participants about how to proceed.

The participatory emphasis of community media means that the starting point of any dealings with new volunteers, or in negotiating with tandem partners (Chapter 4) takes account of their situation, their point of view. Above all, learning how to work in community broadcasting is learning by doing, and learning the eminently transferable skill of how to work in a group.

ADULT EDUCATION AND COMMUNITY MEDIA

Turning to adult education policy, a convenient indicator of the areas covered within CCV and DD is the set of priorities to which projects were expected to contribute under the Socrates Programme. The two projects could claim to be contributing to the following:

- *Approaches to promoting and developing individual adult education demand and to stimulating self-learning.* The above discussion, and Chapter 3 throughout, touches on this point.
- *Co-operation between formal and nonformal adult education systems.* The partnership of the University of Sunderland with a women's center and with a temporarily licensed radio station is an example of cooperation of this kind.
- *Cooperation among educational, cultural, and social organizations/institutions.* The tandem training partnerships described in Chapter 4 and the "cooperation partnerships" set up by Freies Radio Freudenstadt (Chapter 7) typify the kind of strategy adopted by community media generally in approaches to local organizations.
- *Methods of achieving greater participation of citizens at local level.* The "stuff" of community radio, its programming focus and concern, is the local social, cultural, and political landscape as interpreted by the social actors—the citizens—themselves.
- *Comparison of methodologies and development of modules for the training of adult educators.* Training manuals (handbooks) for each of the "actions," translated into several European languages, were an outcome of the two projects. The experience has led directly to a third project, current at the time of writing, and undertaken by largely the same team, to develop a course of training for trainers.[1]
- *Identification of ways and means of involving less educationally oriented and otherwise disadvantaged target groups.* This was the central purpose of the two projects.

The continuation in the new *META-Europe* project of the training approach used in *Creating Community Voices* and *Digital Dialogues* can certainly be classed as an outcome of the two projects and raises the question of the longer-term results of community media training and experience. A picture can be built up from details, not all of which are mentioned in the preceding chapters. At one level, one can note the interest of organizations in continuing to be associated with the activities begun in the projects: a school in Freiburg wants to schedule repeat sessions on web site creation; a Stuttgart-based youth organization, despite the geographical difficulties, remains involved with the *soundnezz* project; the companies and agencies that run the annual Apprenticeship Fair in Freudenstadt want to repeat the coverage of the event by FRF; youth bands, after having been familiarized with the web site experience in the *soundcheck* project (Chapter 8), themselves organized, on their own initiative, a Newcomers Festival; a local association has been formed to manage the future of the Panni archive, and there is an intention to create a similar autobiographical archive in a neighboring town (Chapter 8). On the other hand, there was not one local educational institution involved in *external* evaluation throughout the duration of the two projects (see Chapter 9).

The effect on individuals is much harder to track. One particular, typical instance and the conclusion from a five-nation study may together stand as a summary of the experience reported and theorized in different parts of this book.

From Radio Robin Hood, Turku, Finland:

> *I am PS (radio trainer). I came here a year ago. I did not know anything at all about radio work, I had never even visited a station. Now I have been completely trained in how to make radio programs. Working as a trainer. . . . I prefer to help and assist others and to transfer skills I have learned to the newcomers who know less than I do. As a positive side I will say that when people come here, it may be that some person is very quiet and makes no contact; then three months have passed, and when the person leaves, the world is open, and a sense of pride is felt, self-confidence has grown through success. Here no one sits all the time beside you and does things for you. No, the trainees have to do things themselves, the best way to learn. It is a limitless feeling of having completed something, when you have made a thirty-minute radio program and it is broadcast. And when your friends come and tell you that it was fine.* (quoted in unpublished report by Riitta Haapakoski, Radio Robin Hood)

From a report for the AMARC-Europe Training Partnership:

> . . . for volunteers of all kinds, whether young or old, men or women, from a mainstream or minority culture . . . radio work brings a spe-

cial sort of reward. Through it, many volunteers acquire for the first time a self-confidence which enables them to aspire to and succeed in getting jobs they would not otherwise have imagined possible—and not necessarily in the radio industry. They have, typically, operated recording equipment in difficult conditions, conducted interviews with a microphone that gave them power over interviewees who in other circumstances were perhaps more powerful than themselves, then further controlled the result through editing to produce a finished, creative piece of work; or as studio presenters they have controlled periods of live airtime. Community radio for these people has truly proved an education and a gateway. (Lewis, 1994, p. 32)

In fact the parallel report for the United Kingdom sector was titled "Community Radio—A Gateway to Employment," because a survey by the government agency responsible for broadcasting employment, Skillset, conducted at that time, showed that 9 percent of radio workers in the United Kingdom's mainstream industry began their careers in community or hospital radio or in independent production. More recent indications from other European countries suggest that the "gateway effect" continues to provide trained talent for mainstream broadcasting organizations—a significant contribution by community radio in the light of the decline in in-house training in public service radio and its virtual absence in the commercial sector.

The *Creating Community Voices* and *Digital Dialogues* projects of course met their share of disappointments and difficulties, from which some of the most valuable lessons can be learned. The reflections of one project partner, drawing somewhat pessimistic conclusions from the training experience, stimulated helpful discussion and some important insights, as well as underestimating her own success

- "Awareness of the existence of community radio and of the [target] group's own potential for social influence is not created in two training days."
- "Community radio training often starts with the presumption that groups . . . are 'ready' [to commit] to the community radio activities . . . and are just looking for the media skills needed to begin broadcasting. . . . A training approach based on this misreading has made the trainees passive by emphasizing formal skills at the expense of goal-directed activities."
- "Citizen groups learning journalistic and technical skills don't change the mass media. Therefore the goal has to be to form the group's own media reality."

- "Personal factors cramp participation in community radio training, eg., low self-esteem, underestimation of skills, passivity,
  short-sightedness caused by life crises, a lifetime of being
  taught to stay quiet etc [mean] it is very important to stress
  media skills are available to all." (unpublished notes in *Digital
  Dialogues* records)

Arguably the most important consequence of the involvement of
social groups in community media is the development of a critical consciousness towards mainstream media. This is arrived at through participation in media production. The experience of public accountability is
new to most participants in community media—the fact that they are
personally responsible for the quality of the information they spread and
for the impressions they create. They begin to realize that news items are
made, not "given," and to observe mainstream media more carefully.
Does the evening news portray the reality *they* have experienced? Which
sources are quoted, which are ignored? What roles and stereotypes are
offered to the audience? Questions such as these typically come up in
community media workshops, more or less directly. There is an ethical
dimension to this growing critical scrutiny as well. Participating in media
means respecting the rules of play that apply to public exchange, and it
also means reflecting on the value of the information presented by the
media and the quality of the interaction they depict.[2]

If, then, community media play as valuable a role in lifelong learning
as the arguments in this book assert, why is there not more official
recognition of the fact? One might look first within the educational systems of countries and ask what presence media education has within
curricula and what role community media projects could play to assist in
media education at every age level: our account shows benefits to
school children through to senior citizens. A partnership between, for
example, a community radio station and local schools would provide
strong motivation for a range of studies and skills acquisition. The resulting educational role for a station could result in a hitherto untapped
source of income. Parallel with this is the question of why interest in
community media is relatively still so rare in college and university courses. Attention by staff and students to the need for external evaluation
would be a welcome and valuable form of partnership.

GLOBAL POSTSCRIPT

If we look beyond the boundaries of nation states, the debate has to take
into account global issues that are mostly beyond the scope of this

book, but of which community media practitioners need to be aware. In recent years the pace and felt presence of globalization have markedly increased. Giddens has defined globalization as "the intensification of world-wide social relations which link distant localities in such a way that local happenings are shaped by events occurring miles away and vice versa" (Giddens, 1990, p. 64). According to him the key characteristics of the concept are the way the dimensions of place and time frequently become detached from our experience of things ("time-space distanciation") and the consequent possibility that our social relations are no longer necessarily confined to a local context. Instantaneous electronic communication has changed global financial and economic relations with very real consequences for daily life in most regions of the world, whether these are experienced as an increase in the range of choices in the social and cultural field, largely provided by the internet, or as increasing poverty and debt. The difference between "two essentially distinct populations . . . the interacting and the interacted" (Castells, 1996, p. 371) has been precisely the concern of the *CCV* and *DD* projects described in this book.

In some of the accounts of the activities in *Creating Community Voices* and *Digital Dialogues*, the global reference has been specific, as in Chapter 6 on *Networking Community Media*, and in every community radio or web site project the technology affords potentially global reach. It will have been apparent, though, that these technical connections are meaningless without the links to groups in civil society, expressed in the projects as tandem training, social or cooperation partnerships. These are relationships based on reciprocity, community media supporting and providing structures for local communication that would ring hollow if not filled out by the microstructures of interaction and communication cultivated in civil groups. The fate of civil initiatives depends heavily on their access to public attention.

The same observation applies beyond the local level. Günnel concluded her discussion of action-oriented media pedagogy (AOMP) in Chapter 3 with the criticism of the method's protagonists that they do not sufficiently concern themselves with "the debates surrounding media politics and media access." At the European level, strategies to counter media concentration have been the avenue through which the case for community media as a means to encourage cultural diversity has been advanced, mostly through AMARC-Europe's submissions to the European Commission. The Council of Europe has also recognized the value of this sector. In November 2004 its Advisory Panel on Media Diversity recommended that "Member States should encourage the development and strengthening of the contribution of community media in a pluralistic media landscape" (Council of Europe, 2004). To be relevant to community media using broadcasting spectrum, "encouragement" would have to include regulatory provision reserving frequencies and space on digital platforms, as well as "ring-fencing" the community broadcasting sector to prevent it being squeezed out of existence by commercial pressures.

That neglect of media politics is not limited to Germany is clear from the urgency of appeals to groups representative of civil society at the global level on the part of media activists concerned with the allocation of spectrum and resources. At the time of writing, this concern is focused on the World Summit on the Information Society (WSIS), an attempt to involve a range of interests, including, as well as governments, international and regional institutions, NGOs, civil society, and the private sector in planning a future media environment.[3] It follows from the argument of this book that there needs to be the equivalent of community media's social partnerships at a global level between media activists and NGOs, or in other words, a process of mutual education about what is at stake in the fight for the "global commons" against the pressures for "enclosure," the contemporary equivalent by private and state interests of the removal of common land in eighteenth-century England (Silverstone, 2001).[4]

A quarter of a century ago, the *MacBride Report* argued for a fairer distribution of the world's media flows and resources (MacBride, 1980). Then, the players were nations and Cold War blocs; now, NGOs have become recognized as important stakeholders, and, although the unequal media trade remains, Internet rights have become an issue affecting individuals and communities of all kinds. It is at least hopeful that the WSIS is officially committed to involving a range of stakeholders, including civil society, in the consultation. "If more civil society organizations (CSOs) get the experience and confidence to begin to lobby and advocate on ICT policy issues at national level, involvement in the WSIS process will have been worth the effort," said the Association for Progressive Communication (APC), launching its guide to ICT policy consultation (*http://www.wsis-cs.org/cs-overview.html*).

APC is one of the groups that are campaigning for a say in decisions about who will wield the power in the "Information Society." A leading group is CRIS, Communication Rights in the Information Society, run from the World Association of Christian Communicators (WACC) in London with support from several NGOs and the Ford Foundation (*http://www.crisinfo.org/content/view/full/226/*). Another, a coalition of media academics and practitioners, was referred to at the end of Chapter 2—OURmedia (*http://www.ourmedianet.org/*).

It will require the energy and attention of all these groups if civil society is to claim its rights in the distribution of the world's communication resources. At stake is the right—of course to communicate to the full extent of those rights expressed in Article 19 of the Universal Declaration of Human Rights—but, to put it negatively but realistically given contemporary global trends, to resist the ideology of the free market.[5] At the global level, no less than the local, it is crucial to guard a space for the expression of cultural diversity and democratic values by citizens themselves.

In the preceding chapters we hope to have demonstrated the importance of digital and web technology in allowing disadvantaged social groups a voice in today's world and the part community media can play. Active involvement in media production often encourages critical awareness of how (and for whom) mainstream media work, as well as insight into the way the uniformity of their operations reduces diversity and turns culture into a commodity. We have dwelt on radio because it is, at one and the same time, simple—in its use of the human voice and of basic tools such as microphone and recorder—and, excitingly, at the cutting edge of convergence, making connection with the internet and mobile telephony. More to the point, it is "the most widespread electronic communications device in the world and community radio is a practical and cost-effective means of reaching and connecting the world's poorest communities" (CRIS, 2003). As a means of expression for a diversity of cultures and social groups, community radio can play a role in strengthening participation in democracy and in the new cultural economy.

NOTES

1. META-Europe (Media Training Across Europe) is a two year project under the Grundtvig program whose outcome is a course for trainers "Media Competency and Cultural Empowerment." Details available from http://www.meta-europe.de
2. The question of a code of conduct for community broadcasting is dealt with in Chapter 7 of UNESCO'S *Community Radio Handbook* (Fraser & Restrepo Estrada, 2001).
3. The first phase of the World Summit on the Information Society took place in Geneva in December 2003, the second phase in Tunis in November 2005. See the WSIS official site http://www.itu.int/wsis/
4. The concept has entered the vocabulary of current campaigns; see reference to "cultural commons" at http://www.mediatrademonitor. org/cris-unesco.php
5. See Buckley, 2004, for a development of these ideas in relation to the positions of UNESCO and WTO.

REFERENCES

Buckley, S. (2004). Cultural diversity and communication rights. www.crisinfo.org/content/view/full/797 (retrieved 9 November 2004).

Castells, M. (1996). *The rise of the network society*. Oxford: Blackwell.

Council of Europe. (2004) *Transnational media concentrations in Europe*. Report prepared by the Advisory Panel on Media Diversity for the Steering Committee on the Mass Media (AP-MD (2004) 7). Strasbourg: Council of Europe, November 2004, available at http://www.coe.int/T/E/Human_Rights/media/AP-MD%282004 %29007_en.pdf

CRIS (Communication Rights in the Information Society). (2003). What is the special significance of community media to civil society? www.crisinfo.org/content/view/full/170

Fraser, C., & Restrepo Estrada, S. (2001). *Community radio handbook*. Paris: UNESCO.

Giddens, A. (1990). *The consequences of modernity*. Cambridge: Polity.

Lewis, P. M. (1994). *Community radio: Employment trends and training needs. Report of a transnational survey*. Sheffield: AMARC-Europe.

MacBride, S. (1980). *Many voices, one world: Communication and society today and tomorrow* (International Commission for the Study of Communication Problems, chaired by Sean MacBride). Paris: UNESCO.

Silverstone, R. (2001). Finding a voice: Minorities, media and the global commons. *Emergences, 11*(1), 13-28.

Contributors

Beatrice Barbalato is a professor at the Catholic University of Louvain, Belgium. She is interested in the interpretation and interrelation of prose, film and theater texts, an area in which she has published several books and over a hundred articles. She is editor of *Vincenzo Cerami: Le récit et la scène* (2005, University Publications of Louvain), her most recent essay is *S'autobiographier dans l'Espace Vidéo* (2004 in ART VIDEO, University Press of Namur). Since 2002 she has been responsible for the *Belgian Archive of Autobiographical Testimony*.

Ann Baxter until recently worked as a Development Officer at the University of Sunderland, UK, in the School of Education and Lifelong Learning. She has been involved with widening access to education through working in partnership with community-based organizations and other education providers for over ten years. She is now working as a Widening Participation Project Facilitator and is based at Newcastle College.

Karin Eble heads the Department of Continuing Education at the Scientific Advisory Institute of the Youth Assistance Organization in Freiburg, Germany. She teaches courses in media, gender studies, and project management at the University of Education and the Catholic College for Social Sciences in Freiburg, at the Technical College in Furtwangen, Germany, and the College of Social Sciences in Solothurn, Switzerland. She has been responsible for coordinating projects such as *Young People on the Radio* and the internet audio platform *www.sound-nezz.de*, and is currently involved in developing the internet portal *www.multiline-net.de* directed toward furthering the media competence of girls and young women. Together with Irene Schumacher, she edited the volume *medi@girls: Medienprojekte für Mädchen* (2003).

Traudel Günnel is a member of the academic staff in the Media Department of the Paedagogische Hochschule Freiburg (University of Education), Germany. She has been involved in community media since 1979 and has been conducting research projects since the mid-1990s, including the international projects *Creating Community Voices* and *Digital Dialogues* supported by the EU. Her most recent publications are *Counteracting the Gap: Strategies for Teaching Media Competence* (2002) and *Experiment Arbeitsweltredaktion, Bürgerradio im Kontext von Medienpolitik, Kommunikationswissenschaften und Pädagogik* (2003).

Susan Jones is a free-lance writer/editor and participates in managing a community radio station in Freudenstadt, Germany, which places special emphasis on work with young people and on equal opportunity for girls and members of minorities. Since 1968, she has taught courses at Binghamton University, NY, at the University of Tübingen, Germany, in adult education programs and journalism workshops. Until 1991 she worked as a newspaper editor and since 1992 has been active in theater, audio projects, and radio broadcasting.

Peter M. Lewis is a Research Fellow in the Department of Media and Communications at the London School of Economics and Political Science. Since 1980 he has taught media and cultural studies in universities in London; before that he was an educational broadcaster, and was manager of one of the UK's experimental community television stations in the 1970s, Bristol Channel. He has written extensively about community and alternative media, including reports for UNESCO and the Council of Europe. He is a founding member of the UK's Radio Studies Network and currently Scientific Coordinator of the EU-funded International Radio Research Network (IREN).

Caroline Mitchell is principal lecturer in radio and coordinator of media undergraduate programs in the School of Arts, Design, Media and Culture at the University of Sunderland, UK. She has been active in promoting women's use of community radio for the last 20 years. In 1992 she set up *Fem FM*—a short term women's radio station which has been a model for women's radio stations in the UK. She has run many women's radio training courses in the UK and Europe. She is editor of *Women and Radio: Airing Differences* (2000).

Author Index

Subject Index

Printed in the United States
116524LV00001B/193-198/A